Making the World Safe for Pornography

Making the World Safe for Pornography

and other Intellectual Fashions

by E. J. MISHAN

Alcove Press

First published in 1973 by
Alcove Press Limited
59 St Martin's Lane, London WC2N 4JS

Printed in Great Britain
by Watmoughs Limited
Bradford and London

ISBN: 0 85657 013 3

Acknowledgements

I am grateful to the publishers and editors for permission to reprint the following:
Some Heretical Thoughts on University Reform (*Encounter*); The Spillover Enemy (*Encounter*); Making the World Safe for Pornography (*Encounter*); On Making the Future Safe for Mankind (*The Public Interest*, No. 24 (Summer 1971), pp. 33–61. Copyright © National Affairs Inc., 1971); Futurism, and the Worse that is Yet to Come (*Encounter*).

Contents

Foreword

Such are the sweeps of fashion in this world of over-developed communications media that, try as one might, one cannot remain a heretic for long. Take up any unpromising cause and, whether you will it or not, very soon you will find yourself in company, not all of it perhaps equally to your liking. My own experience is even more remarkable. Recently, through no fault of my own, I have been slipping into orthodoxy. Five years ago, even three years ago, a sub-title *Essays in Dissuasion* might have been wholly appropriate. Today it is not quite. And though the theme of these essays may be aptly expressed by the critic as "The case *against*", the growing unease of the public in all that concerns the future offers some insurance against dismissal of my repeated forebodings as no more than the vindictive soliloquies of some solitary defiant.

Of course, being consistently against so much that was popular not so long ago may indeed stamp one as being, or at least as having been, something of an eccentric. But eccentricity, in the simple sense of deviating from usual character or practice, does not really come into it. The opposition of my views to what was once prevailing opinion is not to be explained in terms of psychology, or rather not in terms of psychology alone. Since my contrary opinions purport to be based on reasoned argument and the evidence of our senses, they are properly to be regarded as an expression of dissent—a dissent, however, that is pretty thoroughgoing and one that aims to draw attention to the inadequacy and inexpediency of the beliefs that have lighted our way over the last half-century at least. These beliefs are just beginning to be challenged and, perhaps, to be challenged too late.

The inexpedient beliefs I refer to are best understood as a continuing part of a climate of respectable intellectual opinion

—what we may call an "Established Enlightenment"—which, though it was never so powerful as to determine the course of events in the face of strong vested interests, could never be ignored by our rulers. Since the 1920s, if not earlier, this climate of intellectual opinion, in Britain at least, has been composed of parts of the ideologies of democracy, socialism, and liberalism, along with a faith in the ultimate beneficence of science, progress, and economic growth. While such sources of ideological commitment could not always produce a single opinion on any issue, they were the ingredients of an intellectual compost from which so-called enlightened opinion and informed judgment on the larger social questions took shape and grew in strength— such opinions and judgments being expressed by the professional classes, the scientific and academic community, by the "higher journalism" and the middle-class "intelligentsia".

A brief word on the contribution of such ideologies to the resulting spectrum of intellectual opinion. The belief in democracy is extended to the idea of increased "participation" in the management of any organisation by all affected by its decisions. It was, and to a large extent still is, believed to be a good thing that workers or students should have more control in the day-to-day running of corporations or universities, respectively, even where their interests are transient, their minds innocent, and their imaginations at times uninhibitedly fanciful. After all, democracy was the word associated with the broad movement to iron out hierarchical differences that appeared to rest on privilege. The element drawn from socialism had little in it of expropriating the means of production from the bourgeoisie. This solution to humanity's problems continues to have appeal only to the very young and those on the extreme Left in politics. This element consisted rather of the idea, as distinct from *laissez-faire*, that the state could and should intervene on behalf not only of underprivileged groups but of society at large in the interests of progress and justice. The contribution of liberalism to the Established Enlightenment has two facets; the more specific economic aspiration toward freer trade, increased mobility of labour and capital, and the more general aspiration toward the promotion of an international community through the exchange of ideas and the removal of residual censorship. The liberal spirit has more recently associated itself, though uneasily, with the movement to extend new freedoms and rights to minority groups within the community—even where the rights demanded by these minority groups affront the sensibilities of others, often the majority.

The idea of progress itself has spawned an impatience with the heritage of the past conceived of as shackles on our journey into the future. It links itself with liberal tolerance in fostering the desire to be "modern" which has expressed itself in the main in reducing discipline in schools in favour of more "creativity", and, more generally, in dissipating moral judgment in favour of psychological considerations. This "modern" attitude, which is for more understanding of (and sympathy with) the criminal, the delinquent, and the perverted, has grown over the last two decades—incidentally along with an increase in crime, delinquency, and perversion.

Progress is, furthermore, conjoined with the idea of growth. Though both ideas can trace their ancestry in the West as far back as the late 17th century or earlier, they have become obsessive since the second World War. Again we can distinguish two senses of the word growth, the narrower sense being associated with the "new economics" of the postwar period, itself a development of the pre-War economics of Lord Keynes. This pre-War economics, however, addressed itself primarily to the goal of maintaining full employment in a liberal capitalist society; the post-War economics, on the other hand, directed itself primarily to sustained economic growth regarded as a prime goal of the economy. This concern with economic growth harks back to Adam Smith. Since then it has been continually reaffirmed and, indeed, achieved some intellectual sanction as a result of the post-War proliferation of mathematical growth models, all building on the narrow foundations laid by Sir Roy Harrod in 1946. As a keystone of liberal capitalist ideology, however, economic growth has to be conceived not only as a direct source of enrichment, but as providing the expanding material base from which all worthy and humane policies are to be attained. The broader sense of growth, on the other hand, can be viewed as an updating of the older idea of progress, as it now has reference not merely to the advance of knowledge generally but more particularly to the advance of *scientific* knowledge and technology regarded as irresistible forces for liberating men from want and drudgery, and offering to them wondrous opportunities for a life of ease, dignity, and pleasure.

Such, in rough, are the aspirations, and convictions, arising from a merging of the elements of older ideologies, and today comprehended by an Established Enlightenment that has had so marked an influence on social thought and action since the War. Despite an occasional touch of irony in my outline of these guiding ideas and attitudes, few readers will fail to recognise them and also to perceive their appeal to the better instincts of men. And yet, as a source of inspiration and guidance, I believe this Established Enlightenment to be wholly inadequate for the world of today and for the future we are moving into.

Only if measured by technological achievement and commercial aggrandisement does our civilisation—the civilisation of the West in the 1970s—rate high. Apart from these undeniable technological and commercial achievements, the sort of progress impelled by economic growth and to some extent guided by the Established Enlightenment looks impressive enough on the surface. Maintenance, until recently, of something close to full employment since the War; a continued rise in "real" income *per capita;* a phenomenal expansion of higher education accompanied by a rise in the school-leaving age; a vast growth in the social welfare services provided by the state; an extension of the suffrage (to younger people in Britain, and, effectively, to many blacks in the southern states of the U.S.A.); a reduction of class distinctions and regional discrimination; an increased recognition of the rights of self-determination of once-subject peoples; a growing awareness of the social disabilities allegedly suffered by women and the gradual introduction of remedial legislation; the appearance in almost every home in Western affluent countries of new labour-saving gadgets and television sets; increased mobility and, especially over the last decade, increased foreign travel for the multitude. In addition, some still controversial but "enlightened" measures have been introduced into a number of countries (and states of the U.S.A.); the abolition of the death penalty and corporal punishment, the abolition of theatre censorship, plus a number of smaller legal adjustments making for a more lenient attitude to juvenile violence and to overtly aphrodisiac literature and entertainment.

The traditional liberal (and, indeed, the non-revolutionary socialist also) might well be excused for feeling very satisfied with the bounty of progress as he surveys these features of national life and compares them with the picture of the social scene fifty, or even twenty-five, years ago. The fashionable intellectual, he is glad to observe, is today quite properly a little guilty at living in material comfort in a predominantly white community, and quite properly touchy on the treatment of immigrants from poorer countries. This same trendy spirit is also, by and large, anti-Victorian, anti-imperialist, condescending toward patriotic sentiment, and with a marked predilection for "debunking" past heroes, national myths, and "the glorious days of old". Withal it exhibits an impatience of reverence, privilege, and ceremony.

Nonetheless, if the advance of a civilisation is to be associated also with order, with propriety, with a refinement of sensibilities, with established norms and procedure, with a sense of things being in place, a sense of harmony and proportion, then the kind of progress we have experienced over the last few decades cannot fail to arouse also a great deal of cynicism.

A society has come into being whose members are encouraged to seek self-indulgence, habitually to make invidious comparisons and to feel disgruntled at not having more—tendencies that are euphemistically referred to as "motivated". Indeed, the momentum of economic growth in the wealthier countries, it is believed, can be sustained only by the unremitting efforts of industry to create dissatisfaction with existing possessions and to promote unbridled covetousness and greed. The resulting restlessness and discontent are accompanied and aggravated by a degenerating environment, and by movement from the villages and smaller towns to the increasingly congested and polluted metropolises and their suburbs. Each year sees more massive office blocks created in our larger cities, cheap, nasty, and depressing for the most part, and once-distinguished streets and squares become tawdry with amusement arcades and sleazy bazaars. The litter of the "throw-away" society is everywhere in evidence, with the means of sex titillation displayed at every corner news-stand and offered in various doses by the greater number of films. Each year some millions or so more rush off like lemmings to places which are rapidly becoming more like the places they want to get away from. The struggle of so many of the young today to look different defies space and time and has reached proportions where virtually "anything goes"; where campuses, and sometimes railway stations, appear at times to have been taken over for a marathon tramp's carnival. As trends go, the number of cars on the roads of Britain is expected to double in the next fifteen years, the noise in the cities to double in the next ten years, and the number of air passengers to double every seven years. The figures for crime and for juvenile violence continue upward. "White collar crime"—business theft, embezzlement, bribery, tax frauds—is rampant in the West. As the young today see it, "everyone is on the make".

A few of these unprepossessing features of modern societies—unbridled greed, degenerate activity, widespread corruption, the popularity of spectacles of sex and violence—may, indeed, be found in one form or another during certain periods in other civilisations, though on an incomparably smaller scale: for means of communication were limited, cities fewer and smaller, and the populations and resources but a fraction of a fraction of those involved today. What is deeply disquieting today, however, is not only their unprecedented scale but the inescapable fact that all the unhappier aspects mentioned in the preceding paragraph are the products also, perhaps the inevitable products, of two hundred years of sustained economic growth in the West. Such an outcome was never suspected by the reformers and humanists of the 18th-century Enlightenment. Nor did such a possibility ever cloud the splendid visions of those 19th-century apostles of progress who, observing everywhere the spread of industry and the introduction of new labour-aiding contrivances, foretold a future of universal plenitude, harmony, leisure and culture.

The symptoms of desolation and anxiety in modern societies are, of course, a product also of having to live with the potential horror of nuclear or bio-chemical warfare, with the nightmare of the "population explosion" and, above all, with the loss of faith by the mass of people in the great myths, and the consequent erosion of a moral consensus.

To expect, to hope even, that some great good will yet emerge from these unpromising developments if only we press on with economic growth, with technological advance, and with "liberalisation", is to make a virtue of wilful blindness by calling it faith. Admittedly, it is extremely unsettling to haul down the mainsheet of beliefs that make up the Established Enlightenment and to think anew each principle and dogma in the light of revealed circumstances. I do not like the idea any more than the reader does. I should much prefer to have been born at some time when society fitted better into its physical environment, when life was more settled, and a moral and artistic consensus prevailed. In such a society, one may beguile the time interpreting life in terms of existing fundamental presuppositions, but one does not spend one's time in a tortuous questioning of them. A growing hyperconsciousness about ends and means, a compulsive scrutinising and rescrutinising of our existing mores, and the ethical premises on which they rest, have something morbid about them. There is a risk of melancholia, a stale and enervating melancholia at that. But there is no doubt in my mind that the risk has to be taken, and that we must start on our iconoclastic pilgrimage in earnest. The alternative is to drift into a perdition being prepared for us by the technocrats, with a strong probability of humanity being annihilated on the way by either one or a combination of causes which I shall touch on presently.

One of the concepts fundamental to the philosophy of liberal capitalism and economic growth is that of the expanding frontier. Up to the turn of the century this frontier was territorial. Since then, the frontier has been chiefly one of scientific knowledge. Without an expanding frontier of the latter sort, indeed without continued investment in expanding such a frontier, the sustained rise in "real" living standards would not, of course, be possible. Further increases in population would then entail a sinking toward some physical subsistence level.

Be this as it may, we are already hard pressed against the tyranny of fact; the fact that the earth is finite, all too finite. Further economic and population expansion, and the increased mobility of peoples, will bring this crucial fact forcibly to the attention of each one of us within the next decade. The magnitude of the problem cannot, however, be properly assessed by a citizen of the modern consumer-oriented society indoctrinated with the idea that superabundance is to be the lot of the future, and that the wonders of technology will never cease to deliver goodies and gadgets.

The question whether we, in the West, can continue in orbit along the growth path—confining our measurement of growth simply to the output of man-made goods, and wholly in disregard of the incidental "bads"—is a question that scientists interested in ecology are now asking themselves. A more discriminating and difficult question would be: what kinds of growth, if any, could the Western countries sustain for what periods of time? More generally, what further growth options, if any, are still open to us? Such questions logically antecede the question I initially addressed myself to: whether a continuation of the economic growth we had experienced in the postwar period was in itself *desirable* or not.

The reason I did not pose the first sort of question, whether and how far continued economic growth was physically possible, is not that it had not occurred to me, but simply because I had no confidence in my ability to make any reasonable conjectures. During the last three years, many books on this subject, or on aspects of it, have been published, and some journals started—in Britain, *The Ecologist* (monthly) and *Your Environment* (quarterly) being among the best known—which were dedicated to illustrating the thesis that the growth path of modern industrial societies is in fact a collision course. If I do not seek to persuade readers of the thesis myself it is, again, simply because I am not competent to assess the validity of the arguments involved. Such arguments, however, turn on the not implausible belief that if world consumption continues to rise—because of rising "real" *per capita* income and/or rising levels of population—then humanity will very soon be faced with two sorts of irremediable scarcity; those arising from the finiteness of natural resources and from the assimilative capacity of the biosphere. On the one hand, it is alleged that if current trends of new discoveries and utilisation are projected, there will be an oil shortage within twenty to thirty years. The market response would be a rise in the price of oil that effectively removes it as a source of energy for mass-consumption purposes.

It is alleged also that within the same period we shall experience an acute shortage of metals today regarded as vital to modern technology and, owing to monocrop culture and excessive use of chemical fertilisers, a decline in the productive powers of the soil. The assimilative capacity of the biosphere, on the other hand, has reference to the constraints on the amounts of those by-products of modern economic activity that can be absorbed by the physical environment, which by-products, when in excess, are recognised as gaseous, liquid, and solid pollution. The concern with pollution ranges from the risk of ozone destruction in the stratosphere (without which layer of ozone life on earth cannot exist), and the more immediate fouling of the air in cities and suburbs, to the poisoning of lakes, rivers, and the ocean itself with oil, radioactivity, and industrial effluent, and the consequent risk of poisoning fish, fowl, plant life and wild life.

Before the War it was possible to hope that advances in technology would somehow prevail. But there are now countervailing considerations. The size and continued increase of the world's population is an unprecedented phenomenon that was not reckoned with. Even if the augmented population could somehow be fed, there is the question of sheer physical congestion, aggravated by the mounting expenditures on automobile and air travel. This ultimate human congestion is something that cannot be handled by technological innovation—not unless we discover another inhabitable, but uninhabited, planet in some far-flung star system of the Milky Way. If we discount such desperate hopes, only a world policy of deliberate population restraint can prevent communal violence and inter-communal warfare.

Another countervailing consideration is the problem of energy. So long as technologists could reasonably assume a virtually unlimited supply of fossil fuels, whether coal, oil, or something else, then they could continue to hope that a future shortage of land, of minerals, or of fresh water might be overcome by man's ingenuity. But once the world's conventional sources of energy, coal and oil, are exhausted, nuclear fission alone remains as a significant future source of energy. And it is not only a question of the colossal amounts of energy required to keep wheels of industry turning. It is also a question of the amounts of waste heat—to say nothing of the disposal of radioactive wastes—that have to be absorbed one way or another by an already impaired biosphere. What makes a virtually qualitative difference between yesterday and today is the unprecedented scale of the current exploitation of the earth's finite resources and assimilative capacity, a scale that cannot continue for many more years without total breakdown.

An exponential curve—more commonly recognised as a curve of compound interest—can be a terrifying phenomenon. If the Indians who sold Manhattan Island to the white invaders for some $24 had invested this sum at 6% per annum, and never withdrawn it, their capital today would exceed the total capital of the United States. The point is that a magnitude increasing at 1 or 2 or 3% per annum can continue to grow for hundreds or thousands of years, and remain comfortably below some critical magnitude. Once it reaches this critical magnitude, however, at which point the curve is observed to rise steeply, its continued growth can threaten to break up the stability of the system of which it is part. And some of the relevant magnitudes today grow at well above 1 or 2 or 3% per annum. The demand for air travel, for instance, is increasing at a rate of 10% per annum, and the world demand for oil is not far behind. This implies a doubling every seven or eight years. Within thirty-five to forty years, unless there is some check on this trend, the demand for air travel and for oil will be sixteen times what it is today. In seven or eight years more, thirty-two times as much, and in another seven or eight years from then, sixty-four times as much as the current world demand. With magnitudes of this order, it should be apparent why existing trends cannot be expected to continue for much longer. Even substantial differences in opinion about, or further revisions of, the figures for existing reserves, and for expected discoveries of new sources of raw materials and fossil fuels, have the effect only of advancing or retarding critical dates by a few years. To the ecologist, the question is not, then, *whether* economic growth rates can continue or not, but *when* and in what manner they will taper off. Counterpoised against these fears is nothing more than a firm faith that continued economic growth and innovation will prove adequate to solve imminent social and ecological problems.

The very idea of the inhabitants of the poorer countries, which comprise three-quarters of the world's population, ever reaching the standards of consumption prevailing today in the affluent West makes economic, or rather ecological, nonsense. If by waving a magic wand such a situation were realised over-night—even assuming no increase in world population and no further rise in the consumption levels of the West—the world's declining resources would be absorbed, on the average, at about five times their present rate, and the rate of pollution of the biosphere would rise accordingly. Again, only boundless faith in the miracles of technology make it possible to believe that the inhabitants of these poorer countries will ever achieve productivity standards comparable with those existing in the West.

There is, finally, the awesome prediction that within the next decade some forty countries will be in a position to wage thermo-nuclear and bio-chemical warfare. In a world of increasing population pressures, overcrowded cities, and resentful multitudes of have-nots, the risk of some fanatical ruler overplaying his hand and starting a world holocaust before the end of the century looks pretty high.

Now I admit that within the last five years increasing attention has been given to such problems by television and by the national press, especially in the Sunday features and magazine sections. But this expressed anxiety about the portentous consequences of unchecked economic growth is to be found cheek by jowl with an equally expressed anxiety, often on the next page, about our slow economic growth performance. On one page, or on one radio programme, society is castigated for its increasing materialism; on another, for its sloth in responding to material incentives. This schizophrenic attitude of our national press and broadcasting system is occasionally papered over by wobbly statements about the need to grow faster in order to solve the problems bequeathed to us by the quickening pace of growth itself. Presumably modern governments subscribe to this uneasy doctrine since the core of official policy is still made up of the traditional endeavours to expand trade and industry, to promote regional development, automobile output, exports, and, of course, to raise economic growth. Environmental or ecological considerations, though recently recognised by governments, remain—in financial terms at least—strictly peripheral to these traditional agenda. For all practical purposes we are pushing ahead as usual, though now with some due-regard-to clauses about amenity or conservation hovering in the official texts.

I might point out in passing that the need-to-grow argument in order to repair environmental damage is quite spurious. As I point out in my essay on "Making the Future Safe for Mankind", the quite orthodox economic case for expenditure on environmental improvement is that, *irrespective* of the distribution of income, and *irrespective* also of the rate of growth— whether zero, positive or negative—"real" national income may be raised thereby. (To be more pedantic, an optimal reduction of polluting activity from its unchecked market level is an economic proposition that is valid for any stage of economic development.)

Turning from the ecological possibility of sustained economic growth in the West to its desirability, my doubts about the latter began when I was a graduate student at the University of Chicago. I recall, in the Summer of 1950, standing on one of the bridges that straddle the Lake Shore Drive and watching, with incredulity, the endless streams of traffic on the six-lane highway below: three lanes, each solid with automobiles, running from North to South—many of them, evidently, holiday-makers— and three lanes running from South to North. I recalled the war-time posters in Britain: "Is Your Journey Really Necessary?" But were these journeys even desirable? Of course, these people, of their own free will, had chosen to make their journeys. And to question their choice was to wander beyond the territory marked *economic*. Or was it? As economics students we had touched upon the concept of *external diseconomies*—the unintended and adverse spillover effects on other people arising from the pursuit of some legitimate business or consumption activity. The price mechanism could be at fault. More generally, institutions could be defective in that they did not offer a wide enough variety of choice. Surely the immense resources required to furnish the population with automobiles, highways, and all the products and services accessory to their maintenance (including police and hospitals) could be used to better purpose, even if the purpose was wholly pleasure! What, then, was the set of circumstances that impelled people to choose the automobile rather than, say, walking, or cycling, or using public transport? Somehow the physical environment has been gradually transformed so that the private motor car had come to appear necessary, or at least desirable!

So I began to ponder on this and related economic phenomena. And as I did so I became less impressed with the marvels of modern technology, and with the vaunted high and growing "real" standards of living in Western Europe and America.

Other than sporadic letters to the press, the first public manifestations of my doubts about the benefits of material progress came in 1958, when I addressed an informal meeting of the Economics Society of the London School of Economics on this topic, and was much jeered at for my troubles by staff and students alike. But though the votes went against me the arguments, I was convinced, went with me, and I was not discouraged in the slightest degree. In reviewing a volume of essays (supposedly relevant for the economic improvement of the poorer countries) for one of the learned journals in 1959, I again questioned the value for the West of recent economic growth. But I was just beginning to warm up. In 1960, a fairly popular article of mine appeared in *The Bankers' Magazine* bearing the innocuous title "The Meaning of Efficiency in Economics". About half-way through it began to sizzle with scepticism, and I ended with a strong argument against economic growth. In a later article in the same journal entitled "Britain, The Economist, and The Six", I was more scathing of the economist as an agent of complacency in a world beginning to disintegrate socially and ecologically. (I was, incidentally, unconvinced of the economist's ability to assess the economic impact on the U.K. from merging her economy with those of the Six.) It is to the credit of my colleagues that they did not write off my then unorthodox opinions as a passing aberration. Looking back today, it seems to me that by producing these two papers I had managed to appropriate for myself the role of the official custodian of the anti-growth seal. From that date on, if ever there was a call for an economist to let off steam against some aspect of modern life, the chances were that my name would come up.

From 1960 on, ominous rumblings in my journal articles and in my reviews of economics books sufficed to assure colleagues that my opinions on the subject had not weakened with the passage of time. The rumblings finally issued in an eruption in 1966, when I had the exhilarating experience of giving unstinted vent to my accumulated misgivings about the value for the West of further economic growth, and to my accumulated contempt for our increasingly vociferous growthmen, in a volume entitled *The Costs of Economic Growth*. Though it was rejected by a couple of editors, Mr Davis-Poynter of Staples Press bravely undertook to publish it, and it was offered to the British public in the Spring of 1967.

In the light of editorial strictures on my MS, which at times came close to bitter condemnation, I was expecting the book either to be ignored or to meet with either contumely or condescension. For I had obstinately refused to make any revisions or omissions, despite pages of detailed editorial criticisms. In the event, I was quite taken aback by the favourable reception accorded to it by the weekly journals and newspapers, and the seriousness with which the themes of the book were reviewed. In 1969, a more popular version of the book was published, entitled *Growth: The Price We Pay* (in America, *Technology and Growth: The Price We Pay*), and in the same year my *Twenty-One Popular Economic Fallacies* appeared. The latter offered a digestible diet of economics and scepticism, and was also designed to convey, among other things, some aspects of the anti-growth thesis to a wider public. From then on, the story is one of modest success, helped along by a sustained growth in the popularity of the anti-growth theme—very little of which is to be attributed to my own making, and by far the greater part to the manifest and continuing deterioration of the environment.

Although the reviews have, on the whole, been generous, some of the inevitable criticism misrepresented some of my opinions—though unintentionally, I am sure. A reviewer is usually hard pressed for time and cannot be expected to read a controversial book with the care that is sometimes taken in writing it. He, too, has his prejudices, and if a slight displacement of the author's position renders it the more vulnerable, it is easily and inadvertently done. It also simplifies the self-imposed task of some reviewers of selecting a political tag. One can only shrug at the triteness of the occasional "reactionary" or "backward-looking", be amused by "romanticist" or "medievalist". "Radical conservative", however, though not felicitous is a little closer to the truth. Though I doubt whether much is to be gained by sifting labels, there is not much lost either by playing along for a minute.

On either side of the broad spectrum of intellectual opinion that I have called the Established Enlightenment, there are non-conforming groups from which it is possible, certainly, to identify a Radical Left. Those factions that comprise this group are united by a persisting sense of disillusion and by their unqualified denunciations of the "whole rotten system", which has to be destroyed—after which, hopefully, the millennial society will rise from its ashes. A Radical Right, sometimes associated with fascism or militarism, may be thought of as polar with the Radical Left, but is so only in a class sense. In their opposition to liberal democracy, in their determination to use the power of the state to suppress opposition, in their political stratagems and in their conviction that the ends justify the means, these extreme groups are sufficiently similar to make the occasional individual transition from Radical Left to Radical Right, or vice versa, relatively painless. In strong contrast in principle to both Radical Left and Right, and to a lesser extent to the Established Enlightenment, is the noncomformist group we might call the "radical pragmatists". Members of this group, which do not yet form a political party, continue to affirm that much is awry in modern society, but not everything. This group is radical only in so far as it is ready to question ruthlessly the existing institutions, and the developments—"trendy" and otherwise—that are taking place, and to do so in the hope of producing a more viable and, perhaps, a more valuable civilisation. It is also pragmatic, while *not* being conservative in the Burkean sense of deferring to a presumption in favour of the emergent laws and conventions of society. For it recognises that, in these cataclysmic times, institutions may have to be rapidly transformed, or replaced, simply as a matter of social survival. If it is conservative then it is so only in its adherence to a core of civilised values by which particular developments of existing society may be condemned, and by reference to which the good life, or at least a better life, may be realised.

If one were to accept these brief sketches of a Radical Right or Left, on the one hand, and a radical pragmatic group on the other—which, as I have just described them, do not look to me to be quite as unbiased as I would prefer—I should place my-self, as the reader suspects, in the latter group. Thus, I acknow-ledge the existence of widespread injustice and corruption in the West; also the inertial power of entrenched interests, material, vocational, and intellectual. Yet in the light of recent history—the history of the last 150 years or so—I believe society can be transformed from within; within, that is, the existing constitu-tions and without a bloody revolution or a descent into anarchy. Not for a moment do I think the task will be easy. The large metropolitan societies today have an economic and technological momentum that is not easy to deflect. But the alternative of placing one's hopes for a better life in the success of a revolution —or, more likely, in subverting the existing order to the point of anarchy—is to offer hostages to misfortune. What has ever emerged from anarchy but mob control and then tyranny?

But having taken my seat among the radical pragmatists, let me return to the sort of criticism that misrepresents the arguments I had employed in defending my thesis.

There are some preliminary and perhaps trivial objections to be dealt with first. There is for instance the popular demagogic question: what right have I, Mishan, to dictate to others what they should want! The answer is obvious. I have never questioned people's right to spend as they please or, for that matter, to vote as they please. What I did question was whether their welfare would rise over time as a consequence of their increasing expenditures—a judgment of fact, not of ethics. My judgment of the policy of continued economic growth may still be a minority view. But a voice urging a minority view is neither absurd for that reason nor, as yet, inconsistent with the operation of existing political systems in the West.

And the answer to those who would confront my scepticism of the welfare value of further growth for the West with the acute observation that people all appear to want to spend more, or that they vote for parties committed to further economic growth, is no less simple. Such observations are evidence neither for the thesis that continued economic growth will enhance people's welfare nor even for the thesis that people prefer a policy of sustained economic growth to conceivable alternatives.

One may *not* infer from the state of affairs resulting from actual economic and political behaviour of people that such a state of affairs is desired by them above any other for the straightforward reason that a large number of technically feasible alternatives, which might be preferred by majorities if their implications were properly understood, are just not understood. There is today, even in the most liberal democracies, a lot of ideological mist about, also dark clouds of prejudice which can easily be stirred in order to obfuscate vital issues. Even if their implications were understood, however, coherent programmes may not be offered to the public by existing political organisations or by the working of the market. There are, in the short run at least, constraints on collective choice just as there are constraints on individual choice.

With respect to the former, the choices offered to the public at any moment of time are limited. Democratic parties are obsessed either with returning to power or retaining power. They are of necessity conservative in their programmes. They address themselves to the same bread-and-butter issues—to a large extent, the current economic issues of employment, prices, balance of payments, growth performance, industrial conflicts and, perhaps, race relations—and think largely in terms of the electoral effect of their speeches and actions in the next one, two, or three years. Of necessity then they are also myopic. Even where the majority of the populace has begun to doubt the conventional economic wisdom, in particular the wisdom of continued economic growth, the launching of a new vote-getting political party—especially in two-party systems—is a Herculean task demanding much time, patience, and vast financial and political resources. The alternative of altering the attitudes and convictions of existing party stalwarts on major issues also takes time, patience, and vast resources.

Turning to the constraints on individual choice, one cannot infer from the fact that each person desires more money for himself in the existing circumstances, that he favours the policy of economic growth for society. A selfish preference for himself in the existing situation is quite consistent with an aspiration for a zero or even negative rate of growth for society. As for the patterns of his expenditure, they reflect his choice only if we take for granted the set of prices (which, as I argued, do not reflect social costs) and the "distortions" in availabilities resulting from the absence of property or "amenity" rights. They reflect also the existing economic institutions, especially commercial advertising, and the belief-system that keeps us all jostling for more.

These considerations tell against a related criticism of my position; that the alleged environmental deterioration cannot be too critical, for if it were people would go to the trouble of stopping it. This conclusion follows from the more general thesis that social problems which go unremedied do so simply because the costs of implementing them are expected to exceed the benefits. This Panglossian view of social ills was no doubt held to be true on the very eve of the French Revolution. But the fact that this thesis is hardly more than a tautology should not deter us from reflecting a moment on the question of the costs of change.

First, a feasible design for some social improvement may not, even where a situation is chaotic, occur to anyone for a long time and, when it does, initiative, effort, and expenditure will be required to persuade others of its desirability. Secondly, greater efforts and expenditures yet may be necessary in order to triumph over highly organised commercial interests and other vocal groups. It follows, as I indicated above, that even if feasible and eminently commendable proposals are advanced, they can founder for lack of funds, political guile, and sustained endeavour.

In order to avoid confusing matters, it should be mentioned in passing that private businesses are admittedly interested in change too, but in change of a particular kind—technical innovation, product innovation, and new methods for influencing consumers' wants—for which task they are admirably equipped and organised. For just this reason their opposition can be formidable whenever a body of reformers seeks public support for measures that are likely to hamper their commercial activities. Estate developers in particular have advantages, incidental rather than deliberate, in that each of their forays into the environment, each of their plans for demolition and rebuilding, for "modernising" and expanding, is by itself too small to actively engage the passions of more than a limited number of local inhabitants and their sympathisers. Piece by piece, then, in each of a hundred small towns and villages, building interests ultimately prevail. Quaint and historical buildings are reduced to rubble in order to create sites for plate-glass offices and supermarkets, for garages and car parks. Roads are widened and extended, traffic lights installed, and detours created, to accommodate the traffic being generated by

27

mounting automobile sales. Thus, within a few years some quiet resort or charming village has been transmogrified at great expense into another area of urban blight through which runs a tawdry, jangling, main street, soon to be strewn with dust and rubbish, bathed in fumes, and shattered by engine noises.

This process, though uncoordinated over the country, is tantamount to a policy of divide and conquer. The cumulative blight that spreads over the face of the country within a decade, which, had it been presented to the public in advance as the widespread features of a coordinated plan, would have been rejected out of hand as an outrage and an insult, manages to slip piecemeal through the meshes of local and central regulation to be discovered later, with incredulity and alarm, as an apparently unalterable *fait accompli*—one more instance of that commercially triumphant philistinism that despite growing public dismay continues to expand, filling the hearts of men with sorrow and despair.

As I indicate in my chapter on "The Spillover Enemy", the chief factors that make this process of rapid environmental erosion so difficult to check—namely, defective public vision, and the risks and high costs of organising opposition to simultaneous acts of commercial vandalism scattered throughout the country—all result from the continued prevalence of obsolete laws that ignore the substantial losses of welfare suffered by the public at large during the last half century, during which commercial and industrial developments have become powerfully instrumental in endangering its health, thwarting its sentiment, and destroying its amenity.

However, the allegation that annoyed me most was that my chief concern lay in defending the privileges of an *élite* of which (of course!) I was a member. It happens, however, to be an allegation that conflicts directly with all that I have written on the subject, and can be maintained only by a particular, and unnecessary, interpretation of the implications of one of my proposals. In general, however, far from ignoring the degrading poverty still to be found within the materially advanced nations, I observed that continued pressure on the growth-pedal does little to lessen their plight while direct redistributive measures can do much. Indeed one of the more telling arguments about the corruption of national character that results from the obsessive striving for more, regarded as a virtue by modern society, is the lack of political will to enact effective relief measures at a time when so large a proportion of its enormous resources are squandered in the production of piteously inane gadgetry.

Moreover, I had stated explicitly that I was concerned *not* with an *élite*, but with the ordinary human being. Those who have read my *Costs of Economic Growth* without skipping pages will have come across passages where I go out of my way to stress the fact that I am not worried so much about the welfare of technocrats and professionals who, if humanity survives, will have some sorts of compensation. "But what are the innate needs of ordinary men?" I go on to ask. My conjecture is that continued technological innovation, which offers him an increasing range of gadgetry and mobility, will also destroy his sources of gratification, his morale, and his self-respect. The last two essays in this volume elaborate this contention.

I was also accused of giving "an unbalanced picture" of modern life when, in fact, not only did I *not* claim to be giving a balanced picture, but I explicitly stated in the Foreword of the book that I should leave the glowing tints in the picture of modern society to the growthmen and "apply myself without compunction, therefore, to daubing in the black spots". After all, I had taken as the text of my sermon, The *Costs* of Economic Growth. In passing, I might add that I decided to let my enthusiasm carry me far from the familiar terrain reserved for the economist. For little reflection is required to perceive that life is more mysterious and perplexing, and fulfilment more elusive, than is commonly represented by those absorbed in the task of "enriching" us with more goods and massive doses of technology.

Even if a miracle should occur and we could escape every ecological hazard, an economic system that seeks to expand appetites in order to meet an increasing productive capacity, that seeks to promote greed in order to prevent surfeit, has nothing to commend it. If residual poverty were eliminated from the affluent society—and economically (though apparently not politically) this is perfectly feasible—the sham *raison d'être* of sustained economic growth would go along with it. Its poverty of purpose could no longer be concealed. It might then be easier to recognise that many things that are utterly rejected by the ethos of the consumer society, such things as hardship, toil, sorrow, frustration, guilt even, are not without redeeming merit. Enduring friendships form in shared hardship; compassion springs from human suffering; love is felt through pain and sorrow. We need the contrasts of dark and light, of heat and cold, of tears and laughter, in order to feel the texture of life. Without toil there can be no real relish of ease. Without taboos there can be no romantic love; without tribulations no moral growth; without the great myths no exaltation. One could go on, but the reader will find other imperfect but disconcerting glimpses of the human condition in the last two essays.

That I failed to offer any satisfactory solution to the problems I discerned was also held against me by a critic. It would appear to me a greater fault of character if, on discovering some insidious threat to society, a man decided to keep the matter secret until he alone had also found the antidote. Nevertheless, the idea of producing some plan outlining a method of transition to a no-growth society does exercise me from time to time. Allowing that the idea will become politically acceptable to humankind in time to avert catastrophe, quite a few economic problems will have to be faced in the attempt, first, to reduce current rates of consumption in the West and, then, to stabilise them at a lower level. I have some notions about how several of the problems can be managed, and I continue to ponder in a somewhat unsystematic way about the others. Perhaps I will decide one day to stick my neck out by offering some imperfect draft proposals, if only to start a debate among economists more competent than I. For the sooner we take deliberate action to veer away from the growth path, the more room we shall have for manoeuvre and the less arduous will be the transition. The alternative is to let the existing momentum continue until we are beset by one or more of a number of crises, any one of which could prove calamitous.

And this brings me, finally, to the sort of criticism that is latent in the affected humility of some scientists and economists. Confessing, almost exultantly, man's woeful ignorance about the magnitudes of an enormous number of complex though crucial relationships, they move in a single step to the illegitimate conclusion that no action ought to be taken until we know a great deal more than we do at present—the implied judgment being that unless mankind perceives a clear and present danger, the policy to be espoused is "business as usual". But business as usual entails a continuing intervention in the ecology, having consequences we cannot properly judge.

It would therefore sanction existing commercial and technological expansion until irrefutable evidence of social injury, arising from the use of any product or industrial process, was established. Since it is widely suspected that a large number of the "newer" diseases, and much social disturbance, arise from a complex of factors connected with modern methods and modern products, such a policy would require that no preventive action be taken until statistically significant relationships have been established, if they can be established. And this, notwithstanding that with the quickening pace of applied science many thousands of new chemical and synthetic products are put on the market each year, and a smaller number withdrawn. Since genetical and ecological consequences may take decades before they are detected, such a policy is virtually a recipe for catastrophe. The costs of reversing certain ecological reactions inadvertently set into motion by men, or rather reversing them rapidly enough to ensure survival, may prove to be prohibitive.

In a world where technology and commerce are having increasing impact, the reverse of this wait-and-see policy is more expedient: that is, unless we have good reason to believe that the continued pursuit of any course of action carries with it little or no risk, we should desist. Such a maxim is particularly apt for affluent societies where doubts exist that further economic growth, even in the absence of familiar spillovers, can make a significant contribution to human welfare.

Indeed, if one extrapolates growth trends over the next

century, one is hard put to make sense of them. Economic growth for 150 years at an average rate of 3%—not considered optimistic by current expectations (Japan has been experiencing growth rates of the order of 10% for several consecutive years)— would produce a *per capita* GNP *one hundred* times as large as that today. Another 150 years of this same rate of growth and there would be *ten thousand* times as much GNP per person as today. Such magnitudes defy the imagination. Where will the energy come from? Where will the materials come from? How will the waste heat and materials be disposed of? How will people be able to spend one hundred, or ten thousand, times more each year than they do today? With the greatest respect to the powers wielded by the wizards of Madison Avenue, how many cars, planes, yachts, houses, machines, computers can a person use? How much travel, entertainment, and education can he absorb? Where is the space to be found? And how will a person find time to use any but a fraction of what he amasses? Already, as Stefan Linder points out in his impressive *Harried Leisure Classes*, people in the West, and above all in the United States, are driving themselves frantic trying to find time both to improve their status and to make some use of the recreational gadgetry they continue to amass.

Thus, even if the economic system were somehow to be purged of all overspill, and if somehow the accelerating pace of change did not exhaust, shatter, and pervert us, there is no presumption that, given the inescapable limits of space and time, the resultant "purified" economic growth could add much to human happiness, which depends above all on a spirit of contentment and acceptance—the opposite, then, to that spirit of perennial dissatisfaction which is the prime condition of sustained economic growth. It follows that the judicious prattle of some economists about the need to determine the right "trade-off" between ecological damage and economic growth— between some loss and some benefit, as it were—is quite invalid. For whereas the increasing environmental damage and the increasing risk of ecological disaster are beyond doubt, there can be no legitimate expectation of countervailing gains.

1. *Some Heretical Thoughts on University Reform*

The 1960s will go down in British history as the decade in which the universities first became uncomfortably aware of a growing threat to their cherished independence and to their long heritage of academic freedom, a threat apparently coming from two directions, from the state and, more recently, from the student body.

The more popular view is that the danger of state intervention in the affairs of the university is an unavoidable consequence of the unprecedented post-War expansion of current and capital expenditure on higher education and therefore of the resulting financial dependence of the universities on the government. The setting up of the University Grants Committee in 1919 (which quinquennially enters into arrangements with the universities to provide them with the public funds necessary to meet their estimated current expenditures) appeared then as a commendable attempt to guard the universities from political influences of the government of the day. But it did not reckon with the post-War growth of university expenditures. In the last year of the quinquennium ending 1967, grants to meet the universities' current expenditures totalled about £140 million. In the same year additional funds for specific capital projects added a further £80 million, bringing the total subsidy in that year to around £220 million.[1] It is hardly surprising that, with public moneys on this scale being handed over to the universities, demands should arise for some control over their efficient use. Nor is it surprising that, after some heated controversy, the decision should be taken to subject both the U.G.C.'s and the Universities' Accounts to the scrutiny of the Public Accounts Committee.

As for the dangers arising from the pressure of students' demand for a greater share of control in the affairs of the

c

university, though aggravated by unruly factions having political objectives that transcend mere university matters, they are seen in this perspective as springing also from the remarkable expansion in the student population over the last few years. With eight new universities founded within less than eight years, with the transformation of ten colleges of advanced technology into universities, and with a vast expansion in the older universities, to say nothing of the multitude of non-degree-granting colleges and institutions, the British student population has increased from about 180,000 in 1960 to close to 400,000 in 1968.[2]

I think this view, which attributes the current malaise ultimately to the extraordinary post-War expansion of higher education, is mistaken—at least if it is taken to imply that the independence of the universities cannot be restored while they continue to spend on so massive a scale and to admit students in such large numbers. Indeed, I shall argue that the current threat to the universities can be removed by simple institutional changes—one requiring no more than a switch to a more rational method of accounts that discloses *the full costs of higher education*, the other a change from the present system of student *grants* to student *loans*. Admittedly the latter proposal is no longer novel;[3] but the weight of argument in its favour has not been fully appreciated by the public.

Moreover, the case gathers strength when placed within a context established by the first proposal and in the circumstances of repeated student excesses and disruption. The proposals, withal, are immediately practical, albeit in a technical sense only. Political resistance to proposals for dismantling any existing piece of administrative machinery is always to be anticipated (and resistance will be the more effective if the inefficiency of the existing machinery escapes notice owing to the absence of agreed criteria). Inevitably those most centrally involved in the old system seek to defend it. If it goes, their accumulated expertise may become valueless, and their status and influence correspondingly diminished. Though social losses of this sort are necessarily incurred in any change-over from one system to another, they are not to be lightly dismissed. In this instance, however, the social gains are substantial enough to enable one to combat political resistance with a clear conscience.

Since each of these two proposals can be adopted independently of the other, it is convenient to consider the first on its own. We can then examine the case against student grants as the second logical step to take on the supposition that *full cost pricing*[4] has been adopted by the universities.

Although the arguments in favour of full cost university fees are independent of the actual magnitude, it is of interest to have some idea of the disparity between fees currently charged by British universities, which often form the basis of calculating the costs of higher education, and the actual costs. Tuition fees for the undergraduate now average about £70 per annum throughout the country. For the British students, they are paid by local authorities which, in addition, contribute to his living and educational expenses by maintenance grants that range from £50 to £370. and average about £250. The true cost to the university of educating the student is, however, many times the tuition fee of about £70, though it is hard to give a precise figure. If we divide the total net current expenditure of a typical university by the number of its students, we obtain a figure of roughly £1,000 per annum.[5] This annual current expenditure obviously includes expenditures on the salaries of the academic staff. But the activities of the academic staff are not wholly devoted to teaching. Part of their time is devoted to independent research. It is sometimes concluded, therefore, that only a proportion of the expenditure on the academic staff should be included in the costs of higher education, this proportion being taken to equal the average proportion of the academics' time that is devoted to teaching or to preparing their lectures.

This proportion is, however, almost impossible to measure. The academic mind tends to be active at all odd hours. The typical don works at home; he debates with his colleagues; he reads the professional journals, assimilates new facts and ideas and contributes to them himself. He may be paid for his published articles, and may indeed act as correspondent to a newspaper or as consultant to business firms or to the government.

Yet all such activities will almost certainly add to his value as a teacher. Certainly the time and effort spent in research is not, in the long run, separable from university education. For the advance of knowledge, which is the purpose of research, is ultimately passed on to the student himself. Though it makes no difference to my proposals, I shall for these reasons continue to use a round figure of £1,000 per annum. Others, if they wish, can substitute a somewhat lower figure.

An increase of university fees from the present £70 per annum to £1,000 per annum does not, of course, involve the country in any greater outlay on higher education—though it makes it impossible any longer to conceal from the public, including the student, the full costs to the community of the subsidy being received by the student, whether British or overseas. The contribution of the local authorities (which is at present guided by the purely nominal fees set by the universities) need not be increased; and, if not, the Treasury will continue to make up the difference. But instead of channelling its contribution to higher education through the University Grants Committee in the form of a *lump sum* subsidy to the university the Treasury, it is suggested, should now pay at the rate of £930 per student[6] direct to the university, so making up in this more revealing way the full university fee of £1,000 per student. The Treasury could, of course, use all this money to make block grants to the local authorities so enabling them, instead, to pay the full fees of £1,000. Alternatively, the Chancellor could transfer to local authorities whatever sums are necessary to enable them to pay on behalf of each student some given proportion or amount. But whatever the formula arrived at, exactly the same number of British students could continue to receive free education at no additional cost at all to the taxpayer. A transfer payment only is involved. The sums that were once paid to the universities in the forms of grants by the U.G.C., and were thus regarded as a direct subsidy to the universities, are now to be paid wholly on a per student capita basis either directly by the central government or by the local authorities.[7]

This financial arrangement is much to be preferred over one in which the central government has used its powers to control fees so as to set them at a figure far below costs. In the process it reduced British universities to complete financial dependence on the state—which is then seen by the public acting as a generous and considerate patron of the spendthrift universities. Allowing the universities to set fees so as to recover the full costs of their services to society would free them at one stroke from their enforced bondage to the state. And once the magnitude of such costs becomes common knowledge, a more informed atmosphere is created in which to debate the crucial issue of loans *versus* grants.

Such a financial arrangement would have a further incidental but by no means minor advantage. It would serve to reform and correct the existing state of affairs in which the universities have no incentive either to ascertain the costs of each of the variety of courses they offer or to ponder ways and means of economising on these costs. Once the universities come to depend on their fees to cover the whole of their teaching expenses, and are thereby brought into competition with one another, they can hardly continue to manifest the present lack of concern.[8]

Turning to the Loans/Grants debate, I consider the case in equity first, following which the question of efficiency will be examined. Over the last few years, however, there have been occasional articles and discussions setting out some of the pros-and-cons of a loans system. We may begin, therefore, by a brief appraisal of some of the more common objections.

Perhaps the most fanciful of these is the allegation that loans discriminate against the marital prospects of the woman student, since by incurring debt—"mortgaging her future"— she brings a "negative dowry" to the marriage. Even in this age of unbridled ambition I find it hard to picture any one of the young people I know—male or female, for that matter— judiciously crossing out one or more names on a short list in recognition of a so-called negative dowry. But this is by the way. For, in fact, the successful woman student who borrows to pay for her university education does not bring a negative dowry to her nuptial partner but a positive dowry. A university training, quite apart from the status and other inherent advantages it confers, does enhance one's value on the market. Under the proposed loan scheme, at least, no student would be inclined to borrow for his education unless he was reasonably confident that the value of the additional advantages exceeded the cost of the loan. It might have made more sense to claim instead that the loan scheme would result in a negative incentive to bear children until a good part of the loan was repaid, or until the graduate was earning more—no bad thing in itself. But if the difference in the annual earnings as between the university-trained and the untrained woman were no less than the annual payments, in the early years of employment this negative incentive to bear children would be no greater for the university trained woman than for the untrained woman—which is, or ought to be, the issue in equity.

Admittedly, the withdrawal of a free good (higher education) will not be welcomed by the student, male or female. But before judging whether the removal of a clear advantage to one group —in particular that currently enjoyed by the freely educated woman graduate over the woman without university education—is socially equitable, it must first be established that the granting of this advantage was equitable in the first place. As for a system which, like the present, allows some women to take up scarce university places (involving about £5,000 of resources over a three-year period) only to settle down afterwards to rear a family, it is, on the face of it, neither fair nor efficient. If the "negative dowry" of a loans system prevents this happening, it clearly redounds to the credit of the loans system.

A more specious defence of the existing system is that in the long run—and provided the graduate does not emigrate—it pays for itself. Higher education raises the earning power of the beneficiaries so enabling the government to recoup its outlays from their consequently higher tax payments. I do not know if anyone has troubled to calculate how much additional tax revenue the government collects as a result of its expenditure on higher education. But whatever the sums calculated they would be relevant *only* if every other borrower of public funds—or borrower of private funds, for that matter—were allowed to treat such loans as *free grants* in consideration of their investing the funds profitably and thereby raising their tax liability. I can think of no one who would refuse a sum of £5,000 or so on these terms. The ordinary citizen who borrows a capital sum to improve his material prospects—whether to invest in a durable good such as a house, or in a capital asset, or in any equipment that raises the value of his services to society—has both to repay the sum with interest and to pay additional taxes on any subsequent rise in his earnings. In fact, irrespective of how his education is financed—whether from a grant of public funds, from private funds, or from loans—the higher earnings of the graduate must certainly raise his tax liability. By switching to a loans system, however, not only is the taxpayer relieved but, in respect of his access to investible funds, *the student is now treated on a par with any other citizen.*

Not surprisingly, it is also contended that the loan system would be harder on the poor student who would have to borrow than on the rich student who would receive the sum as a gift from his parents or guardians. So long as our society tolerates inequalities of income the children of the richer members will continue to enjoy some advantages over the children of the poorer members. And if we had thought to remove this particular inequity by a grants system we seem to have overlooked *the far greater inequity that has resulted.*

The grants system as it currently operates in Britiain is manifestly regressive. Only about a quarter of the student population come from working-class families. The remainder are from lower or upper middle-class families. This would be bad enough if the bulk of the taxes collected by the government came from the higher income groups. But today, the greater part of the public revenues is obtained from the taxation of families in the lower income brackets.[9] Ironically, this typically socialist scheme has produced a situation (already depicted by Colin Clark) in which *the working classes are effectively financing a predominantly middle-class student population.* On a more fundamental plane, however, there are gross inequities in the meritocracy towards which affluent societies are now moving in response to the democratic ideal of "equality of opportunity".

So long as differences in inherited wealth are the chief causes of large differences in material comfort, then it seems plausible to believe that increasing equality of opportunity tends to equalise individual well-being. With rising standards of material comfort for the bulk of the population, and with inherited wealth being relegated gradually to a minor source of differential earnings—the result partly of heavy taxation but, more importantly, of the spread of technology and the consequent trend of aspiration towards expertise and status rather than to mere claims to wealth—the remaining inequalities from inherited wealth become more tolerable. At the same time, however, the forces released by the greater equalities of opportunity are bringing us face to face with a more basic and less tractable form of inherited inequalities. We are moving into a world in which men born into talent will be no less fortunate than were men, before the War, born into wealth—perhaps more fortunate. For the security and status conferred by the training of natural talents cannot so easily be lost by a sudden change of economic climate or expropriated by a new political régime.

But is the man who happens to be born into talent inherently any more deserving of the material rewards of this world than the man who happens to be born into money? Indeed, considerations of justice would suggest that talented people receive smaller earnings than ordinary mortals to offset in some measure their higher status which, in the meritocracy, contributes to their greater satisfaction. One might go further. If economic considerations were less dominant, it would be clearly more equitable to use whatever funds were available for higher education primarily in improving the minds and the material prospects of the less talented members of the community. For the just society is one that acts always to counter the arbitrary distribution of inherited advantages whatever form they take, so contributing towards greater equality of earnings and status.

Yet considerations of economic efficiency are today unquestionably dominant. In a society able to direct only limited resources into higher education and, in pursuit of economic efficiency, allocating these resources among the more promising talents, genetical good fortune becomes compounded by deliberate policy. Indeed, the inequity goes further. For the rest of the community is compelled to finance from their own earnings the vocational training of the privileged group, so procuring for its members far higher earnings and status than the tax-payers will ever enjoy.

If we have to pursue economic efficiency, the change to a loans system at least removes the social anomaly whereby the community as a whole is made to finance its privileged student group—in particular when it so happens that the student body as a whole is wealthier than taxpayers as a whole.

Without wishing myself to subscribe in any way to the cult of efficiency, I shall accept it as one of the current objectives of modern society, and ask simply whether the existing grants system realises this objective better than a pricing system for higher education based on full-cost fees with loans supplanting grants where necessary.

It cannot be too often stressed that the introduction of an appropriate pricing mechanism to deal with an economic problem is not to be thought of as substituting an economic solution for a political one. The present system of direct grants is no more than one means of realising desirable social ends. The use of a price system is but another means of doing so, though one with a general presumption in its favour resting on the virtues commonly associated with a well-functioning competitive market—cheapness, self-regulation, and allocative merit. The actual solution reached by either means is to be judged in the last resort, however, by reference to the political ends pursued by society. Yet these political ends in respect of higher education have been described only in vaguely beneficent terms. One hears about the "enrichment of society" or (in equally vague economic terms) about "the needs of industry" with occasional references, perhaps, to graduate ratios in the U.S.A. or the U.S.S.R. True, the view I would suggest, that society adopt some "optimal" amount and composition of higher education, makes no contribution to a definition of social ends. In fact, it borders on the tautologous. But the notion of an optimum does direct attention to the possibility of formulating, in lieu of a precise statement of social ends, some widely acceptable criterion of efficiency and one by which the present system and the proposed system may be judged.

At all events, in the absence of such a criterion, the present guide-lines will appear to many as arbitrary and lacking the sanction of any self-evident and rational criterion. For the kind of thinking that lends support to the prevailing system appears to draw its inspiration mainly from such concepts as the existence of a latent "Pool of Ability" and, as its corollary, the fear of "Waste to the Nation" in not fully harnessing this potential. These are ideas made popular by the Robbins Report of 1963. That the student population before the War was about 50,000 compared with around 400,000 in higher education today (of which over 200,000 are in universities) is accepted as clear evidence not only of social advance, but of economic wisdom—of a vital contribution to the economic potential of this country.[10]

The weakness of this aspirational approach to the economic problem of higher education is easily exposed when its logic is pushed a little further. While success in scoring two A-levels may be taken as a rough index of ability to benefit from a university education, surely it is not being argued that other school-leavers could not also benefit if not from the existing curricula of our universities at least from two or three years of full-time higher education of some other sort, whether in a technical subject or in the liberal arts. Why, then, is this *wider* pool of ability not also tapped in the interest of the nation? Surely there is evidence of immense waste here?

The tentative answer to this leading question, that it would not "pay"—and clearly no other answer would be socially acceptable—provides us with the lever needed to prise off the pseudo-rationale of the existing system. For we can no longer evade the question: How do we know that higher education for the present student body does pay? Or, more exactly, how can we know that the existing size and composition of the student body are optimal? If we have to invoke economic criteria to exclude the majority of young people from freely enjoying the advantages of a full-time higher education suitable to their abilities, we cannot with any pretence at equity refuse to apply such criteria also to assessing the efficiency of a system that is used to admit the existing body of students.

An economic criterion for additional investment in education, like the criterion for investment in any other yielding asset, may take either of two forms.[11] A calculated excess of benefits over costs is required—benefits being the present value of a future stream of differential advantages expected from higher education, costs being the present value of the output the student could have produced during his university years had he, instead, entered the labour force. Alternatively, it is required that the rate of return arising from the benefits of higher education be greater than the rate of return yielded by alternative (say, industrial) outlets for current saving. Should any supporter of the existing system reject this standard criterion, economic assessment of the present methods of selection is still possible once he makes explicit the criterion by which he justifies the exclusion of the bulk of school-leavers from the benefits of full-time higher education. In the meantime, I shall adopt the latter form of the common criterion since we already have some quantitative estimates in this form.

Reforming the System

There are three ways, however, in which the value of the benefits may be calculated. In order of sophistication (and of increasing difficulty) the benefits will entail *(1)* only the competitive market value of the education as measured by reference to the excess gross earnings of the graduate; *(2)* the (pre-tax) net advantages of higher education as reckoned by the candidate himself; or *(3)* the net advantages to society at large of the student's higher education. Under certain conditions all three estimates of benefits would give identical results. But for thoroughness (and also because some of those opposing the employment of economic rationale in matters of education have a propensity to invoke discrepancies between social and market values in defence of the *status quo*), I shall set myself the task of revealing economic waste or misallocation arising from the existing system using, in turn, each of these three methods for estimating benefits.

1. As indicated, the quantitative estimates that are available measure benefits by reference only to the expected earnings of the beneficiaries themselves. On this method the rate of return on higher education appears to be not greater than $6\frac{1}{2}\%$.[12] If we take the gross yield of relatively safe industrial investment to be between 10% and 12%—a conservative estimate—we must conclude there is over-investment in higher education. On this measure of benefits then there is a *prima facie* case for directing investible resources away from education and into industry.[13]

2. The market value of the benefits of higher education reckoned as their differential gross earnings may differ from the value set on them by the beneficiary himself. For one thing, he may be far from indifferent to the two paths ahead—spending his first three years after leaving school at a university, or spending those years instead in full-time employment (even if there are no pecuniary advantages whatever accruing to higher education). For another, the intellectual disciplines learned and the professional status acquired are generally regarded, albeit in varying degrees, as advantages in themselves. They may in some cases more than compensate for a rate of return lower than that obtainable by investing the outlay instead in some commercial enterprise. Yet bringing these non-pecuniary advantages into the calculus does not reduce the likelihood of there being *substantial misallocation* under the present grants system.

First, there is a proportion of the candidates who are admitted to higher education who would not have elected to apply for it unless it were provided free—certainly not if students, or their families, were expected to pay full costs from their own or borrowed funds. Whether the students in this group are conscientious workers or whether they are content to drift along and settle for a third-class or pass degree, and whatever the future earnings they anticipate, there is no net advantage, on their *own* evaluation, from investing resources in their education. They would not use their own funds, or borrow at the market rate, for the purpose of obtaining a higher education—though of course, they are content enough to receive it as a free gift from the taxpayer.

No one has estimated how large this group is. But I should be surprised if it were less than a quarter of the wider student body or, in round numbers, less than 100,000. On the criterion adopted, their education involves a waste of the country's scarce economic resources. On the other hand, among the several thousand eligible candidates each year who (because of the places taken up by some of the former group) cannot be admitted to the study of the social sciences or of medicine there will be, under the present system, a proportion excluded, the members of which are prepared to pay the full costs of their education, borrowing the money if necessary.

More important yet, there may well be large numbers of school-leavers who at present go straight into the labour force but who if they cannot fully avail themselves of a university education, would be able in their own estimation to profit from two or more years of full-time further education, technical or liberal. The advantage would be enough to make it worth their while paying full costs provided that loans were made available. At present insufficient provision is made for this group which can only hope for part-time technical instruction or extra-mural lectures. Members of this group have no option but to join the labour force and to contribute by their earnings to widen the gap between themselves and the intellectually privileged. Under a loan system, the opportunity to enhance its status and material prospects would be extended to this large group of young people also. A loan scheme would therefore act *to close the rift, encouraged by the present system, between an educated élite and the rest of society.*

Moreover, in response to this new demand from school leavers without the requisite university qualifications, one could anticipate a greater diversity of institutions offering a wide variety of technical and liberal subjects. Of those who go on to these new institutions for two or more years, some proportion will be able later to provide satisfactory evidence of capacity to benefit from university education and, if necessary, will be able to borrow funds to do so. A loan system not only provides a means of moving away from élitist tendencies inherent in the existing grants system, it also promotes educational mobility.

3. We must, finally, take account of the possible difference between the annual earnings of a graduate, which he himself enjoys, and his annual value to society. On this potential source of discrepancy there are five things to be said.

First, that it is commonly misunderstood. And since much of the confusion has arisen from a misunderstanding of the relevant economics, I can see nothing for it but to risk exposing the interested reader with an aversion to economics to some slight tedium in the next two or three paragraphs—which are, however, crucial to the main argument.

On this oft-mooted discrepancy between market and social value the point to bear in mind is that an ideal allocation of the economy's resources endowment does *not* require that the members of each distinct group of productive agents—different kinds of labour and capital—be paid the full value of what they add to the national product. In fact, since members of these different groups necessarily cooperate in the production of any good, the contribution made by those of any one group cannot be separated from those of the other cooperating groups. Indeed, the members of any one group could claim the whole of the output jointly produced on the argument that if they withdrew their services the other groups could not produce any of it. The problem of sharing the output among the cooperating groups is, however, solved easily enough in the market. In particular, a competitive economy tends to produce a workable solution. Irrespective of their allocation in different occupations, the same earnings, received by (equally efficient) members of any one group, are equal to their *marginal* value—the difference made to the total earnings of the group by an additional member. And, as a basic economic proposition has it, this marginal value (and consequently the pay of all members) eventually diminishes as the numbers in the group grow relative to those in other groups.

It is this reduction in the pay of all the *intra*-marginal members of any group consequent upon an increase in their numbers that clearly constitutes a gain, or transfer payment, to the rest of society. Yet these transfer payments, which necessarily accompany changes in the relative size of the various cooperating groups, are perfectly consistent with a necessary condition of all ideal allocations. This requires only that the *marginal* value of each group of productive agents be the same in all occupations. More specifically, if (because of diminishing marginal value) an increase in the numbers of Engineering graduates adds more to the value of the national product than they receive as earnings, the implied transfer of product to the rest of society is quite consistent with this ideal marginal condition being met. One cannot infer from this familiar economic phenomenon any discrepancy between his market earnings and the engineer's marginal value to society; and there is no warrant on this account for raising the pay of engineers or increasing their numbers further.

This ideal marginal condition may not be met if there are barriers to competition or if, even with perfect competition, the marginal earnings of any group take no account of incidental services (or disservices) produced. If the personal appearance and conversation of Arts graduates were such as to give particular pleasure to people, their marginal value to society would exceed the market value of their direct services. An ideal allocation of resources would require that more Arts graduates be produced than would emerge in a competitive full-cost educational system.

Second, there can be no general presumption of significant differences between the existing earnings and marginal value of the services of graduates in industry. It is an accepted convention in economics that the burden of proof lies with those who allege that there are such differences. No specific instances appear to have been investigated—which is not surprising, as those who are quick to point to differences between market and social valuation in defence of economically arbitrary schemes (*e.g.* the existing educational system) have usually misunderstood the allocative argument discussed above.

Third, economic research may yet disclose significant discrepancies between graduate incomes and the marginal value of their services to society in a number of vocations. But such disclosures do not of themselves strengthen the case for *existing methods* of selecting university entrants. The discovery of such discrepancies may reveal the existing system to be more arbitrary, rather than less, when compared with the results of some ideal size and composition of the student body.

Fourth, and what is more to the purpose, the incidence of such discrepancies does not in any way vitiate the effectiveness of using the price system as a means of meeting an agreed economic criterion. Once such discrepancies become the subject of economic investigation (rather than political rhetoric) they are taken out of the realm of private speculation, which forms the basis of informal though politically biased judgments. The corrections that need to be made to the market outcome can then be made effective in a systematic and quantitative manner.

Fifth, it is simpler, more accurate, and more discriminating, to bring about any necessary adjustments to the market outcome by operating directly on the prices of the end-products of higher education than by the indirect method of attempting adjustments at the student-intake stage—whether by financial incentives (or disincentives), by direct control of numbers, or by exhortation.

It is simpler because it obviates the need for and expense of continual calculations. If, for example, it were established that the earnings of Scientists as a whole, though equal to their market value, were below their marginal value to society by an average of some £500 per annum, there would be a *prima facie* case for increasing the country's stock of Scientists until this discrepancy vanished. The method of direct approach, which entails a transfer of some £500 per annum to Scientists, simultaneously corrects the discrepancy and provides the exact incentive. The indirect method, if we ignore popular exhortation and appeals to patriotism, must depend upon making science courses more attractive by offering them below cost and/or offering loans to science students on cheaper-than-market terms. The difficulty arises in having to make estimates of the likely response of entrant numbers to combinations of the differential advantages offered to science course students.

It is more accurate because if £500 is the exact measure of the discrepancy between the social and market value of the Scientists' annual earnings, once this sum is added to their market earnings no further intervention is called for. The stock of Scientists that the market tends now to realise can be wholly justified on our adopted criterion. The indirect method, though it cannot do better than this, can do worse; indeed it is likely to.

Economists' estimates of response coefficients—whether they refer to production, consumption, or trade—are notoriously unreliable.

Lastly, the direct method is more discriminating because the same university training may lead to a variety of occupations while the discrepancies that require correction may be found in only one or two of these occupations. If for any reason it was commonly accepted that the market earnings of Teachers of English Literature or History were below their marginal value to society,[14] either throughout the country or in special areas, the direct method would pay the appropriate subsidy to all Teachers of English Literature or History, or to those only in the special areas. It would not, as would the indirect method, provide financial inducements to potential housewives, journalists, civil servants, businessmen or playboys who, for any reason or inclination, chose to read for a degree in English literature or history.

Of course this allegation of the social benefit of higher education exceeding graduate earnings may be made quite general: that Society benefits from the more stimulating environment that is a product of all higher education.[15] This in itself is a doubtful proposition: higher education is largely vocational. Today it scarcely guarantees literacy, much less learning or wit. It is doubtful also if, apart from those having intellectual pretensions, many really believe this. But if many did, it would imply only that the uncorrected market solution was one producing too few graduates—which certainly does *not* imply that the existing grants system produces the ideal number. Indeed, if people are convinced that indirect benefits flow from the enriched personalities of graduate students generally, it must mean that they place some value on such benefits. The necessary correction is then easy to make. Once this incidental value per student is ascertained, this sum is to be paid out as a direct subsidy to each graduate student, leaving total student numbers to adjust themselves to their resulting "true" social value—market value plus social premium.

If the preceding arguments have been assimilated the most common objection to a loan scheme—that it acts to discourage higher education—calls for little additional comment. A switch-over to a system in which students have to pay full fees, borrow-ing if necessary, will undeniably reduce the attractiveness of a university education as compared with a scheme which offers higher education free. But if society were concerned to make higher education yet more attractive, it could be done in many obvious ways: it might, for example, promise a new Jaguar free to every graduate student. Efficiency is not, however, always coterminous with expansion. Having proposed a mechanism whose operation can be justified by reference to *the broad social aim* of economic efficiency, any resulting reduction of the student population must be deemed consistent with that aim.

This much, I think, opponents of a full-cost loan scheme can be made to concede. What apparently they cannot stomach is the further implication of the scheme: that the resulting per-centage reduction of students of working-class origin is likely to be higher than the overall percentage reduction. This expected consequence is held to be undesirable in itself and to run coun-ter to current democratic trends. Higher education is envisaged as a ladder of opportunity extended to the nether regions in-habited by working-class denizens, enabling some of the more talented among them to climb upwards towards the sunlit pastures of middle-class professionalism. The more of these ladders of opportunity the better. But this belief in the social merit of providing working-class children with the means of escape from a working-class environment is surely a peculiarly middle-class intellectual's view of the aspirations of the working class. Intellectuals are a good deal less envied than they seem to imagine.

In any event the proportion of working-class children—however one defines that category in a society where most people think of themselves as "middle-class"—that make the transition to higher income and status via a university training is very small, barely 2%. If as much as one-quarter of them opted out of the university under a loans scheme the resulting change in the fortunes of the working class—1.5% of working-class children at universities instead of 2%—would hardly be such as to warrant pangs of conscience.

I must admit, nonetheless, that this plea for social perspective springs from a personal judgment about the relative importance of this loss to society, and to the working class. But what of the question of principle? Suppose it were universally agreed that although a university education is a good thing in itself it becomes a specially good thing when imbibed by youths of working-class origin. So long as the number of university places are as limited as they will be in the foreseeable future, we can "push" the working-class student only at the expense of the other students. But what is the "ideal" proportion of working-class students? Clearly, economic criteria cannot help us here. I should ask those who favour greater working-class "representation" in the university to disclose the formula they employ to determine this just proportion, and also the social rationale, if any, of the formula. It would be a coincidence if they all agreed, and a greater coincidence yet if the *existing system* had after all managed to produce just the right proportion.

But even the prospect of provisional agreement on some "ideal" (or some "reasonable") proportion of working-class representation in the universities hardly clinches the matter for a grants system. It is necessary to provide reasons for believing that a grants system making provision for the "ideal" $x\%$ working-class representation offsets all the advantages shown to be associated not merely with a loans scheme *per se*, but with one which—in deference to a widely accepted social aim for greater working-class representation—could be supplemented in one of several ways so as to make provision also for $x\%$ working-class students.[16]

Turning from the issue of working-class students, I should add that I see no strong objection to supplementing the loans scheme with *special grants for deserving cases*. Since ideas of what constitutes "a deserving case" are likely to vary widely, it would be preferable to allow the universities to offer scholarships and other prizes on their own conditions and from their endowment revenues rather than to leave the choice of deserving cases ultimately to the political process by paying for them from public funds.

Finally, and in connection with the question of efficiency at least, it is not hard to reveal that the so-called graduate tax scheme favoured by some economists[17] (a scheme whereby the university graduate pays some proportion of his earnings as an additional tax for the whole or greater part of his working life), though superior to the existing grants scheme, is distinctly inferior to a full-cost loans scheme.

Such a graduate tax scheme involves setting up public machinery for collecting these additional taxes; whereas the loans scheme can be operated by the present banking system with the initial encouragement of the central government. The finance for higher education under a loans scheme is therefore provided almost wholly out of private funds in contrast to the graduate tax scheme which, although it may become partly self-financing, would continue to require public funds. Again, under a loans scheme emigration poses no particular problem, though obviously there can be a number of dishonest students who may hope to escape the long arm of the law by leaving the country. Certainly there would be no call for control on the graduate's movements, and no call for special arrangements between this country and others, principally the U.S., to which graduate students are likely to emigrate.

Far more important, however, is the fact that the proposed graduate tax scheme forgoes all the allocative merits of the loan scheme. This additional tax (calculated as a percentage of the graduate's income, or as a percentage of the differential earnings attributable to his university education) is to be determined, presumably, by what seems "reasonable"; in other words, arbitrarily. Whatever the initial agreement on some formula for arriving at this percentage (which apparently is to vary as between one type of student and another, and as between male and female), in an economic climate of creeping inflation it would almost certainly become very soon the subject of perpetual political controversy.

I do not dismiss the possibility of the occasional student overestimating his abilities, although there will be an obvious incentive under a loans scheme, in contrast to the existing system, for both him and the lender to assess his chances carefully in advance. A failure to take a degree—the probability of which is not high by current university standards, and likely to be lower still under a full-cost loan system—may well place a financial burden on the hapless student notwithstanding his having presumably received some benefit from his three- or four-year sojourn at an institute of higher learning. To allow such people an automatic waiver of their obligations would open the loans scheme to abuse and inevitably reduce the incentives for the borrowing student to make the most of his time at the university. Such contingencies could, however, be met in several ways. One would be to set up a semi-government agency which, in consultation with the university authorities, could agree to meet some portion of the loan, in special cases the whole of it, along with conditions relating to his future earnings. Without going into detail, we can agree that there can be, and should be, ancillary schemes to avoid hardships of this sort in cases of genuine miscalculation.

Equality v. the Intellectual Élite

There is, in addition to these more enduring advantages of a full-cost fee system, another arising from a more recent social phenomenon. There can be many opinions on the chief causes of student unrest, but one need not analyse them all before proposing remedies.

Certainly, the increased dependence of the universities on public funds has provided an air of specious legitimacy to student demands for more "participation" and control. The general impression, shared by the public and academics as well as students, is that the universities, being financed by the public purse, are *de facto* public property. The affairs of the university are therefore as much the business of the students who are its customers, so to speak, as they are the business of the staff hired to serve in them. Both student and staff are seen, through this distorted vision, to be equally vulnerable—both apparently being dependent on public funds—and the question of apportioning authority between senate, staff, and students seems a proper subject of debate, negotiation, and ultimately of struggle. Any successful defiance of the university authorities by sheer physical pressure of student numbers acts on them like a heady draught. And since agreements, open or tacit, are known to be grounded in expediency rather than in mutually accepted procedures, they are regarded by all as temporary only. An atmosphere grows in which it seems that virtually anything can happen, with publicity always close at hand. In the circumstances, the activities of a faction of extremists, ready to take the initiative at a tactical moment, exercises an immoderate influence on the student body.

This question of students' rights along with the occasional rowdyism and incipient violence will, I believe, resolve itself once the universities take their place in society as self-supporting and independent institutions, their full costs of research and teaching covered by fees supplemented by their endowment income. As a private corporate body each university will be free to use its revenues as it wishes and without requiring the consent of any public authority. It will make its own rules for regulating the behaviour both of the staff it hires and of the students it chooses to admit.

The legal position at least will be incontestable. The university premises are private property. No part of them can be used by any group without explicit authorisation. Alternatively, the university can hire out its rooms for students' extra-curricular activity on its own terms. Student privileges are those laid down in the regulations of the university, no more, no less. If a student finds them onerous, he is not entitled to break them: he is entitled only to go elsewhere. However, once the second proposal is adopted and students are obliged to pay fees from their own resources, with access to loans if necessary, calls by the militants for student solidarity, for "strikes", sit-ins, or sit-outs, will have less appeal. Paying something like £1,500 a year on tuition and maintenance costs will provide them with a strong incentive to limit their youthful excesses.[18] In any case, if they do waste money it will not be the tax-payers, it will be their own.

To conclude, the independence of our British universities can be completely restored, and without additional cost to the Exchequer, simply by allowing them to charge fees that cover their expenditures. This would cost the country no more than it is currently paying. For the Treasury would now use the funds, once disposed of by the U.G.C., to pay subsidies on behalf of the individual students (directly or through the local authorities)—rather than to pay them as lump sums direct to the universities. The universities would then be seen as financially solvent and as responding to the demand for university places irrespective of whether this demand is financed from public or private moneys.

This brings us to the second proposal. If the resources available for higher education are limited (and they are), then it is surely *wrong* that only the members of an "intellectual *élite*" be provided by the rest of the community with the means of raising further their status and earnings, so widening the gap between themselves and the less fortunate members of society. Since the ideal of extending appropriate educational opportunities to all young people is economically impracticable, the only tolerable and viable solution is that of making higher education of some sort available to all at its cost, along with a system of loans for all bona fide students unable to meet the costs out of their current resources.

True, only in a completely equalitarian society would the outcome be unexceptionable. While appreciable differences in wealth persist the real sacrifice in buying any asset, including a university education, is smaller for rich families than for poor ones. But the greater real sacrifice of the poor in buying higher education, which sacrifice does however bring its reward, is far less inequitable than *a system under which the unprivileged working class is in effect compelled to finance the education of the well-off majority of students.*

In addition to the case in equity the arguments for efficiency in the use of our resources tell strongly against the existing system with its arbitrary and non-economic methods of student selection.

We certainly do not have to reject a loans scheme for fear, simply, of inflicting hardship on unsuccessful students, or of reducing the ratio of working-class students. Particular safeguards can be tacked on to the main scheme without surrender of the essential allocative mechanism of the full-cost loan system.

But if we do reject the full-cost loan system, we should be quite clear that we are forgoing the opportunity of using an inexpensive self-regulating mechanism; one which is able simultaneously to select the total number of students in higher education and to allocate this number among the variety of courses being offered; one which will tend to produce results that accord with comprehensive and widely accepted economic criteria.

Remaining with the existing grants system we choose in effect to remain eyeless in Gaza.

A Postscript

I would like to avail myself of the opportunity to strengthen a couple of weak joints in the structure of the main argument which have been kindly brought to my attention by friends and colleagues.[19]

The first has reference to the calculations of the full cost of university education. I had opted for including the full salaries of teaching staff in the costs of higher education on the grounds that any time spent in writing papers for publication adds to the value of the university teacher, and that the knowledge he thereby contributes to his subject is ultimately passed on to students. This is largely true, but on second thoughts I recognise that it is not, strictly speaking, an economic argument.

Why do highly trained men become university dons in Britain when for many of them opportunities elsewhere appear much more lucrative? One answer is that in a university they will have time enough to engage *(a)* in research that further enhances their reputation and market value, and/or *(b)* consultation work which is highly regarded and highly rewarded. Unless the university afforded them the leisure to engage in these pursuits it would be unable to buy the teaching services of skilled, and often gifted, individuals at government-determined rates of pay. I doubt whether any senior member of a reputable university would agree—given the existing range of opportunities at home and abroad—to devote his full time to teaching at an unchanged salary. So long as the preference among the more intellectually active dons is for using more of their time for research and writing rather than for teaching, their salaries can be regarded as the supply price necessary to provide the current level of teaching. Raise the teaching load of dons and, unless the salary scale is raised, some of the more intellectually active will move out of British universities. Lower the teaching load, and you can attract more dons at the present salary scale. In short, then, although some qualification and elaboration may permit a more precise statement to be made, it accords with the economic facts of life to regard the salaries of university dons, at least those of the senior and more distinguished dons, as the costs of teaching alone.[20]

The second point concerns the question of equity. I alleged that under the existing grants scheme the working classes were, on balance, being taxed in order to provide free education for the children of middle- and upper-class families. I provided no statistics to support this allegation and rested my case on the existing tax structure. This, I admit, does not constitute a proof of my allegation. A proof would require that the tax revenue for the £250 millions or so spent on higher education be traced back to the tax-paying groups. We must be in a position to say, "of this increment of tax of £250 million, needed for higher education, £200 million was raised from the working-class group. . . ." But in a single integrated budget it is not possible to attribute revenues collected from particular groups to particular expenditures. If we were today to reduce public expenditure on, say, higher education, the taxes to be reduced or abolished could be distributed among the taxpayers in any way the government determined.

Nevertheless, we can reason as follows once definitions of "working-class" and "middle-class" have been settled. If working-class families are, say, three times as numerous as middle-class families, and if middle-class students are three times as numerous as working-class students, then—in order for the middle-class family to pay no less on the average than the working-class family for each pound's worth of educational benefit—the middle-class family would have to pay, on the average, about nine times the increment of tax paid by the average working-class family. This seems to me a highly unlikely outcome.

But we need not stop here. In order for the marginal tax per family paid for a given pound's worth of higher education to be *proportional* to the gross earnings, the middle-class families should on the average pay a marginal tax that is $9R$ times the average tax paid by working-class families—R being the ratio of average middle-class family income to average working-class family income. If this ratio is 3, the increment of aggregate tax would then require middle-class families to contribute 27 times as much as the incremental tax paid by the average working-class family. Obviously a *progressive* tax would require the average middle-class family to contribute *more* than 27 times as much as the average working-class family. If 9 times as much marginal tax is unlikely, more than 27 times as much is inconceivable.

Now, so long as one cannot attribute a part of the revenues collected in any year, from all taxpayers together, to a particular item of public expenditure, one cannot assess the distribution of the burden of financing higher education alone. For all that, it is meaningful to argue that, contrary to expectations, the scheme has been inequitable and "regressive". For there was a time when the nation had the option of financing higher education, or more of such education, by full-cost fees paid directly by predominantly middle-class families, wanting to buy education for their children, as an alternative to financing it by additional taxation. It was apparently believed (on what evidence?) that the latter alternative was the more *equitable* and *progressive* one, one extending educational opportunities to the underprivileged. Whereas if it were possible to go back and determine in each period just how the *increment* of public revenue necessary to meet an augmented public expenditure (augmented, that is, to include provision for more university education), was raised, one could show, in principle, that the reverse was true.

The question can, then, be meaningful without there being much hope of answering it by recourse to the facts. Hence the usefulness of hypothetical calculations such as those above in serving to overcome the strong political (or, rather, ideological) objections to the proposals for a change-over to private finance of higher education.

2. *The Spillover Enemy*

"Greedy Men, abetted by a complacent Government, are prowling over Britain and devastating it," wrote Mr Anthony Crosland seven years ago in a bitter and comprehensive onslaught on the erosion of the British scene, town and country. So when the Prime Minister made him Secretary of State for Local Government and Regional Planning in the recent shuffle Mr Crosland could—and indeed did—check back on his book "The Conservative Enemy" to find, gratifyingly, that he had himself proposed just such a Ministry to combat the neglect of years.

His name for it was the Ministry of Town and Country Planning, but its functions were identical with those he now has: to coordinate transport, housing, location of employment and development planning. But there are snags. His new department does not take over the executive powers of the Ministries of Housing and Transport. It simply acts as their overlord and Ministers with such vaguely defined federal powers have often come to grief for lack of effective authority.

But if Mr Crosland can really get to grips with his new office and if his machine can really make an impression on Britain, what sort of direction will he push in? "Although in this country we have had one of the slowest rates of economic growth in the world even the growth we have had has been achieved at an appalling cost in terms of the environment.

"I would like to redress this. For instance, the country does still slope down from the north to the south to an unhealthy degree. We have had too much laissez-faire over building in the past. I'm preservationist by instinct. But don't put me down as an aesthete who is only interested in preserving old buildings."

Interview in The Sunday Times *(London)*

If men really believed they controlled their destiny, they would not talk of what the future would bring: instead they would debate the kind of future they wanted. Quiet skies, clean air, traffic-free towns, an unspoiled countryside are certainly technically feasible. We could have the lot if we wanted them in earnest—and survive comfortably withal. What, then, prevents a major political party taking seriously a programme designed to create for us all "a green and pleasant land"?

The short answer is the power of myth over mind. In his novel *Chance*, Joseph Conrad describes how the clue to the character of an age can often be found in a single word to which the age pays tribute. In the inter-War period, the word was *thrift*. Such was its hold on the imagination that, at a time of widespread depression and unemployment, people were being exhorted by Ministers to spend less in order to save the country. Today the magic word is *growth*, and it is an article of faith in the Establishment that faster economic growth is the sovereign cure for all known forms of social and economic ills. It is enough merely to hint that a proposed measure favours growth to ensure a respectful silence at any Committee meeting. Nothing, save perhaps "export performance", can vie with it in power to intimidate the innocent citizen.

The era has thrown up another word, *challenge*, a companion piece to *growth*. Indeed, the Common Market was floated into public favour largely on a wave of "challenges" that rolled over all specific objections and dissolved itself in streams of froth about "dynamic" long-run advantages. However, when *challenge* is used together with *growth* it can be depended upon as surely as a two-headed coin. While *growth* is used to sanctify the claims of the technocrats, *challenge* pulls the carpet from under the feet of the opposition. This technique, often displayed in television or radio debates, is illustrated by the following dialogue:

TECHNOCRAT: The growth of automation offers enormous opportunities for increased leisure, enjoyment, education....

PHILOSOPHER: But work is not pure disutility. Through work people find the solace of companionship. Even a routine job provides a sense of security and belonging. Again, a large number of people do find interest in the tasks set them by industry. And surely all men like to feel that their work matters to society; that they are needed. . . .

TECHNOCRAT *(quietly but firmly)* : Ah, but man must adapt himself to face the challenge which automation poses.

And there you have it! The future is apparently pre-empted: and willy-nilly we must be moulded to fit in. But by a lucky coincidence it is all for the best, provided always that we "move with the times", wean ourselves from green fields and uncluttered skies, and learn to love the computer.

The technocrat as "con-man" is, moreover, aided and abetted by the ad-man, who creates unwittingly, but none the less unerringly, a world of growth-spun fantasies. The ad-man is dedicated to fostering discontent in the hearts of men. By tapping repeatedly at their greeds, anxieties, envies, lusts, he seeks to bring their expenditure into line with industry's rising output of consumer gadgetry. And while the daily promptings of the ad-man impel them slowly to the belief that the things that really matter in life are the things that money can buy, they will hardly be noticing that the environment in which they live is becoming submerged in a sea of floating sewage. But let us look at another man's predictions.

Among the more gloomy forecasts for 1983 made recently by Dr Mark Abrams were a population increase of some 5 million, nearly 50% more cars, and uninterrupted aircraft noise. He was incidentally addressing himself to the Town and Country Planning Association. One might infer from this circumstance that the proper procedure was first to predict the worst, and then to make ample provision to accommodate it. Certainly, there was very little said there about *choice* over the future. Not that there is in any case much incentive for any respectable forward-looker to choose a pleasanter future rather than an uglier one when choice of the former, he can be sure, would be ranked below the latter by any index of Gross National Product. This index, as economists know, is an artless though effective device which can be counted on to register some economic gain for almost any country from one year to the next. For the principle employed is simply that of totting up the values of all man-made goods while assiduously ignoring all the man-made bads that are produced simultaneously. These bads (or "spillovers" as they are commonly called) include development blight, the erosion of the countryside, the accumulation of oil and sewage on our coasts, contamination of lakes and rivers, air pollution, traffic congestion, and shrieking aircraft.[1] Indeed, it is to these spillovers that our growth-minded political leaders should look for really gratifying examples of post-war growth.

To the economist, however, they pose a particular problem because the nature of a spillover effect—noise, fume, pollution, and the like—makes it difficult to fit them into a decentralised price system. When these noxious by-products of industry or of industrial goods are thrown off, segments of the public are constrained to absorb them and for the most part without compensation. A topical example is air travel which produces services for the passengers while simultaneously producing prodigious dis-services, aircraft noise, for large numbers of the population. And it is fallacious to assert that man has chosen air travel despite the noise nuisance simply because people have never had any critical choice in the matter. In weighing up the pros and cons of an air journey the citizen considers only the advantages of air travel as compared with fares. He can do nothing about the noise to which he resigns himself, accepting it as a feature of the environment over which he has no control.

Some choice could be provided by a system which offered to each of us the option of air travel at a price, along with the accompany noise, or that of no air travel along with quiet skies: more choice still by a market that allowed each of us to buy air travel at a price and, quite separately, allowed each of us to sell our right to quiet at a price. For in a more accommodating universe, in which a person could somehow lock out these spillovers from the space surrounding him, he would be able to charge for admitting them into his private space just as the owner of private property charges for the use of it. But in the nature of the existing universe the prospect of extending the market in this way is just not open to us.

Let me consider, then, some of the methods put forward to control spillovers.[2]

First, and most obviously, we can adopt a system of Government regulation. This is a scheme, however, which the liberal economist will frown upon. It extends bureaucratic interference. It is costly to operate; and it is likely to "overkill" the spillover. After all, it is better to have some of the good in question along with its associated spillover—for instance, some air travel along with some unavoidable aircraft noise—rather than go without it altogether. Pursuing this idea, the economist comes up with a formula for discovering an "ideal" amount of the good, say air travel. Beyond this ideal amount of air travel there is less to be gained by some additional service than there is to be lost by the additional noise accompanying it. Below this ideal amount of air travel, the reverse is true; more to be gained by the additional air travel than is lost by accompanying noise. Although this ideal amount is always smaller than that produced by the unfettered market, the bureaucrat, it is believed, is as likely as not to reduce production below this "ideal", or even cause the industry to fold up by insisting on the installation of costly preventive devices.

If the liberal economist is, in principle, opposed to a system of direct controls, what scheme does he favour?

It goes without saying that he will give his blessing to any freely negotiated settlement. If a factory producing dye-stuffs starts pouring effluent into a stream, it is likely to spoil the taste of the whisky produced by a distillery located farther downstream. The distillery may cut its consequent losses by financing the installation of a purifying plant for the dye works or for itself, or by moving elsewhere. Alternatively it may bribe the dye works to locate elsewhere or to reduce the level of its output, and therefore its effluent, to a point at which the effect on the quality of its whisky is unnoticeable. Since such mutual arrangements are voluntary, the presumption is that both parties are better off with such arrangements than without.

But such mutual arrangements are practicable only as between highly organised groups such as the two firms in our example. If instead the damaged group is a large number of families dispersed over a wide area—the victims, say, of aircraft noise—such negotiations are not practicable. Any private person who takes the initiative in an attempt to organise the victims of aircraft noise, in order to negotiate on their behalf with the air-line authorities, must be prepared to incur virtually unlimited expenses and trouble while knowing that his chances of success are slight.

In these circumstances the economist may propose levying a tax on each unit of the product or service equal to the social damage it causes. Such an excise tax—equal in value, say, to the damaging spillover effects caused by air travel—would seem to be satisfactory. So would an excise tax equal to the spillover effects arising from the use of the private automobile. In this connection, however, it should be noted that the system of taxes or tolls favoured by many transport economists is calculated by reference only to the mounting costs of time and fuel lost by the motorists themselves as the traffic builds up. In other words, given the existing road system, the toll or tax is to be regarded as an ideal device for rationing scarce road space. It is, therefore, set equal to the estimated loss of time and fuel, etc, imposed by any one additional vehicle on all the existing motorised traffic.

One can agree that there should indeed be such a Traffic-congestion tax. But there should also be a Pollution tax. There should obviously be a Noise tax, and for that matter an "Agony tax", too—even though the grief of a spouse or parent cannot be stilled by any sum of money. And come to think of it, tens of thousands killed a year on the roads and some ten times that number crippled is quite a price for modern nations to pay for their apparent preference for the private motor car over public transport. Finally, there should be a "miscellaneous tax" to cover a host of irrevocable consequences—such as the tendency of the motoring interest to produce cities like Los Angeles which, having dedicated itself to the automobile, now lies prostrate without heart or centre beneath the tentacles of its freeway system, or its tendency to transform the countryside into a wasteland cemetery of gasoline stations. If all such taxes could be calculated and imposed the problem would disappear —along with the greater part of the traffic.

Now why are such taxes on automobiles not in fact levied?

If he disregards charges of vested interests and political conspiracy, the economist might well come up with the argument that the fact of such taxes *not* being imposed is prima facie evidence that the mere cost of calculating them would be prohibitive, or at any rate greater than the potential gain from some resulting "ideal" traffic flow. In other words, the cost of acquiring reliable information about spillover costs is so great that persistence with a tax scheme could result only in a net loss to society. This conclusion (which may be extended to other spillovers) is less plausible, however, if we recognise that the admittedly heavy costs of acquiring information arise from aiming at standards of accuracy that are unnecessarily stringent. Some rough work plus inspired guessing might suggest a tax resulting in a traffic flow which was, say, 10 or 20% off the mark either way. Yet the response to such a tax is likely to be a vast improvement over doing nothing at all.

Analogous remarks apply to the now fashionable technique of Cost-Benefit analysis. But while an excise tax aims to ration the use by vehicles of scarce roadway and scarce amenities, the question of whether or not to invest in adding something to the existing road system is settled by reference to the outcome of a cost-benefit study. And if the transport economist ever troubled to make adequate provision for the costs to society of the familiar spillovers generated by motorised traffic, it is certain that we should build fewer roads.

It is also important to realise, in this connection, that however the tax is set, or however Costs and Benefits are estimated, such economic calculations take no account of equity. *Those whose welfare is adversely affected are not compensated.* This might matter less if such people were to be found among the wealthier groups in society. But the reverse is more likely to be the case. Building a flyover through a poor neighbourhood—and they are seldom built through wealthy neighbourhoods—benefits motorists as a group at the expense of the welfare of the families in the poor neighbourhood.

Yet these inequities are not the end of the matter. If the motorists availing themselves of the flyover are *not* in fact charged for its use—and this is the practice in most countries—

their disposable income is not reduced. Since a proper estimate of the motoring benefits is derived from what motorists can afford to pay for any contemplated "improvement", it is obvious that if, instead, they *were* made to pay for the facilities in question, the estimated benefits of investment in additional flyovers or road-widening schemes would decline. But, as indicated, motorists do not in fact pay taxes or tolls for these motoring facilities (other than an annual motoring tax, and generally as a taxpayer along with the rest of the community). The estimate of what they can afford is insufficiently diminished, and successive projects continue to *appear* economically feasible.

Be that as it may, by far the most serious defect of such Cost-Benefit analysis is that already mentioned in connection with excise taxes: a variety of damaging spillovers continue to elude measurement. As several conscientious economists have pointed out, the outcome of all too many cost-benefit studies follows that of the classic recipe for horse-and-rabbit stew which is made on a strictly fifty-fifty basis—one horse to one rabbit. No matter how carefully the rabbit is chosen for its flavour, the taste is sure to be swamped by that of horseflesh. The horse, needless to say, represents those *"other considerations"* which seldom take up more space than a sentence or two in a footnote, or in the preamble, in contradistinction to the expert's detailed and quantitative analysis which is the scientific rabbit, one invariably having all the earmarks of exacting professional competence. On this recipe, standard for practically all transport studies, I should have no difficulty in producing impressive estimates of net benefits over costs for almost any conceivable traffic project in the London area, beginning with a four-lane highway through St James's Park and a ramp over Buckingham Palace. The more the city is carved up and twisted about to encourage the use of the private automobile the easier it becomes, on the standard formula, to contrive net benefits by further highway investments.

Turning to a specific instance, consider the attempt of the National Trust to prevent the Ministry of Transport from building a six-lane highway through Saltram Park, Plymouth.

Notwithstanding that the land was "inalienable", the Trust suffered a serious defeat at the hands of Parliament. Members were sad to see it go; but being "realists" they bravely turned their backs on sentiment and bowed to "economic necessity". Certainly, the Minister of Transport can produce convincing figures to justify his decision. And it is equally certain that the premises on which the calculations are based follow the horse-and-rabbit stew recipe.

The loss to the country as a whole of the destruction of rare natural beauty weighs only as a single consideration to be borne in the mind of the Minister. In times like the present, where there is growing pressure to be seen going about doing things, this consideration is not likely to weigh too heavily in the balance. But is it possible to attach a figure to such intangibles?

The answer is: yes, in principle. A conceptually exact measure would add together the minimum sums each family in the country would be willing to accept to reconcile it to the destruction of this area of natural beauty. And not only each family now living. As the destruction of natural beauty is virtually irreversible, the loss suffered by future generations of families would also have to be added to the total reckoning.

Such calculations are currently impracticable. But even the most conservative guess of the total loss on this principle—which is, strictly speaking, the correct economic principle—would swamp any measure of net traffic benefits the Minister could come up with. By the same logic, a conservative guess of the social costs of the supersonic booms would be enough to reverse a decision based on a conventional cost-benefit study.

But there is no need to pin our hopes on guesses about minimal compensation to deliver us from further follies. For there is one simple proposal which, if implemented, would effectively check this rake's-progress sort of growth that successive governments have wantonly produced; and that is an alteration of the existing law. Change the law from being in general permissive of spillovers to being repressive of them and the justly admired market mechanism will tend to a solution that seeks to avoid spillovers. For under such a repressive law the "unmeasurable" spillovers are effectively transformed, in the first instance, into legal claims for damages. And such claims enter directly into the economic costs on a legal par with payments for the use of other people's property and services.

The Market and the Law

And why should the law not be altered? To assert that such alteration "interferes" with the proper working of the Market would indicate a misunderstanding of the issues. After all, the term "market" in economics means no more than an organisation for the voluntary exchange of goods and services. It can operate, therefore, only within a legal framework that enforces contracts freely entered into.

The most ardent advocate of *laissez-faire*, moreover, concedes the need for government "intervention" in the economy if only for the purpose of defending the realm against the Queen's enemies and of assuring the maintenance of law and order within it. Again, it is allowed that, in order to prevent debasement of the currency, the issue of coins and notes comes under the strict control of the state. One can go further. Most liberal economists hold that the state should restrict free enterprise in other ways. On moral grounds slave labour is to be outlawed; in the interest of internal security the sale of fire-arms is to be controlled; on grounds of efficiency, and in order also to promote the decentralisation of economic power, monopoly is to be regulated and competition encouraged. The Market, then, is not regarded by economists as in itself desirable any more than private enterprise with which it is usually associated. For the more grasping and heartless men are, the better the Market will work. The Market is favoured by liberal economists on the grounds simply that it is a relatively inexpensive mechanism which, *when constrained by wise legislation*, can be made to serve desirable, though limited, social ends. And if with the passage of time and changing circumstances its operation is revealed to be defective in any respect our first recourse should be to the law.

It is interesting to remark in this connection that the arguments for extending existing legislation to cover men's rights to basic natural amenities are *no different in kind* from those used in defence of men's rights to private property, in particular those turning on equity and economic efficiency. With respect to equity, it is a cardinal liberal tenet that every man should be allowed the freedom to pursue his own interest *provided* that in doing so he inflicts no harm on others. The post-War eruption of environmental spillovers forms a classic instance of the most blatant infringement of this crucial proviso; an instance, that is, of severe and growing damage to the welfare of innocent people as a by-product of the pursuit by others of profit or pleasure, for which damage there is at present no legal redress of any value. For this reason alone the classic liberal doctrine could be interpreted to favour extending the arm of the law in protection of a man's rights to such basic amenities as quiet, privacy, clean air, unpolluted waters—though allowing him the option, along with other people, of accepting compensation from private firms or governments for permitting a designated range of spillovers in his vicinity.

With respect to efficiency, once the costs associated with adverse spillover effects are a charge on the production costs of the perpetrators of spillovers then, unless they can reach agreement with the affected groups, they have to desist entirely from producing the spillover-generating goods. Thus an airline company would have the option of continuing all its services provided completely effective anti-noise devices were installed, or, to the extent that they were not completely effective, of paying full compensation for all the residual noise thrown on to the public. Under such a dispensation the costs of operating the *Concorde* over Britain would have to include compensation for inflicting on us a plague of sonic booms. As an economic proposition it would be a dead duck.

It is to be noted in passing that under the new law the costs of negotiating agreements with members of the public have to be borne entirely by the airline companies. If these costs were so heavy that the residual profit, if any, was too small to enable them to bribe potential noise victims to put up with even a limited number of air services, all air services would have to be withdrawn. And under an anti-disamenity law, the fact of having to do this would be regarded as prima facie evidence of net social gain in abandoning air services.

For all that, such legislation may not go far enough for at least two reasons.

First, there may be insufficient information on the range of consequences arising from the spread of the spillover in question. A citizen who agrees to put up with a certain type of spillover effect in return for a bribe may do so in ignorance not only of the risks to which he exposes his person and his family but also in ignorance of the risks to which he exposes an unknown number of people or humanity at large. The unpleasantness he experiences from being surrounded by exhaust fumes may be only a fraction of the damage ultimately inflicted. Similar remarks are pertinent to other forms of air pollution, to effluents poured in river, stream and lake, to the discharge of oil in the high seas, to the use of chemical pesticides and, above all, to the present creation of radioactive elements by peace-time nuclear reactors.[3]

Secondly, there are spillover effects that are experienced not only by citizens alive today but by future generations as well. Some of those effects mentioned in the former category can be included also among this type of spillover.[4] Other outstanding examples are development-spillover and tourist-spillover, both of which involve the virtually irrevocable destruction of woodland, coastline, lake districts, and places of rare beauty and magnificence. In consequence not only is the present generation deprived, but the keen pleasure and solace offered by such scenic beauty is denied to future generations also. In such cases the State, in its role as custodian of the future, is obliged to overrule the narrower interests of any group of private citizens, and either wholly to prohibit or severely to limit the spillover activities in question.

I need hardly trouble to point out a number of preliminary difficulties, since one can depend upon entrenched interests to supply most of them. But no measure of radical reform can be established overnight. The practical problems of administration are solved only with the passage of time and with the accumulation of experience. What is required first is that, in response to widespread public demand, the principle of Amenity Rights should be formally recognised by law.

The subsequent and more detailed legislation which would result in industries having to set prices to cover their full social costs need not, however, trouble them for long. For they would now have a powerful incentive to re-direct their research into removing the chief technical causes of spillover arising from the operation of their factories and from the operation of their products. Following such legislation there would, for example, be an immediate market for noiseless automobiles, lawn-mowers, power saws and so on.

Yet even prior to the passage of such legislation much can be done. Any government at all concerned with the welfare of its citizens can take the initiative in a number of fairly radical but realistic experiments. It can, for instance, make a start by promoting a scheme for a number of large residential areas through which no motorised traffic would be permitted to pass and over which no aircraft would be permitted to fly. It may be true (although I doubt it) that only a minority would care to live in such amenity areas. But the market under existing legislation will never present it with the *choice*. Municipalities in their turn could do much to improve the pleasantness of the environment simply by keeping motor traffic away from *some* large shopping centres at least, from narrow roads, from cathedral precincts, and from other places of beauty or historic interest that can be enjoyed only in a traffic-free setting.

In our larger towns and cities we could begin with a ban on all private traffic except perhaps for a taxi service (allowance being made for commercial deliveries during the small hours, say, from 3 a.m. to 7 a.m.). In exchange, and at very much lower cost, the public could be offered a quiet, frequent and highly efficient public transport.

No sprint in the growth rate, no stirring export achievement, could confer so immediate and palpable a benefit to the inhabitants of these islands as schemes such as these, radical enough to restore some measure of dignity and humanity to our cities that have so long lain crushed beneath the roar and fume of motorised traffic.

A "Green and Pleasant Land"?

It is not impossible that the reader, though in the main sympathetic to my views, will from habitual response to endless debate about export performance, gold reserves, growth indices, and the like, coupled with daily warnings about Britain's "falling behind in the race" or "our struggle for survival", treat my arguments with half-conscious reservations. While admitting their force he may feel a distinction should be drawn between what is urgent and what can wait, and (uneasily perhaps) between a hard-headed or "masculine" economics on the one hand and, say, a "soft" or "sentimental" economics on the other.

The first distinction is obviously a valid one, but the familiar order of priorities is wrong. The day-to-day problems of managing the economy, the concern with industrial disputes, depressed areas, the level of overall employment, indices of prices and production and—so long as governments continue to be wedded to fixed exchange rates—the balance of payments, have been the staple preoccupation of governments for decades and, indeed, have provided a good living for any number of economists, financial journalists and civil servants. Both the preoccupation and the industry that thrives on it can be depended on to continue unabated into the foreseeable future.

The country's desperate need to produce more exports "vital to our survival as a nation", a favoured *cri de coeur* among our stout-hearted "realists", puts one in awe of the power of current myths. Exports, however, can be spoken of as vital only as payment for vital *imports*. But our imports consist not only of essential foodstuffs and raw materials. An annual average of between £300m. and £400m. of our imports is foreign securities ("export of capital"). Over one billion pounds of our annual import are luxuries, fashion goods, or close substitutes for domestic goods and materials—desirable perhaps, but expendable enough.

Whether a modern economy happens to have a favourable or an adverse balance of payments, whether its supposed growth rate is rising or falling, whether employment is increasing or decreasing, whether its foreign reserves are rising or falling, there will be no respite from the day-to-day plotting of the ups and downs of a variety of key figures. Over time this snakes-and-ladders economics has so fascinated the players that they have long lost sight of the significance, if any, of the moves being made.

My other objection to this game is that it is played in public before a captive audience whose responses over the years have become so attuned that, like those of financial editors, their spirits rise and fall along with the latest figures on the chart. Let the news be of a further decline of our place in the international growth league, or of a decline in our exports, and people feel obliged to mutter darkly and shake their heads at each other in token of disgust and resignation. Let the news be of a record rise in real income or a bumper export surplus, and the atmosphere is thick with discreet self-congratulation. Since the direct impact of these events on our lives is slight—in the complete absence of economic reportage we should be unlikely to notice them or if we did so we should, in the absence of suggestions to the contrary, accept them philosophically—there is much to be said for the establishment of what might be called a Ministry of Misinformation (to borrow "Lord Haw-Haw's" facetious misnomer) to keep our spirits soaring. In our new and buoyant mood, freed from the sense of crisis and impending economic catastrophe, we might feel less ashamed to protest at the manifest deterioration of the environment and to insist that the government take action.

Economic crises, maxi or mini, real or apparent, have been the rule since the War, not the exception. In the circumstances we must regard "the immediate pressure of economic events" not as a mid-stream crisis that has to be overcome before the country can attend to otherwise worthy but less urgent proposals. Economic pressures and urgent crises are now apparently unalterable features of our society, something which will continue through prosperity and adversity, whether or not we make the legislative alterations proposed above and whatever the initial impulse they give to the indices.

The second tentative distinction, that between a "hard-boiled" economics and a "soft-boiled" or "sentimental" one, is not valid. The impression, say, of a casual observer in the U.S. watching an endless stream of forty-ton trucks hurtling through the night, from East to West and from West to East, is that here, indeed, are the visible manifestations of economic power and prosperity. The freight, however, ranges from dish-washing machines to electronic bugging devices, from electric tooth-brushes to plastic baubles, and from cosmetics to frozen TV-dinners. Much that serves simply to gratify the thoughtless whims of people slouched disconsolately before a television screen serves also as the foundation of vast industries whose outputs form a sizeable proportion of the nation's annual product. For in measuring the nation's output one does not rank goods according to any criterion of human need, nor does one weigh its utility as between rich and poor. The 25 cents spent on pretzels chewed listlessly in a cinema by some over-weight matron enters the grand computation on the same terms as 25 cents spent on a bowl of soup by an emaciated pauper.

To this extent at least, the conventional economic procedure for measuring total product, or total value, is admittedly unsatisfactory, and the case I put could be strengthened by departing from it. Yet nowhere have I moved outside the conventional economic framework. If a person is, or can be made, willing to pay a dollar for a good x I infer only that it is worth at least a dollar to him; and that by permitting him to buy x for a dollar he will believe himself to be better off than if permission is refused. These are orthodox economic premises, and the logic raised upon them is equally orthodox. Thus, the spending of 25 cents on a packet of aspirins to *reduce a "bad"* (say, a headache) as compared with spending 25 cents on *acquiring a good* (say, an ice-cream) may have philosophical implications, but no *economic* distinction can be drawn between the two cases. It follows from this that *preventing* a person from acquiring a good is, in economics, on all fours with *compelling* him to receive a "bad". In either case he is constrained to accept a situation different from that which he would otherwise have chosen, and his welfare is reduced accordingly.

Nevertheless, it can be observed that the liberal economist reacts sharply to the first form of "coercion" and remains comparatively unmoved by the second. If the State proposed to ban the sale of tobacco, or chiffon nighties, in certain areas of the country, the howl that would go up would shatter the windows of the Palace of Westminster. And who would doubt that economists would lead in caricaturing the alleged rationale of such proposals? Yet if the State passes legislation which has the effect of compelling people to bear with disutilities of a serious order—or, to put it otherwise, to deprive them of the choice of such goods as "peace and quiet", and for all practical purposes without redress—the public and the economist are not unduly perturbed. How does one explain this asymmetric response? The hue and cry in the Press in the name of freedom if the State threatens to deprive a man of the enjoyment, say, of pornographic literature, and the relative unconcern if a man is deprived of his enjoyment of the free gifts of nature?

The explanation resides perhaps in a "misplaced concreteness" which, despite occasional disclaimers in our more civilised moments, tends to associate utility, or value, with *market* prices. But if all that is priced has value, the reverse is certainly not true. For this reason the economist interested in welfare can devise a rule for putting a price on those things that for one reason or another escape the price mechanism; yet a rule which follows in every respect the logic of the Market.

A worker offering his services to industry receives in exchange a sum of money that is at least sufficient to compensate him for the "bad" or "disutility" he has to endure—or, to put it more positively, for the good (say, leisure) he has to give up—the sum received being entered as part of the cost of the final product to which he contributes. By the same logic any person who in consequence of another's activity suffers additional noise, pollution, or other disamenity, should receive in exchange a sum large enough to compensate him fully for the "bad" or "disutility" he has to endure or, put otherwise, for the good (say, quiet and clean air) he has to give up. Such payments are also to be entered into the costs of the enterprise. Thus, the total cost of producing an article or service can be regarded as the sum of payments required to compensate others for the losses they would otherwise have to sustain.

If consumers are now prepared to pay for the finished product, or service, that creates these "bads" or "disutilities" a price that equals or exceeds its social cost, one must infer that they are willing to pay enough, or more than enough, to compensate all those who have given up something to make the product available. The economic rationale of the commercial rule that price should equal or exceed total unit cost is, then, simply this: that those who gain are able to compensate, or more than compensate, those who lose.

This "overcompensation" (or net benefit criterion) is the crux of the matter. It transpires that it is the only criterion of economic efficiency that is implicit in the orthodox literature on resource-allocation and is at the base of all popular techniques—cost-benefit analysis, mathematical programming, project evaluation, the lot.[5] If any business enterprise is to vindicate itself as an economic proposition, it is ultimately by reference to this criterion. For this reason all the allocative arguments I make use of rest firmly on it. If the victims of spillovers, like the workers mentioned above, are fully compensated for the "bads" they are required to endure—or for the "goods" they must part with—such compensatory payments necessarily enter the total cost of the product or service produced. And if the cost of the product or service so computed is covered by the price it fetches on the market then, indeed, the criterion is met; otherwise, as under the existing system, there can be no presumption that it is met.

The introduction of Anti-Disamenity Legislation of the kind I have outlined can, therefore, be regarded as an effective means of repairing the currently defective allocative mechanism of the Market so that it can operate tolerably well within a private enterprise or mixed economy. My main contention has been that of all the alternative methods so far proposed for correcting the growing allocative distortions of the post-War period—direct controls, group bargaining, excise taxes and subsidies under the existing law, or alterations of that law—that of legislation specifically contrived to bring commercial criteria into line with current economic criteria is easily the most equitable and efficacious.

Having grasped the essentials of the argument the reader should have no difficulty in recognising the basic irrelevance of objectives turning on, say, a country's trading relations with other countries. I do not argue that the proposed legislation entails "fewer imports" or "more exports"—if this could be shown to be the more likely outcome, I would not avail myself of its appeal, for in the context of allocative improvements it is neither here nor there. Nor do I argue that there are far simpler ways of overcoming the apparent imbalance in a nation's international payments position than those currently employed by governments whose horizons are bounded by ideological and political commitment. For the simple point to be made is that, notwithstanding the present near-obsession with trade and currency movements, the state of the balance of payments does not, of itself, provide an independent allocative criterion.

Like any other market, that for foreign goods and services can be out of equilibrium for some time. Without disputing the importance of this market and (given the fetish of fixed exchange-rates and incompetent government intervention) the greater difficulty of restoring equilibrium there, the significant proposition to grasp is that, within an allocative setting, a country's international trade tends to an acceptable pattern only in so far as its internal pricing mechanism is working correctly—as at present, it is not. Once this internal pricing, or costing, mechanism has been corrected, through legislation designed to include the costs of all spillover damage, any consequent reduction or increase of our imports can be fully justified on our economic criterion as an allocative improvement.

To the question, therefore, of whether or not we can "afford" anti-disamenity legislation, the answer is a categorical yes. And it is so, not for the more obvious reason that if we *choose* to live in a greener, pleasanter land it is technically quite feasible to do so—provided we forgo in exchange some technological hardware. It is so for the less obvious reason that the increased greenness and pleasantness would be one of the by-products of a better economics.

If it serves to reassure the reader further, I shall hasten to dub my proposals "progressive" lest another call them "reactionary". If he likes it better, I can insist that they are "forwardlooking" rather than the reverse, or assert that they "face the future" rather than the past. Certainly the magnitude of the post-War eruption of spillovers is a new phenomenon in history, and it would be a novel departure for any country to introduce far-reaching legislation to curb them.

Yet there is perhaps more to be said for avoiding these tired clichés. The idea of using "the future" as a guide to action springs from a view of history as a record of man's inevitable progress from darkness towards light. Both the cause and the effect of history are thereby misrepresented. If instead we regard our destiny as something within our own power to control, and conceive of history as the outcome of choices made by men alone, we are impelled to assume a responsibility for both the present and the future. It should be obvious that we can discharge that responsibility more rationally if—ignoring popular debates about whether any contemplated policy turns clocks back or forward, or faces change or not—we seek only to uncover the full range of choices facing us at any critical juncture and pick our course of action only after a cautious assessment of the likely consequences, in so far as we can anticipate them. At all events, in putting the case for legislation against spillovers, I have turned my back on the ideologies of predestination, technological or otherwise, and have argued throughout as though we are, ultimately, free to choose the sort of future most congenial to us.

I hope I have dispelled some of the doubts in the reader's mind that the arguments I deploy against the official tolerance of adverse spillover effects are not every bit as orthodox and as hard-headed as are general economic arguments for establishing new industries, encouraging economic development, or building dams, tunnels and bridges. It need hardly be added, however, that any movement outside the framework from which a strictly economic criterion emerges would only strengthen further the case for legislation against spillovers. Economic considerations aside, common justice would surely proscribe any self-regarding activities that destroy the amenity of others—

at least in the absence of adequate compensation. A little further reflection about the world would suggest also that the incidence of the more familiar spillovers, aircraft and traffic noises and pollution, falls most heavily on the lower income groups who have not the wherewithal even to attempt to "get away from it all". The distribution of welfare is thus more regressive than the distribution of income. And, if we permit ourselves the luxury of value judgments, it may be asserted that it is more important to reduce existing avoidable suffering than to extend facilities for further indulgence; and that a rapid proliferation of technical gadgetry and plastic knick-knacks will not compensate for a rapid erosion of environmental amenity.[6]

None of the considerations broached above can be construed as an argument against economic growth *per se* but only as an argument against an insensate pursuit of economic growth that is heedless of the associated social losses. Alterations in the law which ensure that these social losses are translated into private costs will go far to bring social welfare into harmony with commercial feasibility. The least that can be said of such a change is that it would make economic growth somewhat less of an illusion than it is at present.

3. *A Modest Proposal to Transfigure the Environment*

In the belief that the spread of industry strengthened the economy of a country and promoted the general welfare, the import of the law has necessarily always been that permitting of some "reasonable" amount of inconvenience which arises in the ordinary course of economic activity. Without conceding that the inconvenience actually inflicted on others by the growth of industry over the last two centuries was at any time wholly justified, there is broad agreement today that the impact on the well-being of the public of industrial overspill has increased, is increasing, and ought to be diminished. In the circumstances, the old permissive doctrine is no longer adequate. Now that anti-pollution legislation has begun to emerge—faster (though not surprisingly) in the United States than in Western Europe—there is among the public at large a greater readiness than ever before to debate any new proposals designed to protect the ambient environment.

The question the economist first asks himself when faced with evidence of some untoward feature arising from economic activity is whether it arises, in the last resort, from some "imperfection" in the operation of the market. Traditionally, the liberal economist's support for a competitive enterprise system rests on his belief that such a system promotes an enlargement of the area of personal choice, and one that is compatible with the preservation of individual liberty. The enlargement of the area of choice itself is regarded as an outcome of the perpetual search for profits in meeting consumer demand, a search for profits that, through the competitive process, acts to lower costs of production and to provide incentives to introduce new products and services. The existence of spillover effects—the injurious by-products suffered directly by innocent parties arising from the lawful activity of others—does not, of itself, warrant a revision of this presumption in favour of the private enterprise system. If the noise or smoke produced by the works of one business concern reduces the productive efficiency of the neighbouring works of some other business concern, a merger of the two firms, or a mutual agreement between them whereby one compensates the other, would in principle satisfactorily resolve the problem. There is, indeed, an incentive for the injured firm, in the absence of all legal redress, to approach the other firm with an offer. And if the offer is accepted, there is *prima facie* evidence of an economic improvement—one in which some people are made better off, and none are made worse off.

But for spillover effects that fall on the public at large, such mutual agreements are unlikely to come into being. The costs of organising opposition to, say, the building of a freeway through a community neighbourhood, or to the building of a nearby airport—in particular where the government is behind the project—is in most cases prohibitive, and the likelihood of the interested public being able to bribe the projected enterprise to move elsewhere is slight. Even if such agreements could be reached, they would clearly be inequitable: the losses would be borne by the potential victims whose welfare is thereby reduced[1] while the enterprise would obviously gain by the agreement. Were such agreements practicable, they would act as a temptation to private enterprise to engage in a form of legal blackmail—firms overtly proposing to set up especially noisy or smoky works close to residential areas.

True, the state, through a system of licences, controls, and zoning laws, stands between the public and the worst abuses. Yet in spite of such controls, the rapid growth of industry, commerce, and traffic is such that over the post-war period urban, suburban, and rural environments have continued to sink in the scale of amenity.

The social consequence is that in so far as man-made goods are concerned there is increasing choice, indeed a superfluous and bewildering choice. In so far as the environment is concerned there is less choice year by year. What is more, the political power and ideology that has grown with the private enterprise system is such that the public is quickly alerted and aroused over any attempt to interfere with their freedom of choice in man-made goods, no matter how trivial. If the government, in a rash moment, decided to prohibit or regulate the sales of beads and bangles, or pulps and porno, not only business interests but self-professed liberals would leap into the fray. Sacred principles would be seen to be threatened. Thin edges of wedges would be discovered. In contrast, the deterioration over the years of the quality of water and air, the loss of quiet, safety, natural beauty—all vital ingredients of the good life we affect to be seeking—continues remorselessly, despite incipient protest and occasional public opposition.

In sum, with the advance of prosperity in the Western countries, the proportion of the national product that takes the form of trivia—which term encompasses not only "expendables", but goods that are either offensive or positively inimical, or else, like the automobile, appear to have defeated the purposes for which they were originally intended—grows continuously. As a result there is increasing choice in all that matters less and less, and in much that is on balance injurious, while in contrast there is a continuing reduction of choice in that which has come to matter more and more—the physical environment in which we dwell.

The *status quo* can be justified by valid economic argument only if the tenor of the existing laws is accepted. The common law, enacted controls, and the law of torts can in some circumstances be applied to check particular abuses. But by and large the law is still permissive of industrial expansion; permissive also of the concomitant overspill generated by industrial plant and industrial products.

It is possible, however, to enact laws that will reverse the general tenor of the law from being permissive of spillover effects to being repressive of them. The principle involved is that in the former, the existent law, pollution continues unless the victims are successful in persuading the pollutor to desist. In the latter, the proposed law, pollution is prohibited unless the pollutors are successful in persuading the polluted to put up with some amount of it. Although, in the simple textbook examples of two or a few people, firms, or industries situated in close proximity, it makes practically no difference to the outcome whether the pollutors have to bribe the polluted, or, more generally, whether the offenders have to bribe the offended—indeed, one can play semantic games so as to make the designations offenders and offended appear ambiguous—it can make a vast difference to the outcome when the pollution in question affects the public directly. The point is, perhaps, worth elaborating.

Under the proposed law the initiative to secure agreement between the interested parties will have to come from the pollutors. One consequence is that those who would otherwise suffer pollution, far from having to estimate the largest sum they can afford to pay the pollutors to curb their pollution in varying degrees, now have to estimate the minimum sum of money they are prepared to accept as compensation for bearing with varying amounts of pollution. In the ordinary way, what people are willing to pay for a thing is smaller than the amount they are willing to accept for parting with it—if only because what a person is prepared to pay is limited by his income whereas there is no operative limit to the sum he can receive. This asymmetry has the following consequence: if mutual agreement can be reached under either kind of law, the social cost of any amount of pollution will appear higher under the pollution-repressive law and, therefore, the agreed amount of pollution will be lower as compared with the agreed amount under the existing law.

More important, however, is the unlikelihood of voluntary agreement being reached between the public, on the one hand, and those creating pollution on the other[2] simply because of the magnitude of the efforts, expenses, and risks that have to be incurred in the hopes of reaching and maintaining agreements of this sort. These negotiating and administrative costs—the economic literature refers to them collectively as "transactions costs"—tend to rise rapidly with the size of the affected public and its spread over a given area. Such being the case, whatever the state of the law, the alternative outcomes tend to be polar:

under existing permissive laws, the production of pollution-creating goods is no more restrained than that of goods which produce no pollution. In contrast, there would be no production of polluting products under a pollutant-repressive law. Either outcome is, then, economically justified under its own law since, under either law, the transactions costs involved in reaching agreement about allowing or curbing the polluting goods exceed any mutual benefits calculable in the absence of such transactions costs. Using words evocatively (and continuing to suppose that mutual agreement on the output of polluting goods is the only method in use), permissive laws would result in a world having "too much" pollution; repressive laws would result in a world having "too little". To be more precise, "too much" and "too little" refer here to the resulting unchecked output and zero output respectively, when either is compared with some hypothetical *ideal*, or *optimal*, output that would have been agreed upon by both parties in the complete absence of transactions costs.

The clear intent of effective anti-pollution legislation should be to protect the public against a wide range of specifically mentioned pollutants, at least above some minimum level, low enough to be negligible. The method of implementing such laws would have to vary with the particular type of pollutant. Mutual agreement between all affected parties would still be allowed wherever such agreements are feasible—that is, where the transactions costs involved are low enough. Otherwise protection could take the form of enforcing minimal standards of purification, a prohibition of certain goods or of certain methods of production, direct regulation of output, taxation of polluting products, relocation of polluting industries, or legal compulsion to adopt more effective preventive technology. The choice of these alternatives is an economic one, the obvious criterion being the lowest cost per dollar of net social benefit.

In order for such legislation to be effective, however, the public at large must be free of any obligation to initiate procedures against pollution offenses. Any infringement of the law that is detected would call for action by the public prosecutor.

A Modest Proposal to Transfigure the Environment

Originally, we might reasonably assert, pure air, clean water, beautiful scenery, tranquillity—or, at least, freedom from assault by engine noises—were a part of nature's bounty. Had man been so far-seeing and so prudent as to have enforced pollution-repressive legislation early in modern history, environmental costs would automatically have entered the economic calculus, and a good deal less of these original gifts of nature would have been lost. For under such laws, no enterprise would have been permitted to damage other people's interests, or their lives, without proper compensation. Nobody could, in effect, be made directly worse off by industry.[3] It is then precisely because the law was, on the whole, benignly disposed toward the progress of industry that a wide variety of spillover effects escaped the economic calculus.

In this regard, the 19th century was something of a calamity compared with the 18th century, and the 20th century a greater calamity yet than the 19th. Though no one today belittles their impact on our environment, our current inability to place dependable values on these unwanted spillover effects—the "bads" that get produced along with the goods—makes it uncertain whether in fact "real" income per person has been growing, say, over the last two decades or whether, instead, it has been declining. It is unnecessary to know the answer, however, in order to justify a change-over from the existing laws to pollutant-repressive laws that—though they cannot of themselves redress the damage already done in the name of industrial progress—can at least check the pace of environmental destruction, and ensure that the social costs of further damage are more than offset by the benefits. A number of considerations would seem to favour this radical change in our legal attitude toward industry and its by-products.

1. Scarcity. Though we cannot measure "utils", it is reasonable to suppose that the annual increments of goods *per capita* in affluent countries are subject to "diminishing utility". In view of the mounting sales pressure necessary apparently to dispose each year of the increments of gadgetry, gew-gaws, and plastic knick-knacks, this is not hard to appreciate. The public is in effect being subjected to disguised methods of "forced feeding". A lot of what it buys, more of it each year, it does not *need* in any meaningful sense. In contrast, environmental quality and amenity become scarcer each year. We could of course say that their "marginal utility" is increasing as they become scarcer. But that would be an old-fashioned way of saying simply that the relative valuation we put on the environment is rising. If so, we should be increasingly concerned not to squander what little remains simply to enable a consuming public to absorb yet more of manufactured goods that are already so abundant as to be almost worthless and often self-defeating.

2. *Ecology.* The information necessary to enable people to evaluate goods and "bads" becomes increasingly deficient, even to the point of being misleading, as we move into an era of rapid technological innovation. Such limited evidence as has come to light over the last two decades should convince the most sanguine growthman that the manufacture and use of an increasing variety of chemical products, of drugs, pesticides, detergents, synthetic materials, have potent ecological repercussions, including the genetic effects on man, that may be irreversible. Yet it will take many years before complex biochemical relationships can be established, during which time additional synthetic products will be marketed about whose *long-term* effects we know nothing, and about which private enterprise, in the nature of things, cares nothing. For this reason economists' cost-benefit calculations, which depend wholly on estimates of people's own valuations, at the time of purchase, of goods and "bads", become less reliable as criteria of net social benefit. Though the risk attaching to any one synthetic product or process may be small, as the number of such products and processes increase the combined risk of some ecological catastrophe occurring before the signs are recognised begins to approach a virtual certainty, the only mitigating circumstance being the possibility that a lesser catastrophe, striking first, will be heeded as a warning.

Although the change of law being contemplated will, if adopted, act to stay the pace of marketing of some innovations, it will not be enough to cope with this source of risk. It will have to be supplemented by far more restrictive legislation than exists at present on the marketing of new products and the introduction of new industrial processes. Since the anticipated gains of such innovations are slight, measured in terms of human needs, and since the risk of danger is to be thought of in terms of human survival, there is everything to be said for requiring a far longer period of experimentation and re-examination before such things are placed on the market.

3. Culpability. The conflict of interest that arises between the pollutor and the polluted does not imply equal culpability. The damage is caused in the first instance by the pollution generated, and is suffered by the victims of that pollution; not the other way round. One has to be careful here. Although the smoke exhaled by the smoker offends the nostrils of the non-smoker whereas the clean air breathed by the non-smoker does not of itself offend the smoker, it may yet be insisted that the *idea* that other people do not smoke can be a painful one to the smoker, and that in principle he, too, ought to be compensated for this reduction of his welfare. But the true liberal position—and here I think it represents a consensus of opinion in modern society— makes no concession to the mere prejudices of a man. It is required that the incidental spillover damage be evident and tangible. It is precisely in order to eliminate the possibility of such sophistry that a pollutant-prohibitive law should direct itself to a specific range of spillovers.

There are, of course, places to which one may go and at which one must expect to encounter what, in other circumstances, would be regarded as particular forms of pollution, or dis-amenity. No reasonable man would feel angered at the yelling and stamping that goes on at a boxing match, or in a football stadium, or at the smoking that goes on in a bar or a pub. But where the individual cannot opt out of a polluted environment, or can do so only at great expense and inconvenience, where noise-levels rise within his neighbourhood or fumes increase in his home town—then there is a *prima facie* case in equity for redress or adequate compensation.

4. Posterity. The idea of our children and our children's

children inheriting a world in which every level bit of land and every body of water has been put to some agricultural, industrial, or commercial use—a world of continuously moving traffic, ground and air—a world in which a person cannot even hope to find quiet, repose, solitude, time for reflection—in which there are no areas of natural beauty left where a man may seek to find inspiration, or to refresh his body and spirit—is something that should appal if not alarm us. Yet unless we act very soon, that world of desolation is indeed what our grandchildren will inherit. Just because no price has been placed on nature's free gifts, they are being wantonly destroyed in the post-War tourist spree. Yet their value to mankind can only become higher as they become scarcer.

It may well be that our grandchildren will not complain at the way we are today plundering our planet. They may know no better, never having experienced anything other than a highly computerised industrial society set in a traffic-dominated environment. Yet they would be that much more frustrated, and that much less human, in consequence.

5. Ethics. In an affluent society, one in which the vast majority enjoy material standards far above subsistence levels—indeed, one in which, given the political will, no family need suffer material hardship—the official priority given to promoting economic opportunity is an anachronism. So also is the economist's emphasis on allocative merit narrowly conceived, as it usually is, in a society whose institutions are such that its members are continually goading themselves into producing and consuming goods from artificially-created discontent and from fretful ambition. How can government officials seriously declaim about the "needs of industry" or the "needs of the economy" when so much of last year's cornucopia of GNP stuff lies mouldering in waste heaps over the land or contaminating the earth, the waters, and the air above, and so much of this year's is no more than candy floss, tinsel, throw-away software, and misinspired technological frou-frou. Given that society is struggling, albeit perversely, with the problem of surfeit, not scarcity, a shift of accent from goods-production to equity is more than overdue.

It would seem right in these economic circumstances that wherever there is a conflict of interest, the avoidance of unnecessary suffering should take precedence over the expansion of opportunities for pleasure or profits. It is, incidentally, a precept to which pollutant-repressive laws give expression.[4]

Any legislative proposal to improve the quality of the environment elicits at least two kinds of objections.

The first, and more common, objection arises simply from a misunderstanding of the economic and distributional implications: it is to the effect that environmental quality is a middle-class desideratum, one that should be resisted since any expenditures on improving the environment necessarily reduce the resources that would otherwise be made available to the poor and underprivileged.[5] No one will trouble to deny that the government could indeed reallocate a part of its revenues from investment in existing slum clearance or (since that has environmental implications) from direct relief to the poor, or from health and welfare programmes, to, say, improving the quality of the air in cities. But to limit one's vision to these (unlikely) possibilities is to forgo perspective. A moment's reflection is enough to recognise that expenditures are maintained and increased on all sorts of goods in the economy, any or all of which—and not merely environmental expenditures—could be reduced to enable the poor to consume more. Before preparing to limit what little moneys are being spent on environmental quality, a recognised "merit" good, we ought first to be willing to reduce expenditures on a great many "demerit" goods, starting perhaps with pornographic literature and entertainment.

There happens to be, however, clear economic justification for reducing unchecked pollution either by curbing output, installing new technology, or by other means. A cost-benefit criterion is met wherever the social benefits enjoyed from reducing pollution to some lower level exceed in value the resource costs incurred in reducing it. The sense of the argument can be made clear by supposing the cost of improving the quality of water in a district costs $2 per 1,000 gallons. This improvement, let us say, is worth nothing at all to Mr Poor but is worth $3 per 1,000 gallons to Mr Rich. If the purification plant were established and Mr Rich were charged $2.40 per 1,000 gallons more than before, he would feel better off. Mr Poor is no worse off, and he could be made better off by giving him a subsidy of 60 cents per 1,000 gallons on his water. Both Mr Rich and Mr Poor would then be made better off, and the cost of the new purification plant covered.

This example may be thought to be of academic interest only, inasmuch as information of this kind is costly to obtain and transfers from rich to poor on each of such occasions would be impracticable. But whether academic or not, the fact that in this example both persons could be made better off (if income transfers were costless) is enough to meet the economist's allocative criterion that a change should be adopted if everyone concerned can be made better off—irrespective, that is, of whether in the event some people are actually made no better off or even become worse off.

The question of whether in fact the rich or the poor benefit or lose from a reduction of unchecked pollution depends on the type of pollution and the method employed to curb it. If manufacturers producing goods used processes that polluted the air, or a lake, were to be taxed accordingly, their products would rise in price. To that extent, the cost of living would appear to have risen. If the sums are done correctly, however, society as a whole is better off (on the criterion stated above), since the benefits of cleaner air or water are deemed, by reference to individual values, to be worth more than the extra costs incurred. None the less, the cost to the poor, reckoned as a proportion of their total expenditure, may exceed that of the rich. Such distributional effects would be regressive, and alterations either of the tax structure or of the structure of public expenditures would be necessary to correct the regressive outcome. On the other hand, anti-pollution or pro-amenity measures can be designed so as to benefit the poor almost exclusively. Deflecting motorised traffic from using poorer class neighbourhoods as through-ways, improving garbage-collecting services, planting trees, building parks, and setting aside recreational and pedestrian precincts, or introducing an efficient public transport service are examples of measures that would have a direct and salutary impact on the lives of the poor. What is more, legislation that prohibits unchecked spillover would act to reduce expenditures on road and highway construction which is, in general, detrimental to environmental quality. And in so far as expenditures on highway programmes compete for limited public moneys with public education and welfare, the effective operation of such legislation would imply a transfer from the community at large to the needier groups.

The second objection is that a change of law that would put the burden of paying pollution costs on the shoulders of pollutors, at least in the first instance, would be tantamount to retroactive legislation. Though one can point out that manufacturers as a whole would tend to pass on the additional pollution charges to consumers, it is far from impossible that firms which have recently invested heavily in mineral rights and equipment under existing permissive laws would find themselves at a considerable disadvantage under the new laws. For this reason, the government should give ample notice of the impending anti-pollution legislation as, indeed the United States government has done in setting the deadline for automobile fume controls for 1975. The period of notice would vary from one type of pollution to another and, indeed, the change-over could be accelerated in some cases by the offer of subventions or tax concessions to corporations taking prompt action.

Although the change-over to firm anti-pollution legislation—or, put more positively, to a charter of amenity rights for the citizen—is a pre-condition of the good life we affect to be seeking, and though it is technically feasible and economically justifiable, a modest understanding of political realities suggests that progress may be slow, and that in some cases (motorised and air traffic, for instance) the struggle for power might become protracted and bitter.

Connections between political and business aims are apt to be strong in the mixed economies of the West, and the advances in technology are not likely to weaken them. Some political representatives accept business patronage when in power and, if successful, may be offered a seat on the board of directors on retirement from active political life (where, it is hoped, they can still pull some strings). More than that, the executive government habitually seeks advice from businessmen regarded as employers of labour, producers of goods and, therefore, as having practical knowledge of the likely effects of alternative government policies on particular industries. There is also an influential body of vocal opinion on both sides of the Atlantic committed to the ideology of private enterprise; and it is easily roused to suspicion by the need for "intervention" on this scale. I say nothing, for the moment, of a consuming and working public long nourished on the pap of expectations of more, ever more, whose commercially cultivated discontent could easily be directed against environmentalists' proposals especially if they came to believe that their "legitimate" material aspirations were being threatened. In consequence, one can anticipate some powerful resistance to the massive and detailed legislation required to cover a wide spectrum of spillover effects.

What is more, the economic resources required to refashion the physical environment on the basis of radical anti-pollution laws designed to safeguard the rights of all citizens would be staggering. It is doubtful whether the use of automobiles or aeroplanes would continue to be an economic proposition under such laws, except perhaps in outlying areas and on a much reduced scale. Today's sprawling metropolises would have to be split up by green belts into smaller towns and cities if the intolerable frustrations, the mounting crime and violence, are to be reduced.

As one of the "Seven Wonders of the Polluted World" (according to a report in the *New York Times*, in September 1971), London—"destroyed by developers" since the War under successive Labour and Tory governments—would have to be rehabilitated. A huge post-War crop of eye-sores would have to come down. Piccadilly Circus, Leicester Square, and other centres of human concourse would have to be freed of traffic, and the rash of sleazy amusement arcades and other offensive enterprises removed from Oxford Street. Space would have to be re-created by removing more recent buildings of doubtful architectural merit in order to provide a dignified setting for our great historical buildings if London is to be made a capital city whose citizens once more can be proud of its architecture; if it is to become a place where people can meet, stroll, mingle on the streets and—freed from today's endless fume, dirt, noise, stench, frantic pace, and traffic danger—enjoy all the art, music and culture that civilisation has to offer.

Factories would have to move to special locations or alter their technology, transistors be forbidden from beaches, and lawn-mowers silenced. One could go on. A livable environment cannot be created, one that would gratify and inspire men, without first undoing an almost incalculable amount of environmental hideousness perpetrated by "developers" over the last quarter-of-a-century.

Finally, some practical problems are sure to arise in the methods used to enforce pollutant-repressive legislation. Certain kinds of spillover, such as noise or smell, appear almost impossible to tax or regulate satisfactorily. First, there is the difficulty of measurement. Recent attempts have been made to measure the value of noise and air pollution by reference to differences in market values that purport to reflect differences in noise and in air pollution respectively. The formidable statistical difficulties are compounded by the fact that, since noise and air pollution have increased and spread rapidly over time, these differences in pollution as between localities are much diminished. Even if the values attributed to perceptible differences in noise and air pollution were believed to be statistically significant, calculating therefrom the value of the loss suffered by a family from the total amount of pollution would be arbitrary. Nor would time data help much, for a house that is over time exposed to increasing amounts of noise and air pollution will not lose its market value if all other houses that could be regarded as close substitutes are also exposed to much the same amount of increasing noise and air pollution. Thus it is entirely possible for the market value of a man's house to remain quite unaffected by rising levels of air pollution and noise, notwithstanding which his welfare can decline drastically as a direct consequence of these disamenities.

On the other hand, information obtained by direct questionnaire methods, while throwing some light on the costs people attach to air pollution and noise, would hardly be conclusive even in skilled hands. It is not merely that people find it hard to place values on such intangibles or that they may not always answer truthfully (there are ways of coping with these difficulties). The fact is that, without some period of actual experience of daily living without noise and air pollution, few people could form a reliable judgment of the worth of living without them.

Again, even if arbitrary standards, set up by engineering experts, were adopted, not only might they be unwarranted by economic criteria that are raised on the subjective valuation people attach to "goods" and "bads", but such standards would be next to impossible to enforce. Noise pollution for instance, is a complex thing, depending not only on decibels, but on the type of noise, its frequency, its suddenness and its persistence. The police and courts would, of course, prefer a single dimensional metric with a reading above some critical figure constituting a nuisance. Measuring offensive smells suffers from similar difficulties. Yet even if these difficulties could be somehow overcome, there is the problem of locating the source of particular noises, especially after dark, and the expenses involved in each case in bringing the culprits to court.

It would be unreasonable to entertain expectations that over the near future such forms of pollution as noise and smell might be reduced to "optimal" levels by taxes or regulations, or kept under control by the police. Despite the clear intent of pollution-repressive legislation there is, at least in the liberal democratic state, the possibility that the levels of some forms of noise and of other spillovers will not fall, and may even rise.

Separate Environmental Areas

Because of the likelihood of strong political resistance to effective pollution-repressive legislation, and because of some practical problems in enforcement, we might be tempted to try another path into a more livable future, one that looks to be quite feasible politically, and one that offers the prospect of some immediate and striking improvements for many people.

The notion of "separate areas", or more generally, "separate facilities", has a positive appeal of its own. Under ordinary economic conditions its economic justification arises from a reconsideration of the meaning of an optimal situation as that in which no person can be made better off without at least one person being made worse off. But such a situation does not in fact exhaust the possibilities for improvement in those cases where such an optimum is realised within an area that covers people having conflicting interests. The effluent poured into a stream by an up-stream manufacturer could well be optimal in the sense that any *greater* pollution would incur social costs that exceed the net benefits of the manufacturer, while any *smaller* amount of pollution entails social costs that fall below such net benefits. A separate facilities solution, in contrast, would allocate, say, a single stream into which all such manufacturers could pour their untreated effluent while leaving other streams wholly unpolluted, a solution which could make everyone better off than if each of such streams were optimally polluted. Again, a large residential area may choose an optimal traffic solution (where account is taken of noise, fumes and traffic nuisance to pedestrians) or else a separate areas solution in which some parts of the area are wholly reserved for pedestrian movement. Another example would be a stretch of beach shared by those enjoying transistors and those disliking them. The conventional optimal solution could be brought about by those averse to transistors paying the remainder to reduce the volume of noise. The separate areas solution in contrast, would allocate to each group a separate part of the beach.

There is a presumption that, in all such cases of conflicting interests, the separate facilities solution increases overall welfare beyond the conventional optimal that is constrained to a single area, since—regardless of which group has a legal right to compensation—neither group in fact requires compensation from the other in order to restore its original level of welfare. If one group no longer has to compensate the other group in order to acquire some concession, it is better off than it would be under a joint arrangement brought about by its compensatory payments within the single area, while the compensated group need be no worse off than before—at least if the size of the separate areas is regarded by each group as large enough for its purposes.

So far I have omitted the question of "transactions costs". In order to establish the superiority of a separate areas solution, it is not enough to show that it confers larger net benefits than does an optimal solution which covers a single area. Such an excess of net benefits must also be shown to be larger than any *additional* costs of creating and maintaining separate areas, as compared with the costs for determining and maintaining an optimal solution within the single area. On *a priori* grounds, however, there is no reason to believe that the former costs are greater.

Ignoring the question of political initiative in both solutions, the costs mentioned can be divided into *(a)* capital costs, if any, in erecting barriers in order to demarcate the separate areas; *(b)* the costs of ensuring that the features particular to one or both areas are maintained; and *(c)* the costs of compensating any of the inhabitants who would not wish to remain in the newly-created "amenity area". Formally, of course, a cost-benefit calculation could vindicate the economic feasibility of setting aside any such amenity area from the main territory. My guess is that a cost-benefit criterion could easily be met, at least if two procedures are adopted: *(1)* that the amenity area be judiciously chosen, and *(2)* that the value of such an area to the potential inhabitants be estimated by reference to the minimal sums they would be willing to accept in order to forgo the advantages to them of dwelling within such an area.

I would hazard a further guess that even if the second procedure is not adopted, a cost-benefit criterion would justify the introduction of a goodly number of such amenity areas, provided that the chief features of such areas were freedom from all engine noises from cars, airplanes, garden implements, etc. If, for instance, only one family in a hundred in the U.K. or in the U.S. was immediately interested in living in such noise-free areas, a population respectively of over half-a-million people, or of about two million, would be potential candidates for them.

Nevertheless, and quite apart from their economic justification, the establishment of such amenity areas, conceived as "merit goods", would surely appeal to the public imagination for other reasons.

Variety. The irresistible advance of Western technology is fast transforming the physical environment inhabited by men into a monotonously similar pattern the world over. Each year that passes sees towns and cities in every country growing more alike, more ugly and "functional" and more clamorous with traffic. In these circumstances, the case for deliberate policies of fostering variety and amenity is too obvious to be laboured. True, the preservation of cathedrals, great houses, and, of course, national parks, has something to offer in the way of respite. Yet such beautiful buildings can be enjoyed largely as museum pieces, relics of a more spacious and leisurely age. National parks, especially in the U.S., offer brief experiences of the great outdoors, accompanied often enough by crowds of other holiday makers whose communion with nature is apparently incomplete without a car, a caravan, transistors, frozen foods, air-conditioning and all "mod. cons.". The devices and paraphernalia of modern living infiltrate the natural habitat and transform it into an adult playground, often a noisy and untidy one. The separate amenity area, in contrast, is conceived as offering a distinctive way of life to its inhabitants, one in which they may take refuge from many of the products of modern technology.

True, if one seeks no more than quiet and communion with nature one can perhaps still find them in Britain in the remoter parts of Scotland or on the Yorkshire moors. In the U.S. there are still vast wilderness areas to which rugged men seeking a simpler more primitive way of living can escape. But the existence of these extraordinary options is not in issue. There are not many people who seek isolation for long periods, nor many who do not enjoy occasional company and opportunities for meeting and mingling with people, nor yet many who are anxious to escape from all the comforts a civilisation can offer. Among the vast majority of people, then, there can be more than

G

just a few who, while wanting to live in some sort of community, would yet welcome the opportunity of opting out of a life dominated by certain technological products. And, what is more, it is technologically quite feasible to enjoy many of the advantages of material progress while at the same time deliberately rejecting an environment believed to be inimical to the good life. In short, there are choices open to us other than all-or-nothing with respect to modern technology.

Social Justice. The "separate areas" proposal is undeniably a modest one. No one is proposing to alter the prevailing technological features of modern life. No one is proposing that automobile production be halted, or that air services be closed down, or that all forms of pollution be disallowed. For the first few years of the experiment more than 99% of the land area of a country is likely to remain unaffected. For nothing more radical is being proposed than that, initially, a few small enclaves of quiet and repose be set aside for the more sensitive souls among us who suffer irritation or distress at certain features of urban life. If our humanity can be moved to the extent of providing reservations for certain species of wild animals, we should find it in our hearts to make provision also for those of our fellows who are, under the existing dispensation, made to suffer needlessly simply because of lack of imagination and initiative.

Indeed, one can invoke the popular doctrine of liberal economics which argues for private enterprise and decentralised decision-making as against collective enterprise and bureaucracy on the grounds that the former extend to individuals greater choice in the things they want. But in the choice of some minimal variety of that good crucial to their welfare—the choice of the physical environment in which they dwell—private enterprise has precious little to offer. Indeed, the market cannot offer significant choices of environment[6] simply because finance and enterprise alone do not suffice; ultimately it is a question of legislation.

The prohibition of motorised implements and automobiles in an area, and of aircraft flights close to such an area, requires legislation and enforcement. It transpires, then, that so far as a real choice of physical environment is at issue, it is collective action rather than private enterprise that offers the means of extending it to individuals. What is also significant in this connection is that a political decision to introduce separate amenity areas, far from negating the rationale of the market, provides the condition necessary for a market in environment to come into being for the first time. For as people learn about these opportunities, and experience living in them, more of some kinds of amenity areas and perhaps less of others can be built in response to the demand for them.

Quality of Life. In his theorems about resource allocation, the economist of necessity takes people's tastes as a datum. But, like everyone else, he is aware that tastes can deteriorate over time, and also that goods which would be rated as tawdry, and possibly inimical, on any civilised scale of values may become objects of mass consumption in response to commercial forces and to continued product innovation. At the same time we are becoming estranged from many things in life that once gave solace and pleasure to our forbears. Insulated in our vast conurbations from the force and rhythm of nature, we do not hear the song of birds, or the running of rivulets. Our nostrils no longer delight in the smell of fresh-mown hay. We do not know and therefore we cannot be moved by the deep silence of the night.

The deliberate creation of areas of more natural environment can go far to resurrect these lost experiences and, perhaps, go some way to bring people closer to the sense of fulfilment and serenity that inevitably eludes us in the traffic-blighted sub-topias that are growing up about us.[7]

Such are the reasons why the creation of separate amenity areas has a strong claim to the public's immediate attention. Granted that the public responds to the appeal, there are a number of practical issues to be discussed. If I appear more tentative henceforth, it is not because I perceive any unusual legal or administrative difficulties. Far from it; one can easily recall the successful launching of far more complex political experiments over the last thirty years. There is an obligation to be tentative at this stage simply because, once the principle is conceded, detailed planning should be guided by informed public debate, one that will turn on three main issues, those of size, location and organisation.[8]

I am concerned chiefly with the creation of amenity areas of largish size—an average size of, say, about four square miles accommodating about a thousand or so families—large enough, that is, to warrant legislation for the purpose, if necessary, of re-routing aircraft and highways, so as to ensure complete protection from engine noise. Nevertheless, it is an essential part of the scheme that local governments be also encouraged to provide separate areas on a smaller scale.

The minimum non-motoring area within a town or suburb would be no smaller than the conventional pedestrian precinct located about shopping centres. In addition, ancient, winding or narrow streets, often of historical interest, within a town or city, along with centrally located squares (sometimes surrounding an area of park) should be set aside for pedestrian use only. Central parts of some cities and towns, obviously the more picturesque or archaic parts, should be cleared of all motorised traffic—and of recent commercial buildings also—in order that they can be appreciated and enjoyed in a traffic-free setting. In a number of seaside resorts, too, traffic should be forbidden along the sea front—at least along the prettier parts. Motorised craft of every sort could be prohibited from the seas and lakes of a number of our holiday resorts, and stretches of beach freed from the omnipresent transistor.

These modest and not unreasonable innovations, simple to enact and inexpensive to maintain, would go far to restore to the ordinary citizen some of the amenity that has disappeared since the war. They have an immediate impact on the quality of life and would do more to augment society's well-being than any imaginable spurt of productivity or further proliferation of gadgetry.[9] And there can be nothing more salutary to the citizen's morale than the dawning recognition that he does have the power to make vital choices irrespective of the direction taken by technology; that he need not be the resigned victim of technological change but the master of it; and that despite the urgent voices of businessmen and the forecasts of technocrats he can, whenever he is ready to do so, choose for himself a style of living more satisfying to his spirit than that which is bequeathed to him by the self-propelled forces of material progress.

The effects of these smaller innovations in enabling people to realise the extent of the options for shaping an environment more congenial to their tastes will, moreover, be strongly reinforced from the accumulating experience of living in the larger separated areas which, as indicated above, cannot be brought about without effective legislation by the central government (possibly by state governments in the U.S.). In view of their key role in the scheme, I restrict my remarks in the remainder of this essay to these larger amenity areas.

Since it may be anticipated that interest in a noise-free residential environment will, at first, be strongest among middle-income and professional groups,[10] most of which are employed in the larger towns and cities, the chances of immediate success are greater if such amenity areas are chosen within commuting distance of them. Exactly how close is partly an economic question depending upon the particular geographical features involved. The closer to the town or the city, the costlier in general will it be, because of higher land values, because of higher costs of re-routing air and ground traffic, and because of the likelihood of a greater concentration of population which is apt to require larger sums in order to compensate the correspondingly greater number of existing inhabitants who would elect to move out. Thus, amenity areas within commuting distance of London would probably not be less than 30 miles from the centre, and possibly more than 60 miles. Given that the area is to be linked to the metropolis by rail, however, a journey of not more than an hour need be contemplated. Should an amenity area be desired that is deeper in the country, or close by the sea, a rail journey in excess of an hour would not, I imagine, be regarded as too high a price to pay.

Since motorised vehicles are expressly prohibited from such areas, a fast rail service to a point close to the boundary of the area would seem to meet requirements. The alternative possibility of building a car-parking lot close to the periphery of the area, with a road link to the capital, would be more expensive and possibly incompatible with the goal of complete freedom from engine noise. It would, moreover, certainly add to the congestion in and about the metropolis.

Some decisions have to be made with respect to features that are common to all amenity areas; others with respect to features that will vary from one area to another.

The first group of decisions covers the administration of the area: the type of local government and the powers vested in it, in particular penal legislation for infringement of the rules by which the character and amenity of the area are maintained. Since the success of the venture depends critically on the maintenance of the standards of amenity offered, I would regard a policy of leniency for offenses, even first offenses, as inviting trouble. For wilful disregard of any of the by-laws specific to the kinds of amenity adopted, expulsion from the area would not, in the circumstances, and bearing in mind what is at stake, strike me as being too severe.[11] The ability to implement such penalities would require that the freehold of all land be vested in the chosen authority, properties within the area being rented or leased to the family for any agreed period—though always contingent upon the family's continued respect for the laws and regulations designed to preserve the character of the area in question.

Included in this first group of decisions are those which relate to administration, policy, education, sanitation and medical care. Detailed planning of these things in such areas will raise a number of special problems, though none likely to pose great difficulties.

The second group of decisions is of more interest and consequence. For a prime aim of the scheme is not merely to provide a refuge from neon lights and traffic-jammed suburbias, but more positively to initiate a wide variety of environments; to offer in effect an extension of the range of choices in a good that is crucial to the enjoyment of life where at present there is, for the ordinary citizen, practically none.

Although such areas need not be large—I have tentatively suggested areas of about four square miles accommodating about a thousand families, although it may prove to be convenient to have some areas much larger and some areas smaller than this—the means of local transport may vary not only as between such areas, but also as between districts within an area. Thus some areas may be wholly pedestrian, the transport of merchandise or furniture being accomplished by hand-carts or horse-drawn wagons. Other areas may choose to admit bicycles and pedalled vehicles only. Others may favour horses and gigs, and still others, possibly some of the larger areas, may admit electric-powered vehicles for the delivery of goods, during certain hours, or for public transport along designated routes. Of course, to technocrats and "forward-lookers" such arrangements will be dismissed as retrograde. But if we are concerned with welfare, not "progress", no defence of an attitude that wilfully rejects some of the new fruits of technology is called for. It is enough that people are ready to cover the costs of living in areas where they are banned.

Turning to other differences as between areas, although motorised garden (and other) implements will in general be banned, one should not rule out the possibility that some otherwise peaceful areas may prefer instead to set aside one day or more a week, or certain hours on certain days, during which times alone motorised lawn-mowers and other garden implements may be used. In some areas, transistors would be forbidden, at least outside the house. And it is not unlikely that an area prohibiting television and radio—and possibly also telephones—might attract enough people seeking to recapture an environment offering a more intimate experience of living than is possible in modern suburbs, and a more direct dependence on one another for their needs, their pastimes and their entertainment.[12]

Architecture, too, will vary from one area to another, and sometimes as within areas. The wider the range of income groups within an area—a wide spectrum of incomes within an area being one of the choices offered—the larger will be the differences in the size of house and garden. Since such areas are primarily peaceful and quiet, otherwise sensitive people may be contented with less seclusion and smaller gardens. Roads, wide or narrow, straight or winding; squares, parks and ponds; the locality of shops, schools and clinics: all have to be decided largely in advance as people attracted to such areas seek to avoid the annoyance and disruption caused by continued and piecemeal development.

A number of auxiliary problems I have forborne to comment upon, my judgment being too tentative. In particular, I have said nothing of the status and composition of the group set up to design one or more amenity areas, the methods of bringing together new ideas for new kinds of amenity areas, and so forth. Once public interest is aroused in the scheme, enough to produce enabling legislation, one would have to be unusually pessimistic to believe that the country lacks the talent necessary to find workable solutions to problems as they arise, and to learn rapidly from the accumulating experience.

Two favourable aspects of the scheme may be stressed. First, it has the virtues of "gradualism". Though the proposal is radical enough, the initial changes are minuscule in relation to the economy at large. The first separate amenity areas to be established should offer complete protection from all ground and air traffic noises. As the demand for such areas grows, new features will be introduced into them and, with the growth of experience and understanding, the face of the country may gradually be transfigured. Secondly, it costs no more in economic resources, and probably costs much less, to create an amenity area for a thousand families than to provide for that number by creating, or extending, a modern suburb or dormitory wasteland crawling with vehicles.

Since the war, *"challenge"* has become recognised as the politician's favourite cliché for promoting policies that carry unwarrantable risks in exchange for illusory benefits. (It has, of course, been in continuous use in recent years in the attempt to swing British public opinion behind the government's determination to conjoin Britain to the Common Market.) Consequently, I am chary of using the term. Instead, I might use the word *promise*—the promise of a better life which requires for its redemption no more than the good-will necessary to overcome inertia arising from long habits of staring at tables of statistics and charts, and refusing to look at the state of the environment about us. For the scheme proposed here offers the means by which, slowly but surely, we can restore to ordinary people the opportunities to free their homes and their habitat from the merciless assault of the more noxious products of technology and commerce.

To punish mortals the gods grant their wishes. Man, inspired by the Promethean myth, was not content to be a part of nature, but sought instead to master it. Today, possessed of a power he can no longer restrain, he thrusts his way into the unknown, covering the earth with his products, destroying the elements that sustain him, fragmenting the communities that cradled and nourished him.

With compulsion and genius man has laboured over the past two centuries to create for himself a utopia of material abundance. But the goal appears to recede faster than he advances, and in the wake of his advance there follows a wasteland wherein his soul parches.

Not all is despair, however. There is the unassailable fact that for lower income groups material standards have risen over the century—a fact which, for growth ideologues, is the ultimate vindication of industrialisation and a clarion call for more technology and GNP. But for many this fact is not consolation enough. The needs and feelings of minority groups should count no less merely because they are not all poor.

What I am virtually proposing is that in this wasteland we have unwittingly brought into being, an oasis be now created; a small thing in itself, but of infinite potential for good. I propose that we relent towards past economic dogma only to the extent of permitting those who wish it to spend part of their time, at least, in an environment cleansed of noise and fume. Let us ask only some forbearance on the part of the worldly-wise, not to mock or to thwart the desire of any of their fellows who choose to move closer in some regard to an older way of life, who with patience and hope seek to recapture in the mysterious and all-giving earth a lost world of sound, sight and scent; a myriad things large and small in endless motion and renewal.

Free once more to wander in quieter purlieus, a man will find time to unclench his brow and to open his heart. And at night he will raise his eyes toward the untroubled skies, and like his ancestors before him, search there pensively for his Maker, and lose himself in sorrow and in wonder.

4. *Making the World Safe for Pornography*

The "permissive revolution" which gathered pace in the 1960s encompasses a number of related aspects, a minor one perhaps being the growing use in popular writing, in pop songs, and in ordinary discourse, of vulgar expressions and four-letter words.[1] The joys of shocking the gentry are drawing to a close however. Obscene words and phrases are now an inescapable part of the flotsam and jetsam of today's admass argot of communication, this being but one of the several consequences of the rapid inter-permeation of Western cultures, styles, customs and techniques, that threaten to culminate in an unrelieved uniformity the world over. In the scramble for taking off, getting there, anywhere, there is time no longer for fine distinctions. The pressures of time (which paradoxically appear to grow *pari passu* with the proliferation of labour-saving devices), the expansion of visual media, the impatience of the current generation with forms and procedures, all combine to breed contempt for linguistic precision and to foster a relish for multi-purpose clichés and the vulgar vernacular.

Permissiveness of dress has an affinity with that of language: both are part of a commercially sponsored "youth culture" that has become a little too self-conscious in its studied defiance of a nanny image of adult authority. Quasi-exhibitionist attire, from being a fashion of the 1960s, appears to have settled down to become a trend. Leaving out the cult of grubbiness, one of the more pathetic forms of protest against "the System", one of the ambitions of the wide-eyed young is that of being seen in the accoutrements of the ad-man's "jet set", enjoying the glossy privileges of the "new Europeans"—coolly smoking the finest Virginian, carelessly leaning against the hood of a high-powered Mercedes, drinking vodka by candlelight, flying to chic resorts along the Mediterranean and, above all, sporting gaudy and daring attire. At the age of peak desire for self-display, the young in an affluent society lend themselves admirably to being a ubiquitous part of the erotic scene.

Never have styles among women during the summer months been so openly flaunting. Knee-high black boots focus the spectator's eye on the full length of a thigh that, through a vestigial skirt, can be seen to merge, on sitting, into the opulent rotundities of the buttocks. As one picks one's way through a railway station, the bouncing jaunt of girls in over-tight silk slacks offers tantalising visions of pneumatic bliss. "Hot pants", with their familiar barrack-room connotations, vie with undulating see-through blouses and, on special occasions, with see-through pants, panties and chemises—vie also with topless or bottomless costumes that are uncertain as yet whether to move from private beaches, restaurants and night clubs into the broad daylight and into the streets. One cannot but sympathise with those members of women's lib who watch aghast a trend that so blatantly submerges the individual character of women in a flesh-pond of sexuality. For men can hardly be expected continually to avert their eyes from the manifest eroticism of fashions that have made of otherwise ordinary females an essential part of the furnishings of the sex-permissive society. Unless a man can somehow become de-sensitised over time, it will remain something of an effort to have to remind himself dutifully, from time to time, that such temptuous flesh-obtruding beings are really "persons" after all.[2]

Another product of the "permissive revolution" is the cornucopia of female flesh currently exhibited at night spots all over the country. Yet the conventional strip-tease act, though it continues to attract a varied clientele, does not rate as daring compared with the live shows—openly advertised in Denmark —depicting a diversity of sexual activities between members of the same and opposite sexes, in couples, threesomes, foursomes and "moresomes", with the occasional animal thrown in as a zesty treat. In contrast, the public cinema has confined itself to more intimate shots of "normal" or heterosexual activity, often discreetly admixed with violence or horror, although the more conventional forms of deviancy such as homosexuality, lesbianism, incest and the sexual involvement of minors are manifestly on the increase. As for books, magazines and blue films, they range from men's magazines, "naughty" sex, and "pop porn", appearing on the news-stands, to those that probe the nethermost fantasies of sexuality, with manuals specialising in the depiction of improbable feats plus photographs of outsize organs taken from every conceivable angle.

It is, perhaps, unnecessary to remark that much of this matter appearing in manuals and booklets is commercially promoted as "educational": *i.e.* case studies in the history of pathologies, and the like, though today such rationalisations are hardly thought necessary. The literature on sexual experience and the psychology of sex has wandered far from the trail left by the earnest pioneering efforts of Marie Stopes or Havelock Ellis. Far from muting the sensory aspects of the sexual experience in favour of the therapeutic, the former are magnified to the point of obsession. The accent is now unabashedly on the orgasmic, on the techniques for the attainment of the uttermost. Even on a superficial plane one begins to feel uneasy, nostalgic almost. For just as the old-time leisurely wayfarer has given place to the tight-scheduled packaged tourist who, with guide-book in one hand and camera at the ready, aims to "do" Florence in one day, and Paris in two, so, it now seems, is the old-tyme lover who followed his impulse and fancy destined to give way to the new sex technician, trained by film and guide-book to save on time, to avoid making "potentially disastrous mistakes", and to master advanced methods which cannot be learned "by instinct or trial and error" but that will enable him "to bring any woman to heights of ecstasy she has never known before".[3]

I confess that my heart falters at the prospect of mastering the athletics of forty-nine different positions, to say nothing of the timing and location of a variety of slaps, scratches, blows, bites, licks and pinches. If the taste for this new high-powered sex catches on, it is goodbye to the old-fashioned notion of sex as one of the nicer pleasures of life, at least as a dependable form of reprieve from the daily hum-drum and stress of circumstance. For this new concern with norms of sexual performance lends itself too easily to statistical charts and self-rating devices in modern technological societies. And the search for maximum sexual satisfaction (or should it be "optimal"?) is likely to add yet another item to the weird list of new "rights" espoused by sproutings of discontented citizenry in the wealthier communities of the West.

What is significant is not, of course, the mere existence of such literature and such entertainment. In different forms they can be found in other periods of history. What is significant is the scale and the "publicness" of the phenomenon: the fact that obscenity now struts openly in the market-place.[4] The latent demand, it could be argued, was always there. But wealth, technology and the aquiescence of the law were required before the latent demand could be made effective, before it could be stimulated and promoted.

As they say up North, "Where there's muck there's brass". Hardly had the law begun to avert its eyes than the ubiquitous forces of private enterprise moved into the field. Quick fortunes have been and are being made. The commercial opportunities for the "dirty" book, film or live show are today brighter than ever. Despite these developments, the movement calling on the law not merely to avert its eyes but to turn its back on all sexual matters, whether of public behaviour or entertainment, has not abated. Is there cause for concern, or is there not?

Since manifestations of the new sex "permissiveness" are so varied, a short essay must of necessity limit itself to particular aspects. In the main I confine myself to the growth over the last decade of the erotic, the "lascivious", the "obscene" and the "pornographic", in literature, art and entertainment.[5]

As distinct from the argument to which they give form, there are also a number of emotional attitudes tending to favour the "permissive" revolution. One of them is commonly to be found among the lower-middle-class and young middle-age group, in particular among social workers, civil servants, semi-professionals, including some educationalists. What appears to be common to such a group is a deep, almost desperate, desire to be associated with things "progressive". Any doubts about the value of a new "cultural" departure are deemed absurd if not reactionary. "The future" itself is a beacon, while "the past" is seen as a long struggle upward through the darkness toward the present. For this group, the highest virtue is tolerance—tolerance of any kind of social deviancy. You name it—they'll tolerate it.

I choose the words "emotional attitudes" deliberately, since much of what is cast in the form of arguments turns out, on brief inspection, to be no more than rhetorical dicta having historic or emotional overtones calculated to confuse the issues. Four characteristic examples have been selected from a recent statement to the Press by John Mortimer, Q.C., the well-known playwright and the defending barrister in the famous *Oz* case (as reported in *The Times*, 9 August 1971). Each example is followed by my comments in parentheses.

1. "I do not think it would be possible to embark on a life as a writer on the assumption that there was any area of human activity which you were prevented from exploring." (The "exploration" of the area of human activity that could be proscribed by law or custom being, in this instance, specifically descriptions of sexual activity, normal and abnormal, his belief is patently false. The greater number of the world's most famous novelists—Eliot, the Brontës, Dickens, Hardy, Flaubert, Stendhal, Turgenev, Dostoevsky, Tolstoy: one could go on indefinitely—all managed well enough "to embark on a life as a writer" even though "exploring" this particular area of human activity, *i.e.* intimate sexual description, was not to be thought of. A more germane question is whether permissiveness to "explore" carnality is producing for us a better society. Irving Kristol argues the contrary and adds, moreover, that it is producing worse novels.)

2. "Obscenity is in the eye and mind of the beholder." (Mortimer is here saying not merely that obscenity is a matter of taste, but that it cannot even be identified. Is cruelty also, then, in the eye of the beholder? Although standards change over time, and although we may approve or enjoy cruelty or pornography in some circumstances, there is generally little difficulty in recognising either. Certainly pornographic writers and film producers have a pretty shrewd idea of what their public wants.)

III

3. "It is part of living to be shocked and nauseated; perhaps it will induce us to do something about it, which is also good for you." (From the fact that cruelty and crime *are* committed, which is a part of living, it does not follow that cruelty and crime *ought* to be committed or depicted. By playing loose with the language of social commitment, Mortimer is confusing the public's shock arising from true *information* on existing injustices, about which remedial action may be taken, with the shock that comes of witnessing, say, cruel or obscene practices simply as *entertainment.* But of what social value is it that people, willingly or unwillingly, be shocked in such ways—unless, of course, it leads to the closing of such shows and penalising the actors and promoters?)

4. "I think it is absolutely necessary that people be outraged. I do not think there can be any progress without people being outraged." (Here, again, language is used to evoke a crusading spirit in a shoddy cause. For it is manifestly untrue that a person, group, or society cannot make any progress without suffering outrage. And even if it is true that *some* sorts of outrage, say those arising from reports of a public scandal, lead to social improvements, not *all* outrages do. I have no difficulty in imagining cultural progress, or the maintenance of a high standard of civilisation, without the necessity of outraging propriety by public displays of sexual activities or sado-masochism.)

A related group are today's pallid liberals for whom sexual morality poses no problem. "Every man to his taste" is the crucial dictum here, with the occasional proviso that nobody be manifestly hurt in the process. Censorship, they point out with impeccable logic, is an infringement of personal freedom. As for what they, as responsible adults, are allowed to see and read, they will *not* be dictated to by government officials. And that's that! A few remarks on the ambiguity of the law, on the incompetence of bureaucrats, a quotation from John Milton or John Stuart Mill or Lord Acton on free speech, and the matter is settled.

Mixed in with these two groups are the "freedom fighters" for whom the promotion of sex permissiveness is part of the unending crusade against those imperishable Victorians; a part of the movement from the dank dungeons of repression into the broad sunlight of erotic freedom and abundance. Among this company are to be found "enlightened" councillors, educationalists and, alas, far too many otherwise undistinguished secondary-school teachers.[6] One is hard put not to suspect that the good fight for some of these teachers is but a part of their personal but futile struggle against their own childhood inhibitions; that their "frank and honest" talks and films depicting cohabitation, masturbation, and an occasional garnishing of lesbianism, provide them with the relief they fondly imagine is being shared also by their captive audiences of somewhat bemused youngsters.[7]

Passing mention should also be made of the art critic who makes a speciality of regarding pornography, and the controversy surrounding it, with detached cynicism. Staring in silence at the heaving flesh of coupled lesbians, or at a threesome in frenzied masturbation, the tight mouths and craned necks of the aficionados leave no one in doubt that their excitement at times verges on the excruciating. By dint of dissociation, however, the journalist or art critic chooses to see it all as a form of charades. As such it is not hard to depict its comic and pathetic features. Let it take its ridiculous course, he says in effect, it won't get very far. As an art form, at least, porno is strictly a limited medium. 'Ere long, we shall all be yawning.

More interesting yet, the assertion that pornographic entertainment will in time vanish of itself is made by those who have come to find the whole thing thoroughly distasteful. One reason for this belief, or hope, is an apparent reluctance to invoke legal sanctions, a reluctance illustrated in the following passages taken from a recent editorial of the *New York Times*.[8]

> The explicit portrayal on the stage of sexual intercourse is the final step in the erosion of taste and subtlety in the theatre. It reduces actors to mere exhibitionists, turns audiences into voyeurs, and debases sexual relationships almost to the level of prostitution.
>
> It is difficult to see any great principle of liberties involved when persons indulging themselves on-stage in this kind of

peep-show activity are arrested for "public lewdness and obscenity"—as were the actors and staff of a recently opened New York production that, in displaying sodomy and other sexual aberrations, reached the *reductio ad obscenum* of theatrical art. . . .

The fact that the legally enforceable standards of public decency have been interpreted away by the courts almost to the point of no return does not absolve artists, producers or publishers from all responsibility or restraint in pandering to the lowest possible public taste in quest of the largest possible monetary reward. Nor does the fact that a play, film article or book attacks the so-called "establishment", revels in gutter language or drools over every known or unknown form of erotica justify the suspension of sophisticated critical judgment. . . .

Far from providing a measure of cultural emancipation, such descents into degeneracy represent caricatures of art, deserving no exemption from the laws of common decency merely because they masquerade as drama or literature. It is preposterous to banish topless waitresses when there is no bottom to voyeurism on the stage or in the movie house.

In the end, however, there may be an even more effective answer. The insensate pursuit of the urge to shock, carried from one excess to a more abysmal one, is bound to achieve its own antidote in total boredom. When there is no lower depth to descend to, ennui will erase the problem.

Of course, journalists can always be found who would allege that live shows are already a bore. After visiting Denmark in August 1971 Peregrine Worsthorne assured us (without, however, describing just what it was he witnessed) that "It was all so unbearably dull", and later surmised that "Left to its own devices, it [pornography] can only slide inexorably down its own slime into the pit of oblivion."[9] In fact, he found the shows not only dull, and lacking in artistic skill, but somehow anti-aphrodisiac: "Not so much disgusting as unpalatable."

On the other hand, Mr Worsthorne found the porno shops in Copenhagen ("which seem to be in every street") far from dull. And the case for permissiveness changes accordingly from porno as a mild soporific to (or in addition to) porno as a terrible warning. The contents of the porno shops, he declared, were a form of evil that every one can understand, not evil disguised or dressed up, but naked and unashamed. May it not be right that we should be forced to live cheek by jowl, as the Danes now do, with the evidence of where our obsession with sex is leading us? . . .

The porno shops *are* awful, and it may well be that a few are corrupted by them. But many more, staring into the abyss they represent must draw back in terror.

The idea of voyeurs, examining the contents of a porno shop, "drawing back in terror" speaks loudly for the imaginative powers of Mr Worsthorne; so does his plea for abolition of censorship so that we may reap the benefits of exposure to naked porno, benefits that take the form of a hell-fire warning to all of us. It is an attitude which is reminiscent rather of those familiar editorial declarations of firmly refusing to withhold from the British public the true facts of the seamier side of sex, no matter how revolting—a policy pursued with relish and success over many years by some of our well-known Sunday papers. None the less, if one values these "warnings" provided by pornography according to their volume and persistence, the rising trends of such enterprise must be morally gratifying to Mr Worsthorne. Perhaps the medicine may work yet more effectively if the government could be induced to subsidise a porno supplement to the family newspaper. Though anticipating later arguments, I must vent my doubts about this sort of reasoning. No country exhibits more crime and violence, actual and fictional, than does the United States today, and the grim and ugly consequences are there for all to behold. Yet living "cheek by jowl" with it has not caused any reduction of crimes of violence, least of all among the impressionable young—nor, for that matter, has it caused a decline in the public demand for the depiction of violence in literature or on the screen.

Be that as it may, the question arises: suppose ennui does *not* set in, or the warning does *not* take hold, or not soon enough, what then? Indeed, is there any evidence to suggest that those who flock to see a "dirty" show become bored, or warned? Although some effect to drop in for a lark, or from curiosity, or as a perfunctory gesture of emancipation, the compelling power of these spectacles of sexual abandon is not to be underestimated. As in the depiction of scenes of violence, murder or torture, it is possible to be revolted, or angered, also by promiscuous sexual display. But not really bored. It is a psychological fact that people do not tire of their fantasies, least of all of their sexual fantasies. And the "dirty" show excites the voyeur just because it projects before his eyes the unswerving camera close-up, or the living flesh reality, of his fragmented fantasies. It would be as reasonable to expect voyeurs to tire of this fare as it would be to expect drug addicts to tire of their "trips", and more reasonable to suppose, instead, that the appetite grows with the feeding. And though I shall not argue the point here, it is not to be supposed either that the majority of adults are "normal" people, wholly immune from such impressions on their senses, whose tastes cannot be debased over time or their character corrupted.

Notwithstanding the complaisant pronouncement of such liberals as Supreme Court Justice William O. Douglas—to the effect that people are mature enough "to recognise trash when they see it" and, in rejecting it for more satisfactory experiences, eventually "to move from plateau to plateau and finally reach the world of enduring ideas"—there is no evidence as yet of any slackening of attendance at sexual performances on screen or on stage. From the fact that people are, for the present, able to distinguish between "art and trash" it does not follow that they will invariably choose art. Berns quotes a woman from Connecticut who protested loudly at the showing of an expurgated version of the film *I am Curious (Yellow)*: "I paid to see filth, and I want filth".[10]

At all events the purveyors of pornography take a more sanguine view of their commercial prospects. According to a recent report in *Life Magazine* (1970):

Behind the torrent of erotica are some opportunistic businessmen, in the U.S. and abroad, some of them backed by money from organised crime. They keep a watchful eye on the shifting tastes of their customers—with good reason, for it is a $1 billion-a-year low-overhead business where profit margins run up to 10,000 per cent. Watching *them* is a whole host of largely baffled government offiicials, local, state and national, who can barely stay informed about what's new on their beat, let alone control it. . . Mail order houses abound, with some 200 firms in Los Angeles alone changing their corporate names as fast as the postal officials strike.

This report, however, provides but a fraction of the evidence that could be documented to challenge such bland reassurances as appear from time to time in the Press, such as "The idea that sexual heresies, way out intercourse . . . are so overwhelmingly attractive . . . that only censoring their propagation can prevent them from spreading . . . seems to me manifest nonsense." The words are those of Peregrine Worsthorne, again, writing in *The Sunday Telegraph* (8 August 1971).

Ironically, the very next week *The Sunday Telegraph* (15 August 1971) carried an article, "The Profits of Pornography", describing the rapid expansion of the hard porn and pop porn industry. Stating that the real money-spinners are not, just now, the epics in the 2,000-seat cinemas but the sex films running in the 250-seaters, it revealed that "Andy Warhol's *Flesh* was made in a week-end for £8,000 and has already earned over £1 million in Germany. It has now been taken up by all the major circuits after playing for 22 weeks to crowded houses at the Chelsea Essoldo." As for uncensored films, they may be shown by "Film Clubs". Apparently this is one of Britain's growth industries. The "Tatler" chain of 35 cinemas has 130,000 members and is still expanding.

After describing the financial success of David Grant's two most popular sex films—"The first, *Love Variations*, had a cast of two demonstrating 69 positions for sexual intercourse, and a number of doctors talking about different aspects of sex. It cost £20,000 to make and has grossed over £600,000 at the box office" —the article remarks that "The moguls of the film industry, though late on the scene, are realising that there is a huge potential audience who would never normally go to an *X*-film but flock to the cinema when they can get 'culture' and sensation."

Can the Law Help?

Along with the hope of some eventual reaction by the public to the "torrent of erotica" goes the belief that the law is in any case unfitting as an instrument of moral improvement. Moral improvement, it is thought, is something which, like personal responsibility, must grow with the passage of time. In a liberal democratic state, the only acceptable censorship is self-censorship.[11] One can perhaps see artists, scientists, philosophers and intellectuals taking this solemn advice to heart, but it is hardly likely to restrain the enterprise of the producers of erotic and pornographic films. To quote the words of David Grant, producer of the film *Love Variations*: "I am not interested in the sort of films I make, I'm interested in arses on seats." (Reported in *The Sunday Telegraph*, 15 August 1971.) There is no reason to doubt that his attitude is typical of other producers of such films.

Nevertheless, self-censorship remains an article of faith among would-be progressives, though one they are most ready to affirm when thinking strictly of sexual morality. They would apparently be less inclined to sit back and merely provide opportunities for moral growth in *other* directions. For it could not be denied, surely, that the virtues of charity and benevolence would have more scope if all state aid to the infirm, the aged, and the destitute, were to be abolished. Perhaps private corporations also ought not to be denied the opportunity of growing in moral stature, or at least in social responsibility, in the expectation that sooner or later they will voluntarily incur all necessary expenses to prevent noise and to curb pollution of air and water. Yet one is assailed by misgivings, for society is not only liberal and democratic, but also commercial. With respect to environmental pollution, there is far more money to be made by a firm ignoring the pollution it produces, wherever the law is permissive of this, than by attempting to combat it. In consequence one can be reasonably sure that little will be done about it until the government takes action. And what applies to environmental pollution applies with greater force to "sex pollution" inasmuch as the latter is not simply an *incidental* by-product arising in the manufacture of a range of goods but is the highly profitable product itself.

Before coming to grips with the real issues let us first weed out some popular but irrelevant arguments.

An argument related to the issue of personal liberty, that of political liberty, arose during the trial of the editors of *Oz* magazine during the summer of 1971. It was alleged in the correspondence columns of *The Times*, and other newspapers, that the trial was really a political trial, on the grounds that the "sexually obscene" matters in the magazine were an integral part of the political protest against the "Establishment".

Now the temptation to choose offensive forms of behaviour or expression to "get at" a society that appears quite indifferent to a protest movement so long as its ideology is explicated in plain language is quite understandable. But it is manifestly untrue to assert that there is, in the plural societies of the West, any censorship on the expression of views, however radical. It is not the expression *per se* of political dissent that falls foul of the law; not, in this instance, the belief or explicit argument that the depiction of scenes deemed lewd and pornographic by society liberates the personality and leads to the joyous life. Just as the law is directed *not* against any statement of the creed of nihilism or of violence, but is directed against the *act* of violence or against the activity (including exhortation) that in the given circumstances is likely to result in violence, so the law does *not* forbid any person expressing his belief that the widespread depiction of sexual scenes of any sort has therapeutic or transcendental value. What the law does—or rather should do—is to forbid sexually obscene actions, or activities, that are likely in the circumstances to promote the spread of sexually obscene entertainment or literature.

I have added the words "or rather should do" in the above sentence in recognition of the inadequacy of the existing laws and of their uneven application. It is a fact, however, that (as I shall argue later) calls for reform of the law, not its abolition.

To assert that any censorship of the Press, or of any form of entertainment, constitutes an infringement of personal liberty is true. Indeed, it is a tautology: restriction on any particular choice of activity is, by the ordinary meaning of words, a restriction on a person's freedom. Factory-owners in the early part of the 19th century argued powerfully against the withdrawal of child labour, against the regulation of hours, against the compulsory installation of safety devices, and so on, all on the grounds of freedom of contract, ignoring that there were principles other than freedom of contract to be taken into consideration. The notion that personal freedom is, or has ever been, the predominant consideration in political decisions is at variance with the facts. The whole body of law, from traffic regulations to the criminal code, from taxation to tort law, constitutes a tight network of restraints on our individual freedom. Without law, there is only the total freedom of anarchy, a state of affairs less secure yet than its counterpart, tyranny.

Every change of the law imposes or removes constraints on some or all citizens in the pursuit of one objective or another. And a law that effectively reduces the area of an individual's discretion properly does so only in the reasonable expectation of some increase in society's advantage, convenience, or moral satisfaction. Whether a new law is to be introduced that undeniably circumscribes liberties hitherto enjoyed is, then, a pragmatic question to be settled in each instance by considerations of the likely effect on the general welfare. Such being the case, a person who opposes legislation designed to contain the movement toward increased sexual exhibitionism and obscenity cannot validly do so *solely* on the grounds that individual liberty is thereby restricted.

Nor can a person properly oppose such measures by invoking the vision of a free market that reflects the diverse wants of the community. The law is not, nor was it ever, indifferent to what appeared on the market or what could be made to appear. Nor, for that matter, can he oppose such measures on the alleged libertarian grounds that any citizen or group, whether a majority or minority, has a *right* to follow its own bent or tastes. Such opposition has to be referred back to our original thesis concerning the balance between individual liberty and the welfare of society. More specifically, in the case at issue, the contemplated reduction in opportunities for voyeurs, and performers and writers of porno, has to be set against the other interests and purposes of society.

By such reflections we are led to recognise Dicey's thesis that, in a constitutional democracy at least, law is the ultimate expression of public opinion. More affirmatively perhaps, the law embodies the expression of the public's moral sentiments—which is as much as to say that the law is a force giving moral direction to the development of society and to the realisation of its aspirations. Thus, provided always that public opinion is behind it, the law can indeed exert an influence on the moral behaviour and, therefore, the moral tone of society.

I pause at this juncture to remark the present popularity of editorial phrases about the government's duty to "lead" public opinion, as distinct, that is, from "following" it.

It is astonishing that a phrase so frequently employed by Lenin and other leading Bolsheviks should be found congenial by today's would-be enlightened liberals in Fleet Street, and in both the Conservative and Labour Parties whenever their views conflict with popular sentiment on critical political issues—as they did, for instance, on the abolition of capital punishment, on metrication and decimalisation, on the *Concorde*, on Commonwealth immigration, and on the Common Market. Irrespective of the merits of any of these policies, the only interpretation of the phrase that can be acceptable to a consistent liberal democrat is that of *leading public opinion to accept one's point of view by reasoned argument*. The alternative interpretation, that has been and (at the time of writing) continues to be practised, implies contempt for the electorate, and constitutes an arbitrary and unwarranted exercise of political power.

It was, therefore, with no little satisfaction that I read in *The Times* (6 March 1971) that the West German government has been having second thoughts about "getting ahead of public opinion" on the subject of pornography. Since its draft to liberalise the law in this respect was published in September 1970, there has been a storm of criticism. Suggested amendments by the Minister of Justice included a ban on the showing of pornographic films in public or on television, and on any sexual acts involving animals. According to Dr Jaeger, former Minister of Justice in Bavaria, 72% of the public want a total ban. "There are things," he said, "which are pretty nice in the bedroom, but nauseating on the stage." The issue as he saw it was whether the Germans would remain a people of culture or sink into "a new barbarism".

Although it cannot make each one of us virtuous, the law can be framed so as to discourage us from activities that are deemed by society to be patently immoral or offensive. And in an imperfect world, one in which there are plenty of people who are selfish, weak, short-sighted and corrupt, one cannot reasonably expect more. The particular methods adopted will, of course, vary with the particular issues and their significance. In an otherwise stable society, it would be as costly and socially impracticable to attempt to eradicate every vestige of pornography as it would be to attempt, say, to eradicate all sexual promiscuity. Only a police state attempts to control what goes on behind closed doors.

With respect to the issue in question, then, what the law can easily do is to stop sexual obscenity flaunting itself openly in the market place. It can make the peddling of pornographic literature difficult and costly. Some porno literature and blue films would no doubt continue to be available, but they would not appear openly on sale in rows of shop windows or at kerbside kiosks in central parts of the city. As before the War, those whose craving for such items is strong enough would have to go to some trouble and incur costs in order to obtain them.[12] But they would no longer be part of the social scene.

To assert that the law can be made effective in curbing the spread of public sexuality is not, however, to deny that the existing laws are manifestly ineffectual. Indeed, the Working Party of the Arts Council of Great Britain, set up in 1968 for the purpose of investigating "the workings of the Obscene Publications Acts, 1959 and 1964, and other relevant Acts . . ." had an invitingly easy target.[13] For the definition of obscenity as "a tendency to deprave and corrupt" serves to obscure the interests and apprehensions of society, and the formula hardly lends itself in particular cases to a clear determination based upon the facts.

The members of the Working Party, therefore, had a field day. They made a picnic of the law's discomforts, enjoyed themselves hugely, and waxed merry in contemplating the problems facing judges and juries. "Apparently," they quipped, "it is fair enough and perfectly acceptable that a man should deprave a few people and corrupt a few more, but not too many. It is for the jury to decide how many is too many. Nor is this the end of the juror's dilemma. . . . He must then ask himself whether an ounce of depravity spreading is more or less potent than an ounce of artistic merit. . . ."

Now as David Holbrook observed in his review article in *The Times* (20 March 1971), officials of the Director of Public Prosecutions cannot cope with the growth of obscenity just because by these Acts they are obliged "to define the word obscene in terms of whether or not they could convince a jury of ordinary people that individuals are likely to be depraved or corrupted—in the sense that they immediately went off and did some perverted act." By such criteria, "for people to simulate masturbation, engage in sadistic titillation . . . for couples to engage in lesbianism and actual copulation on the public stage in *Council of Lovers* was not obscene."

But, as indicated above, from the correct judgment that the Obscene Publications Acts of 1959 and 1964 make very poor law, it does not follow that a system of censorship of works believed to be obscene, in the ordinary use of language, cannot be made to operate in a satisfactory way. The Arts Council's Working Party makes too much of the difficulty of "founding a law that can be accepted on so subjective a concept as obscenity". Indeed, it went so far as to recommend that other relevant acts containing such words as "indecent" and "profane" be amended or repealed on the grounds that they "are no more capable of definition than 'obscene' ".

But it is surely not the ambiguity, or not *necessarily* the ambiguity, of such words that makes censorship of obscene works difficult, but simply the method of leaving it to a jury to decide whether *as a matter of fact* a particular work "tends to deprave and corrupt". A board of censors, surely, would not find it unduly difficult to decide whether a work was obscene or not. Or if in a particular case it did find some difficulty, it would not be because the word obscene is hopelessly ambiguous or "subjective". Words such as "indecent", "profane", or "obscene" are defined well enough in a good dictionary. And if judgments differ as to whether any particular work is obscene or not, the same can be said of a large number of other terms strewn liberally throughout the Working Party's Report, such as "vital", "breach of taste", "ordinary sexual desire", "social reprobation", "artistic merit", "repression", "common sense", "great insight", and so on. It is possible to go on being awkward in this way indefinitely in a civilisation where the larger number of adjectives in ordinary discourse derive from personal judgment and assessment.

The dividing line between any attribute and its negation can seldom be ascertained in all circumstances, and if the application of the law were to depend on its prior and exact determination we should dwell forever in anarchy. Cases have come to light in which medical men were unable to agree whether, at a particular time, a man was dead or alive—notwithstanding which we are, for most practical purposes, able to decide whether a being is alive or dead, or, for that matter, whether he or she is awake or asleep. And although it is also true that history and geography operate, within limits, on people's customs and values, every viable civilisation has some awareness of a difference between decent and indecent, between order and disorder, between sacred and profane, even though they may prefer the latter, and even though controversies may arise in particular cases.

Thus the degree of consensus in a society should be large enough to ensure that a body of disinterested citizens could, from day to day, pass judgments on the question of obscenity with a tolerable degree of consistency;[14] allowing, that is, for occasional disagreements between members of the board of censors, or as between the board and other groups in society. If, out of a sample of a thousand works of fiction some thirty were branded as obscene, but agreement could not be reached by the board on three others, it would not matter that much. Three or so books out of one thousand wrongly suppressed would not deprive the public unduly. Good literature over the ages is available today in such quantity that no one person can possibly hope to read more than the tiniest fraction of the total.

And, for whatever it is worth, I am amenable to the argument that no great damage would be done either if the three books in question were wrongly released. Provided that censorship of obscene works is, in principle, believed to be desirable, an inevitably imperfect system of censorship can ensure that the more flagrant examples of obscene works do not appear on the market, and that those eager to make a fortune by promoting the spread of the wantonly offensive are duly discouraged. Only in a society in which a consensus on, say, sexual obscenity has wholly disintegrated does censorship become unworkable. And if at times it seems as if we are moving toward such a society, the mushroom growth of pornographic entertainment and literature over the last few years is clearly an aggravating factor, one which could surely have been checked by the maintenance of stricter censorship.

Should the Law be Invoked?

So far I have suggested that the trend toward increasing sexual obscenity in literature, and on the stage and screen, is unlikely to reverse itself either as a result of eventual boredom or as a result of moral improvement—which moral improvement, as some have curiously alleged, will come only after our being steeped deeper in pornography—but that it can be contained and reversed by appropriate legal sanctions. We now come to the heart of the matter. Granted that the trend can be reversed, do we wish to reverse it? Since there are many who would not hesitate to answer in the negative, let us briefly appraise the arguments in favour of letting the movement toward increased pornography drift on.

The dogmatic opposition to any infringement of personal liberty has been touched on earlier, and it is no more impressive in this context. Confining the doctrine to freedom of expression, and taking a purely abstract view of the issue, we can perhaps be persuaded that censorship in any form is unwarrantable. Our minds have a habit of going back to the trial of Socrates, to John Milton's noble plea in *Areopagitica*, to John Stuart Mill's elegant reasoning in his tract *On Liberty*, and so forth.[15] Yet in so far as the specific freedom in question is that of depicting, or enacting, scenes of sexual titillation it must be admitted that it is hardly one to stir the hearts of men, or to raise them to heights of eloquence. Such a cause, if not ignoble, is certainly pathetic. And it is symptomatic of the times we live in, where moral paralysis passes for tolerance, that apparently intelligent people can bring themselves to think of the removal of any residual censorship of sexual obscenities in terms of a consummation of a heritage of liberties.

Regarding the matter in this light, the question of *quis custodiet ipsos custodes* is hardly significant. The worst that can happen is that some works will be censored that are not overly effensive, or left uncensored when they are. Either contingency can be comfortably borne within a society already having at its disposal a surfeit of good literature and art.

Nor can an affected alarm about thin edges of wedges be taken seriously. As well one might discern a potential homicide in a man using an insect spray. The freedom to articulate radical political views (always provided the language is not obscene) has existed for over two centuries in Britain and America and, up to the last few years, existed along with the legal suppression of the sexually obscene.

We may also dispose in passing of a high heap of euphoric verbiage with the word "healthy" at the apex. A typical example of its use is found in the opening remarks of a Dr G. B. Barker in his "Evidence relating to the Effects of Literature and the Arts". According to Barker "Sex and nudity are now much more openly portrayed on film and described in literature, and nudity is now accepted, if in context, on the stage. This would seem to me utterly healthy." The phrase "utterly healthy" has about it an uncompromisingly affirmative ring. Yet the discreet proviso "if in context" should not be overlooked. Is sex and nudity properly in context in the show *Oh! Calcutta!*, in the films *Flesh*, or *Pork*, or *Love Variations*?[16]

In addition to "healthy" we have "natural", "beautiful", "God-given", "artistic", "stirring", "strangely moving" and, of course, "exciting", often mingled with heroic metaphors about "pushing open doors", "breaking down barriers" or "reaching into new dimensions", plus a lot of trumpety sound that can mean almost anything; to wit, "There is nothing obscene whatever in the portrayal, however explicit, of the erotic as such. The erotic is something to be enjoyed. . . ." Or "The heart of the sexual revolution in our time is that potentially now we have within our grasp a freedom *over* sex, as over the rest of nature, undreamed of before. . . ."[17] Such vacuous declarations contribute nothing to the debate, however, and we need not tarry to contemplate them.

The case for drifting further into "sexual permissiveness" wants for something more than simpliste arguments and engaging metaphors against an alternative policy of tighter censorship, and more is provided.

Let us move on then to consider the connection, if any, between "obscenity" and art. Two common allegations may be distinguished. One is implicit in the arguments for the defence in the case of *Lady Chatterley's Lover*, of *Ulysses*, and of similar works commonly acknowledged to have some literary value: namely, that because a work has literary value or artistic merit it cannot be, or *should* not be, judged obscene.

I should have thought that if Rembrandt had a mind to depict sexual orgies he would have made an excellent job of it. Judged by artistic standards, such pictures would have been acclaimed masterpieces, notwithstanding which they could have been sexually obscene by any standards. A work of unparalleled artistic execution is therefore altogether compatible with its simultaneously being a work of undiluted pornography. And if it is the case that the circulation of pornographic works does tend to deprave and corrupt in some sense, then in that sense the public exhibition of such pornographic masterpieces would also so do. The cases that come to public attention, however, are more usually those of high or modest artistic accomplishment that are "marred" by occasional obscenity (which is invariably alleged to be "essential" to the narrative). Since we are chiefly concerned with the profusion today of works that are unambiguously crude, salacious, or obscene, and having no redeeming merit whatsoever, we can bypass the question of criteria for the selection of works that are both artistic and obscene.

The other allegation is basically semantic: that pornography be recognised as an art form in its own right on the grounds simply that it affords pleasure and excitement to some people— a brazen but hardly an attractive proposal.

Neither form of assertion, incidentally, has any bearing on the substantive issue, the effects on society. The former allegation, in effect, demands of the public that it withholds judgment on the pornographic elements in a work whenever the pundits agree to perceive artistic merit in the work as a whole. The latter allegation is tantamount to the proposal that the criterion of art be extended to cover the depiction of anything that succeeds in stirring our feelings, apparently *any* feelings. Grant but this, and art will encompass the uttermost in what is sick and sordid. For who denies that scenes of homosexual copulation, scenes of sadism and physical torture, the crucifixion of squealing girls, scenes of unhinged bestiality, do not pluck at the raw ends of the nerves. On this criterion, the concentration camp at Auschwitz during the last War would have to be accounted as a veritable power house of artistic achievement.

"Pornography Can Do No Harm"

On the substantive issue concerning the social consequences of the spread of the erotic and the pornographic, two opinions in favour are offered by "permitters": the strong opinion that it is positively beneficial, and the more cautious opinion that the growing availability of such stuff does no harm—or, more cautious still, that it does *no more* harm than a number of other things that are socially acceptable. Let us examine these beliefs in that order.

Supporting the first opinion is the *Report* of the Arts Council's Working Party: "The so-called permissive society may have its casualties: the repressive society almost certainly has a great deal more.[18] Repressed sexuality can be toxic both to the individual and society. Repression can deprave and corrupt." In this connection, as one might expect, the hapless Victorians come in for ritual abuse.

Like so many of today's insular liberals, the authors of the Report tend to judge their forbears from the lofty, albeit shaky peaks of permissiveness, in today's affluent and welfare states.

The apparent optimism and self-satisfaction of the Victorian middle classes at a time of Britain's industrial pre-eminence was but one side of the coin. Turn it about and one discerns the unease and alarm at the cataclysmic changes taking place in the towns and cities. Above all, there was the fear, particularly among the lower-middle classes, of losing their precarious hold on the edges of respectability and of being drawn into the morass of vice, misery and destitution left in the train of rapid industrialisation. The costs of economic growth did not begin with post-War affluence.

None the less, the Victorians are damned as hypocrites since, despite the seeming need to maintain a façade of respectability, and to subscribe to strict codes of sexual behaviour, they managed well enough to enjoy their sex in discreet ways. The Dr Barker of the *Report*, for instance, talks righteously of "the flagrant existence of a second world of illicit sexuality on the part of men . . ." (not being quite up to date with his history, he makes no mention of the "illicit sexuality" of the women).

It is hard to take this sort of condemnation seriously. Indeed, to do so would suggest that our Victorian forebears knew just what they were about. After all, secrecy adds an element of excitement to sexual adventures—at least according to the Working Party's *Report*. For, in recommending more openness (p. 34), the members tell us that "custom and acceptance are great anti-aphrodisiacs". And when they add gratuitously that "Nothing could be more antiseptic sexually than a nudist colony",[19] one is left uncertain whether such statements are in praise of, or in condemnation of, "more openness".

Be that as it may, let us return to the emphatic assertions about the evils of "repression". I place the word in quotes because it is not properly indicative of psychological malaise. As understood by psychiatrists, repression is a mechanism for dealing with emotional phenomena—memories, desires, impulses, fantasies—a mechanism whose proper function is necessary to a person's mental health. It is *over*-repression—which is what people usually mean by the word repression—that entails emotional maladjustment. So also does *under*-repression.[20]

However, under- and over-repressions are not social but

J

individual maladies. Over-repression of sexuality results in a reduced ability, or total inability, to enjoy physically the sexual act. Its causes lie deeply embedded in the psyche. Though it can sometimes be treated successfully by psychiatry, so far as I know, exposure to erotica, or pornography is not reckoned by the profession to be an essential part of the treatment. On the contrary, although the over-repressed individual might well become a voyeur, such exposure can only aggravate his sexual frustration. No matter how "permissive" the cinema or theatre becomes, no matter how vividly copulation is depicted, sexual gratification eludes the victim of over-repression. While those well enough adjusted to enjoy sexual activity are not unduly arrested by erotic images, these can have a pathological attraction for the sexually unfulfilled.[21] Yet hope springs eternal in the human breast, and if repeated failure depresses, it can also feed an inner fury that seeks somehow to force egress into the citadels of sensation. But drinking the salt water of pop porno, gazing fixedly at live shows, contemplating photos of swollen proportions, staring orifices, and bizarre postures—all act on the victim's fevered imagination, generating exaggerated visions of sexual gratification quite unrelated to that which is naturally attainable, so adding further to his frustrations and tempting him into sado-masochistic practices, or into intemperate attacks on his image of a grudging "establishment", in the vain hope of release.

Indeed, if it is true, as the publisher John Calder argues,[22] that "violence is always the direct result of frustration", the growth of pornography has much to answer for.

To sum up on the alleged virtues of "permissiveness" in contrast to the so-called toxicity of "repression": if the stricter proprieties of the Victorians presented no real barrier to sexual adventure (though one was well advised to have decent regard to the established hypocrisies of society to get the best out of it), it is perhaps unnecessary to seek "liberation" by the defiant cultivation of sexual "permissiveness". What is more to the point, the causes of frigidity and sexual despair are manifold—over-repression being rather a loose way of referring to some of them. And there is no evidence whatsoever that their incidence has diminished along with the growth of erotica and pornography. Frigidity and other forms of sexual failure may yield to medical and psychiatric skills. They do not yield to public manifestations of increased "sexual permissiveness", though they are likely to be aggravated by them.

On the more cautious proposition that the spread of sexual content in literature and public entertainment can do no harm, three things may be said.

1. The "evidence" from the Danish experiment is worthless for two minor reasons: *(a)* that the data on sex offences cover too short a period to have any statistical significance; and *(b)* that comparability with the years immediately preceding abolition is invalid for the simple reason that what were once recognised as sexual offences *ceased* to be so under the new laws and conventions. The study of the Danish experiment is worthless for the major reason that the damage to the social fabric envisaged by the opponents of abolition does not take the form of a rise in the incidence of sexual offences but of other and more far-reaching consequences which I will touch on presently.

2. The so-called "cathartic theory" advanced, though somewhat awkwardly, by the members of the Arts Council's Working Party is controversial, to put it mildly. Again we have the urgent voice of Dr Barker—whose representations we are meant to take very seriously since the Report naïvely asserts that he had "plenty of clinical experience behind him"—declaring roundly that the sadistic material read by his patients did have a "cathartic effect", and that a withdrawal of the aforementioned sadistic materials "would cause tension", by which phrase he means, presumably, that if they were deprived one bright day of their customary quantum of pop porno they would clamour for its return.

This gem of evidence, plus a Mr Wedmore's fumbling speculation about the effects of witnessing the enactment of violence: that "there is a slightly stronger suggestion that we sleep and even behave better after witnessing scenes that 'get it out of our system'," is about all that is offered in support of the by-now discredited catharsis hypothesis. In contrast, members of the Working Party made a point of emphasising that the statement offered by a Mr James Halloran—pointing out that experimental studies in the United States offered no support for the catharsis theory but rather for the contrary theory—was to be regarded as tentative only.[23]

3. Finally, in asserting that "Nobody can demonstrate that anybody has been depraved or corrupted by a particular obscene article" (p. 72) Professor Jackson is batting on a safe wicket. It is obviously going to be extremely difficult to prove that after reading a particular piece of sadistic literature—or, for that matter, watching a bear-baiting show or a public hanging—a certain person became "depraved and corrupted", if only because depravity and corruption are attributes that do not lend themselves to fine measurement.

To go further than Professor Jackson's ultra-cautious statement, however, and to insist that, say, a reading of literature in general can *never* do harm is to take up an indefensible position. For it is commonly believed by those who condemn censorship of art and literature that they can do a powerful lot of good. Taken at its face value such a position amounts to the belief that, although art and literature can do a great deal of good, they can never do any harm—reassuring, perhaps, but hardly convincing. They knew better than this in ancient times. If Plato would ban poets from the ideal city it was because, aware of the power of art for good and evil, he did not wish to risk the stability of society in order to entertain the populace.

It would be more convincing, then, if those favouring the abolition of all censorship explicitly acknowledged the influence of art and literature, and also of the screen, theatre, and television, in moulding people's behaviour and character. They could reasonably add that, in any particular case, the resultant effect might not be clearly perceived; that one might not always be able to determine in advance whether the impact of certain works would be benign or otherwise. But they could hardly avoid the conclusion that continued exposure to some sorts of art and literature was better than, or worse than, others in their effect on the character of people and, therefore on society as a whole.[24]

Just for the record, it may be noted in passing that the members of the Arts Council's Working Party also go over to the attack, though only by brandishing the still weaker argument that the art and literature of porno-violence is *no more harmful* than many widely read and justly famous works. To quote them:

> Is there no tendency to corrupt in a handbook for pick-pockets, such as Dickens incorporated in *Oliver Twist*? What about the multitudinous thrillers that offer guidance on the disposal of corpses, or of "Westerns" whose hero is pre-eminent in violence and slaughter? (p. 19).

It went on to include some canvases by Goya, newspaper reports of robbery, rape and violence—and who would disagree with them here? Surprisingly, it did not include children's fairy tales although other abolitionists have attacked them as fair game, and made much of bloodthirsty giants and granny-eating wolves.

Since a consideration of this favourite, though superficial, argument would take us out of our way, being directed more toward the effects of violence than pornography, I have placed my comments on it in a Note at the end of this essay.

The Pornographic Society

Familiar arguments used to persuade us that the growth of sexual permissiveness has wholesome effects on the personality, and increases the capacity for enjoyment, are, to say the least, inconclusive. Those who attempt to persuade us that, no matter what the degree of depravity in a work, it cannot really harm anyone are wholly unconvincing. It is time, therefore, to bring some thought to bear on the harmful consequences society may suffer if current trends toward increasing pornography continue.

I begin by acknowledging the fact that not all those favouring the abolition of censorship are equally comfortable at the turn of events. Some are prepared to admit that things have gone too far, or far enough. Yet, as indicated, they continue for the most part to repose their hopes for containment or improvement on some eventual recoil from current excesses, or on some re-assertion of an imagined natural law that is latent in liberal democracies, or, in the last resort, on the gradual onset of ennui. However, since there is no evidence at present of any slackening in the growth of the market in pornography, hard or soft, it is just possible that—unless the state takes action—our innocent sex libertarians will be proved wrong by events. If so, the question of the consequences for Western societies of an un-arrested trend toward increased public pornography becomes very pertinent. In addressing myself to so large a question, I admittedly enter the realm of speculation though without, I hope, forsaking the conventions of reasoned discourse.

In order to avoid tedious qualification at every turn in the argument, let us project existing trends and think in terms of an emergent "pornographic society", one in which all existing restraints have vanished: there are no legal checks on any form of erotic experience, "natural" or "unnatural", and no limit with respect to place, time, scale or medium, in the depiction of what today would be called the carnal and lascivious. Neither are there any limits placed on the facilities for auto-eroticism, or for participating in any activity, heterosexual, homosexual, bestial, or incestuous, sado-masochistic, fetishistic, or just plain cruel. Provided actors, audience and participants are willing, provided there is a market for the "product", no objection is entertained.

Any who would accuse me of being an alarmist merely for proposing this concept as an aid to enquiry would surely be revealing also that, were such a society to come into being, there would indeed be grounds for alarm. Since, however, they would reject this possible outcome (in the absence of state ac-tion) it would be of some interest if they could be more articulate on the nature and strength of the forces they believe can be depended upon to stem the tide. It would be of further interest to know just how far they expect society to travel along the primrose path to all-out pornography. How far would they themselves wish to travel along this road or, to be more fastidious, what existing or possible features would they wish to admit or prohibit, extend or contract? In short, where would they wish to "draw the line", and, having drawn it, on what principles would they defend it, and by what sanctions? Finally, if they could be persuaded that the forces they once relied upon to restore some sort of equilibrium are too weak to operate, what measures would they favour now in order to stay the pace of movement toward the pornographic society?

Perforce we leave open these questions until the abolitionists stir themselves to think on them. The really crucial question of whether such a society could be realised, or if realised could endure—whether, that is, such an altogether amoral dispensation is compatible with the minimal degree of sanity and order to allow a society, especially a highly technological society, to function at all—I shall also leave open for the present.[25] Notwithstanding doubts about its viability, the concept serves the useful purposes attributed to it in the preceding paragraph: by reference to it, each of us can define his own position.

A caveat has to be entered before we enter the domain of conjecture. Those who distil their complacency about the future from historical gossip, whether true or otherwise, about the "goings on" in past civilisations are as likely to deceive themselves about the course of events as economic expansionists do when they look back upon the dismal prophecies of the last two centuries concerning diminishing resources, growing population and fears of pollution. Such phenomena today have an altogether different scale of effect than their counterparts before the last war. It has begun to dawn on us during the last decade that the earth, or at least the biosphere on which we depend, is indeed finite, if not as fragile also as the civilisations dwelling within it.

While no person can speak with authority of events covering a period of recorded history going back 4,000 years, there does seem to be a consensus on some broad features. The fertility rites of primitive peoples would strike us, or our fathers, as sexually exotic if not weird. But they were not searching to extend the bounds of promiscuity. The fertility rites or their sexual aspects were an essential part of the life and religion of such peoples. Apart from such ceremonies for encouraging the harvest and propitiating the gods, tribal sex life was for the most part closely regulated by custom and taboo. A golden age of innocent sexual abandon was no more than a part of the dream world of the latter half of the 18th century. The vision of such an age has never faded, though its chronology has been altered by the more impetuous from a remote or mythical past to a future toward which we are moving.

Again, the idea that public orgies or spectacular displays of sexual practices were commonplace in Antiquity bears no relation to the known facts. Although sexual conventions differed from those of the West today, there was, in Islam at least, apparently no pornographic literature. As for ancient Greece, the sexually obscene went little beyond the familiar bawdy matter found on some vases and in popular plays such as those of Aristophanes. And if there was something like a pornographic literature circulating during various periods of the Roman Empire, its circulation was rather limited and never such as to cause much stir.

But even if my impressions are mistaken, or if evidence were to be unearthed which suggested that there were, indeed, from time to time, public orgies or public exhibitions of carnal virtuosity,[26] no reassuring conclusions could validly be drawn about our own future. For there were in any case natural checks in the past to the spread of sexual promiscuity among the masses that no longer operate today in the affluent societies of the West.

1. In all earlier periods the vast majority of the inhabitants lived, not in the towns and cities, but in villages and farms. Even of those who dwelt in the cities, by far the greater number, in daily toil for their livelihood, had neither the time nor the money for regular attendance at sex carnivals, even if they were available. Clearly this is no longer the case in the West. The growing excess of "real" income *per capita* above comfortable subsistence levels now enables people to indulge their appetites, without financial strain, for all the forms of hard and soft porno the market can offer.

2. Illiteracy among the masses limited the size of the public for erotic reading matter. And while today's cinema and television can bring their quota of sadism and prurience right into the home of every humble hamlet in the country, the scope for such entertainment in other ages would be limited to the occasional private and local performance.

3. Up to the middle of the 19th century distances were vast and travel slow. What happened in one town or in one country had little immediate influence on other towns and other countries. Thus the aberrations started in one civilisation were not easily spread abroad. Today, in contrast, we are part of a network that enmeshes the globe. And the more violent, obscene, bizarre, or perverse are the events or activities in one part of the globe, the more surely and the more fully will they be reported in all parts of the world.

4. In older times the mass of population lived close to the earth. Innately conservative, and far removed from the temptations and the artifice of the cities, their lives passed slowly, regulated by the rhythm of the harvests, by kinship, and by ancient custom. In contrast, the mass of Western populations are today urban dwellers, uprooted from the earth, cut off from all sustaining tradition, mobile, chronically restive, ready to be blown hither and thither by any commercial breeze and sweep of fashion. An easy prey to promises of new forms of titillation and exciting experience, their resistance to insidious cults is minimal.

It is time to turn over in our minds some of the facets of the problem posed by the concept of the pornographic society: namely, whether such a society is compatible with the good life, any good life.[27]

Allowing that family life will continue in such a society, what are we to make of the effect on the child's psychology of his apprehension of a society obsessed with carnal indulgence? It has been alleged, occasionally, that children are immune to pornography; that, up to a certain age, it does not signify. Though this allegation cannot draw on any evidence since they are not in fact exposed, when young, to sexual circuses, we need not pursue this controversial question here because, presumably, there does come an age when they begin to understand the significance of what is happening about them. It is appropriate then to question the effect on the child's emotional life, in particular his regard and feelings for his parents.

Is it not just possible that the child needs not only to love his parents but to esteem them? In his first gropings for order and security in a world of threatening impulse does he not need to look up to beings who provide assurance, who appear to him as "good" and wise and just? Will such emotional needs not be thwarted in a society of uninhibited sexual device? I do not pretend to know the answers to these questions, but no one will gainsay their importance. In view of the possibly very grave consequences on our children's children, would it not be an act of culpable negligence to allow current trends toward an increasingly promiscuous society to continue without being in sight of the answers?

Consider next the quality of love in such a society. Three closely related questions arise.

Treated simply as a physical exploit with another body, and divorced from the intrusion of sentiment, is sexual fulfilment possible?[28] David Holbrook, for one, has doubts whether this is possible. Indeed, he concludes that the so-called sexual revolution is "placing limits on people's capacities to develop a rich enjoyment of sexual love by reducing it to sexuality".[29] Nor has Professor Kristol any brief for the more visible manifestations of the sexual revolution: "There are human sentiments . . . involved in this animal activity. But when sex is public the viewer does not—cannot—see the sentiments. . . . He can only see the animal coupling. And that is why, when men and women make love, as we say, they prefer to be alone—because it is only when you are alone that you can make love, as distinct from merely copulating in an animal and casual way."

The second question that comes to mind in this connection is whether romantic love will become obsolete in a society of unfettered sexual recourse.

The "savage" in Aldous Huxley's brilliant satire, *Brave New World*, who commits suicide in despair, tried for romantic love but could obtain only instant sex. There might well continue to be sexual friendships, sexual rivalries, sexual jealousies. But the sublimation of sex, thought to be the well-spring of creative imagination and of romantic love, would be no more. One of the great sources of inspiration of poetry and song, of chivalry and dedication, throughout the ages would have dried up. To the denizens of the pornographic society the story of *Abelard and Heloïse*, or even Stendhal's theories *On Love*, would be implausible, if not incomprehensible.

The third related question is about the quality of love in general that can be expected to emerge along the road to such a society. One wonders if it would really be possible to love other people very much, or to care for them as persons very much, in a world without opportunity for sublimation. Can such virtues as loyalty, honour, compassion, sacrifice, charity or tenderness flourish in an environment of uninhibited public exhibitionism and pornography?

Taking a wider perspective of the scene, one wonders whether it is possible to unite unchecked public sexual indulgence with the continued progress of any civilisation—thinking of civilisation in terms not merely of increasing scientific advance and technological innovation but in those, also, of a refinement of taste and sensibility. Let the reader ponder on the question at his leisure, bearing in mind the reflection that whereas the emergence in the past of a new civilisation, or of a new age within the matrix of an existing civilisation, has indeed always been associated with a rapid displacement of old conceptions, values, and purposes by new ones, it has never been associated with a mass movement toward unbridled sexual licentiousness. For, aside from the sexually neurotic elements at large in Western societies, there are in each of us—among "normal" people, that is—infantile and regressive elements that are for the most part dormant though deeply imbedded. "Emotional maturity" is a frail plant that can sustain itself only by clinging to an appropriate social structure. Familiar taboos that place a variety of constraints on freedom of sexual practices reflect a society's desire to guard against the activation of such elements. Until recently the laws of all Western societies sanctioned and reinforced taboos against an unlimited sexual freedom that, if actively sought, could be destructive of organised society.

Thus a first experiment of this kind just might be the last experiment ever. Goaded on by the predatory forces of commercial opportunism, expectations of carnal gratification—aroused by increasingly salacious spectacles and increasing facilities for new sexual perversions—would soar beyond the physical limits of attainments. In the unrelenting search for the uttermost in orgiastic experience, cruel passions might be unleashed impelling humanity into regions beyond barbarism. One has only to recall the fantastic sadistic barbarities of the

Nazi era—and to recall also that in 1941 the Nazis were within an ace of winning the War—to accept this conjecture as neither far-fetched nor fanciful, and to recognise that civilisation is indeed but skin-deep.

Finally, and returning to this question of the viability of such a society, we are led into thinking about those things that hold together the members of a tribe, a folk, a race, or nation—a fondness of the myths that tell of their origins, a pride in their common ancestry, beliefs about kith and kin, an esteem for their traditional institutions, a concern for their survival as a people and, sometimes too, a confidence in their future.[30] Such sentiments wax and wane with the passage of the years and centuries. Whether they will survive the growth of the scientific spirit and the unifying forces of technology is a moot question. But (since we are nowhere in sight of any form of world government that would command our allegiance) once such common feelings vanish, and there is nothing but self-interest to move people, society itself will surely disintegrate. Although, for a time, the forces of law and the power of bureaucracy may preserve it from anarchy, without a common myth, without a common pride and sense of purpose, the vitality of such a society ebbs, and it lingers on like a body wasted by disease, a prey to internal convulsions and external aggression.

Is it not likely, then, that the universal and daily display of pornographic activity will contribute toward the destruction of a people's image of itself? Today an educated man may sympathise with those given to voyeurism, to homosexuality, or to more perverted sex practices, without however being altogether indifferent to an increase in their numbers. He may shrug at the sight of long queues of "Peeping Toms" shuffling with impatience to gorge their eyes on live flesh performances. He may, if determinedly and indiscriminately libertarian, affect a tolerance even of the spread of the "little shops", of sex boutiques, sex fairs, and sex supermarkets, all waxing prosperous from the sale of blue films, fantastic photographs, porno-literature and sexual gadgetry; a tolerance also of the overt sexual advertisements and hyper-erotic billboards. He may stubbornly continue to assert that "in matters of taste there can be no debate". For all that, he would readily admit that such sights do not inspire him. They are not such sights as to sustain in a man, much less produce in him, a sense of civic pride. Well might he ask: are these the sort of people for whose society he must stand ready to make sacrifices? Do they comprise a nation in whose defence he should be willing, if necessary, to take up arms? Can any one *care* very much what happens to a society whose members are continually and visibly obsessed with sexual carousal—to a society where in effect the human animal has been reduced to a life-style that consists in the main of alternately inflaming itself and relieving itself?

Such questions need not be regarded as merely rhetorical. They may be thought of as genuine questions. But unless the answers to them are quite other than what I suspect they are, there are clear and present dangers in the current drift toward increased sexual permissiveness.

It may be as well to summarise the main features of my argument. I began by indicating some of the varied manifestations of the "permissive revolution", and the emotional attitudes of those who welcome it. Those less happy at the turn of recent developments, however, seem unable as yet to reconcile their libertarianism with a return to stricter censorship. Despite all evidence to the contrary, they continue to hope for a reaction by the public arising from disgust or, in the last resort, from eventual boredom—a reaction, however, that would not need to invoke legal prohibitions.

After examining briefly some of the more familiar arguments against the censorship of sexually obscene matter, and finding them wanting in substance, I affirmed the view that the law is ultimately an expression of the moral sentiments of society. Though the law cannot instil virtue it can discourage vice. While conceding that the existing Obscene Publications Acts in Britain make very poor law, there was no reason to doubt that the law could be made more effective in reducing sexual obscenity in literature and entertainment if we so wished.

The arguments favouring the trend toward increased "permissiveness" were then considered. I dismissed the idea that great art could never be obscene; also the idea that, just because it could stir people's emotions, pornography should qualify as a legitimate art form. The familiar allegation of abolitionists that the current trend toward greater sexual permissiveness has therapeutic value was challenged as being both implausible in itself and at variance with the limited evidence at our disposal. Nor was it possible to take seriously the proposition that art and literature can never be injurious to the character of society.

Moving on to speculate on the nature of the corruption to society, I first gave reasons for believing that the experience of history, however we interpret it, would not be relevant to our own times. I then raised the question about the provision for children in a pornographic society; about the effects of such a society on our ability to love, care for, cherish and trust one another. Finally, I pondered upon the sources of conflict between, on the one hand, the aims of the good life and the needs of civic virtue to sustain society, and, on the other hand, the trend toward manifest obsession with orgiastic experience promoted by the spread of pornography in the market place. Without answers to such questions we cannot tell just where the "permissive revolution" is taking us. But we cannot rule out the possibility that, if it is given its head, it will take us past the point of no return.

Decisions in the Presence of Uncertainty

If a crucial social decision has to be taken in circumstances of great uncertainty, how do we proceed? The answer is that the procedure, and the solution it yields, will depend almost wholly in such cases upon which of the two opposing principles we adopt. The first principle, put bluntly, says: *Make the change* if there is a chance of some gain, even though there is also a chance of some loss. The alternative and opposing principle takes a conservative form. Put bluntly, it bids us *not to make the change* if there is a chance of loss, even though there is also a chance of gain.

To take a topical example, diesel exhaust gases contain the carcinogenic substance 3.4 Benzpyrene which is suspected of causing lung cancer. Under the existing dispensation, however, the first principle is adopted. We accept the risk of increasing the number of deaths by cancer rather than reduce technological progress or commercial activity, and we continue to do so until evidence that people are dying from diesel fume pollution has been established beyond reasonable doubt. What is more, both industry and government are unwilling to invest as much in research on such health hazards as on technological innovation and product-promotion.

We may say, in general, that the first principle is operative in a society whose material development is guided in large measure by criteria favoured by private enterprise, especially in a growing economy. For the prospect of profits can induce the production of "goods" that have harmful consequences for society at large, even though few ordinary people would have much difficulty in branding as trivial, if not positively inimical, many existing products in large demand. Apart from the fact that the marketing of some goods produces serious environmental damage, a growing range of chemical products that may prove, over time, to be highly toxic continues to be offered on the market simply because the existing evidence—often of a short-term and experimental nature—of damage to health is not conclusive. Since the newspapers have impressed us recently with some of the more distressing consequences of these business norms, it is unnecessary to labour the recent findings on such diverse items as DDT and other chemical pesticides, cyclamates, detergents, radio-active wastes, tranquillisers, and such drugs as Thalidomide. The harm done to a species, to human beings, or to parts of the earth's surface, is sometimes irrevocable. Yet just as rapid technological innovations entail unforeseeable ecological and health hazards, so also can rapid "cultural" innovation produce unforeseeable social hazards. In an age in which technology is gaining pace and power, the determination of our actions by this first principle exposes us to grave risks.

The second principle has an affinity with the method adopted in the sciences. Despite occasional disclaimers, the practice has been to hold on to an existing scientific view or theory until evidence in favour of a new view or theory has so accumulated as to be overwhelming. Whatever the importance we attach to this methodology, there are particular reasons for adopting the more conservative principle where the issue is that of a "sexual revolution" whose consequences we cannot foresee. No civilisation, as far as we know, has ever left the choice of sexual morals or propriety wholly to the discretion of the individual.

Indeed, in the last resort, it is this same principle that stands —or ought to stand—between society's acceptance of homosexuality as a form of experience and love on equal terms with those of heterosexuality. Nature produced heterosexuality as humanity's mechanism of survival. Physically, psychologically, emotionally, we have been fashioned by an evolutionary process for heterosexual intercourse, not homosexual. Culturally too, and through the centuries, *romantic* (sexual) love has been exalted in song, sonnet, art, and great literature, as that which springs between man and woman; not between man and man or between woman and woman. Homosexual love and practice can, then, be properly regarded as an aberration from nature, from culture, and from custom. Notwithstanding "newspeak" terms like "gay liberation", there is nothing healthy or heroic, nothing virile or beautiful, about homosexuality. At best it invites sympathy, as being the symptom of a pathological condition—one, incidentally, that can be induced in lower animals by experimentally exposing them to "unnatural" or stress conditions, sometimes by over-crowding.

The common libertarian assertion that if a particular indulgence affords pleasure of some sort to consenting adults, and does no obvious harm to others, society should have no further interest in the matter, has then only a superficial appeal. And to contend further that *there is no reason why* sexual activity should be prescribed according to gender amounts to an appeal directed to the first principle. It is equally valid to argue that *there is no reason why* sexual activity should be prescribed according to animal species.

This second and more conservative principle views the question in a different light. Confining oneself only to historical experience, a decision to abandon sexual mores that have endured for ages, mores on which the family is based and which have shaped our thought, language, literature, and culture over thousands of years, is surely a matter deserving of prolonged and serious reflection inasmuch as the consequences for society can be far-reaching and perhaps irrevocable. So momentous a social and legal change, one that recognises homosexuality as in all respects on a par with heterosexuality, can be contemplated with equanimity only by the ultra-doctrinaire, the light-headed, and the sexually afflicted.

No one should infer from such considerations alone that such an alteration in our laws should never be undertaken, but simply that it is up to those who propose it to provide arguments in its favour potent enough to satisfy the natural apprehensions of those having an abiding concern for the future of mankind and aspirations toward the good life. Until this condition has been met, the law should act to uphold custom and that which for ages has been accepted as normal and natural. Exactly how the law is to be applied, whether with severity or lenience, is an auxiliary question to be decided in the light of prevailing circumstances.

There is no reason to feel much confidence about the outcome of such "permissive" experiments undertaken in the fevered atmosphere of the post-War world. We can hardly describe the age we live in as the natural inheritor of the Enlightenment that began in the 18th century. The upsurge over the last decade of sadistic, prurient, and obscene literature and entertainment cannot seriously be considered as marking a further advance in our liberties. Such developments have taken place during a period that has witnessed the emergence of the beatnik, the provo, the drop-out, the hippie, the skin-head, the yippie, the Weatherman, and a number of smaller but even more exotic movements, to say nothing of the revival of witchcraft in Britain and America. It is a period that has witnessed an intensification of racial strife the world over, not unrelated to the "population explosion"; a period of growing student unrest and intolerance; a period of direct-action movements, of near hysteria and, most insidious of all, of the growing popularity of violence and blackmail—and this not merely among delinquents, but among otherwise intelligent, idealistic and well-meaning people. For they have come to regard violence, and threats of violence, as a

K

legitimate means of asserting their claims, and of promoting good causes, in societies grown too large and bureaucratic to respond flexibly. Such a period is evidently not one in which to discern the culmination of a heritage of liberties.

To put the matter more assertively, the view that we are living in a stricken society, a sick society, a dissolving society, fits the observed facts better. At all events, it is a society in which the great religions, and the great myths from which mankind once drew inspiration and comfort, have been eroded by the spread of secular knowledge and scientific "objectivity". With the easing of economic circumstances in the West, and with the growth of the Welfare State, the older virtues of frugality, stoicism, moral responsibility and self-discipline have more limited scope and more limited appeal. What is more, the sense of community is being irreparably fractured by the developments of modern technology, by automation, computerisation and motorisation. Everywhere, and not only in the West, there appears to be a growing restlessness and discontent. In the expanding cities and suburbs frustrations continue to mount, and the sanity of ordinary citizens is being increasingly threatened by the unabating assault of mass media, and by the inescapable noise, fume and traffic congestion. It is all too likely that we are becoming unhinged, and nearer to social disintegration than we dare imagine.

Seen against this backcloth, the current obsession with sexual gimmickry may be properly regarded also as a symptom of the growing frustrations that have brought about a new crisis of confidence in the West. Gate-crashing into sex is not too surprising a response of the denizens of the consumer society, long reared in institutions dedicated to bloating men's appetites; a foredoomed attempt to combat their growing despair and the stresses produced by being subjected to, and having to keep up with, rapid technological change.

To generalise thus is not to deny, however, that over the last few years we have also witnessed the beginnings of a movement of profound concern for what we have done, and what we are continuing to do, to our lives and to our unique planet in the name of progress. Many in this movement reject the idea of a future society impelled by technology, and shaped by economic growth and currently operating market forces. From this movement there are emerging the first uncertain attempts to formulate a philosophy that will break with the ethos of the last two hundred years and will, instead, create institutions designed to promote a social order more attuned to men's instinctual needs and more in harmony with the ambient ecology of our planetary home.

But these are as yet tender shoots struggling for life in an urban civilisation growing in on itself and made callous by the habitual commercially-inspired clamour for speed and spice, and by the inveterate strife between sect and colour, between haves and have-nots. Alas, there is no historical law or transcendental dialectic to assure that the new forces of understanding and humility will prevail in time against deeply entrenched interests, financial, bureaucratic and technocratic.

In any period other than the present, a failure to check the commercial pressures impelling a community toward overt pornographic spectacles and revelry would, indeed, cause the rot to set in. It would destroy the morale and vigour of the community, leaving it a prey to tyranny or to foreign conquest. In the world of today, however, a world lurching toward a variety of ecological crises, and moving closer over time to the perils of a nuclear Armageddon, the exhilarating descent into the pornographic maelstrom can be more aptly regarded as but one more insidious form of distraction added to the many that already blind the fast-scurrying members of the affluent society to the impending holocaust of the human species.

A Note on the Prevalence of Violence in Folk Tales
The vision of some aspirant of the underworld today scouring the pages of *Oliver Twist* for hints on "how to do it" is surely a bit far-fetched, though it is not impossible that an ambitious criminal might glean some new ideas from a close reading of Agatha Christie's murder mysteries. None the less, information on *how* to do it does not necessarily make a person *want* to do it. And it is certainly not information, or not information alone, that is provided by the literature of sex obscenity and violence. The

assertion that repeated exposure to brutalising scenes can brutalise a person, or make him more callous of the suffering of others, depends for its force on the character and the purposes of the protagonists and upon the moral implications of the story.

No one will deny that the *Iliad*, the *Aeneid*, parts of the Old Testament, the Norse Sagas, and the legends and fairy tales from all over the world are richly strewn with incidents of cruelty and violence. Yet they are unreservedly accepted as an integral part of our culture. Wherein, then, lies the difference, if any, between such literature and the modern literature of violence, of sadistic violence or what we might call porno-violence?

Consider, first, the fairy tale. Whereas wolves and witches and giants do seem to be addicted to unfortunate eating habits, the fact that these creatures are wolves and witches and giants does tend to place them in a world of make-believe and of long ago; at any rate in a world outside the child's immediate range of experience. The world of porno-violence, on the other hand, though it occasionally harks back to some historical period, is for the most part recognisable as the here and now. The characters are credible enough, and not too different from the types of people we read about in our newspapers.

Again, if there are wicked stepmothers and fierce dragons, there are also good fairies, faithful servants and brave princes who—the child soon realises—can be counted upon to tidy up the most unpromising situations; to slay the cruel monster in a single stroke, to rescue the fair maiden, and to live happily ever after. Invariably then good triumphs over evil ere the tale is done with. In the fiction of porno-violence, however, good cannot be relied upon to conquer evil—if only because there may be no good characters in the story. In the more blatant pieces of this genre, the hero, or rather the anti-hero, is a depraved specimen distinguishable from the other characters, if at all, only by his being more cunning and ruthless. It is unlikely that a normal child would accept such a story as a reasonable substitute for a fairy tale.

Finally, while granny is indeed gobbled up by the bad wolf (later to be released intact, and apparently unruffled), and the giant is frequently depicted as joyfully crunching up little children in his hungry jaws, the cruelty is but a prelude to the retribution that is sure to follow. It is a pattern of narrative that is apparently very satisfying to children, and to adults too. The sort of ritual violence in such tales has the significant psychological effect of helping the child to come to terms with his inner conflicts of love and hate in which inevitably, though on an unconscious level, his parents, brothers and sisters are involved.

For in almost every tale, the conflict is satisfactorily resolved. Envy and cruelty are clearly recognised, and are sometimes perhaps a little alarming. But goodness and love prevail in the end. The fairy tale points a moral, and provides much-needed assurance for the child that all will end well. For, though only vaguely apprehended by him, such tales act over time to strengthen the child's confidence in his own good impulses, notwithstanding the fears arising from his more primitive and cruel urges.

In today's popular pulps laden with sadistic violence, all will not end well. It does not aim to reassure. On the contrary it aims to excite, alarm, and disturb. Far from being affirmed by the narrative, the moral order is repeatedly violated by it. Such "literature" sets out to shock, to impart savage sensations, to whet sadistic appetites, the successful repression of which is one of the preconditions of civilised living. The relish with which there is depicted in such writing the uses and abuses of human beings as wonderfully tormentable things, instrumental to the degraded appetites of another, excites both fury and lust, confuses identity, and can aggravate emotional conflict and disorder.

Now much that has been said of fairy tales can be said also of the world's myths and sagas which are, after all, only fairy tales for "grown-ups". True, there is violence, bloodshed, cruelty, and endless battles, feuds, and tragedies. There is also the anger of the gods, inter-tribal hatreds, and sworn enmity between men. But though there are apparent injustices through the caprice of the gods, the narrative as a whole tends to move with the moral grain of man's psyche, and not against it.

The course of events is never such as to weaken the reader's compassion or to confuse his loyalties. Even among scenes of carnage, the heroic narrative speaks loudly for those attributes of men that span time and space; of comradeship and courage in adversity, of sacrifices willingly made in the common cause. The traitor is spurned, the coward scorned, the victim pitied. Honour and justice are recognised and applauded. And, above all, there is eloquent testimony to the enduring power of love.

Such qualities do not, however, emerge in the literature of pornography, sadistic violence, and crime.

5. *The Economics of Sex Pollution*

If I were asked for a private off-the-cuff opinion on the causes of the post-War explosion of sex obsessiveness, I should hazard the view that it was one of the several symptoms of incipient social disintegration, a consequence itself of a global ecological eruption which, despite our growing concern, is gathering pace and amplitude. Experiments with lower mammals have revealed their striking reaction to contrived changes in their environment. Crowding, or noise, above certain levels causes normal animals to become neurotic—to become vicious, to become homosexual, to kill and even to devour their own offspring. It may be thought presumptuous to infer men's behaviour patterns from experiments on rats, pigs, and monkeys. But if such crude evidence alone is unacceptable, so also is the thesis that man, of all mammals, can somehow transcend his environment. Who would maintain that if technology made possible an increase in world population to the point where privacy was no longer possible, where people were almost literally treading on each other's toes, physically frustrating each other's movements, people would not soon be reacting in violent and perhaps perverted ways?

It is not merely the size of the global population, however, but its distribution trends and its degree of mobility. The sheer size of modern urban centres, which yet continue to attract population, makes them vulnerable to any disruption of essential services, accidental or deliberate. Large cities today are, also, growth points for crime, drug addiction, and delinquency. As for international mobility, the enforcement of immigration controls, in the West, against the pauper multitudes of Asia and South America is on the way to becoming one of the big problems of the near future. And if it is going to be hard to contain this sort of mobility, it is going to be equally hard to continue to expand another sort, travel for pleasure. Apart from the growing congestion problems the tourist-industry, packaged and unpackaged, cannot continue to expand much further without running the risk of outbreaks and rioting by local populations. The terrible truth we are finding so hard to believe is that the earth is indeed finite, and that at last we are coming smack up against the fact.

It is in the cities and metropolises of the West that sex obsessiveness—or "sex permissiveness" as it is euphemistically referred to by witless "liberals"—has taken root. And it is the cities and conurbations of today that are the breeding grounds of every form of psycho-pathology—not surprisingly, of course, in view of the endless noise, traffic jams, mounting queues, and of the feverish jostle and pace, the over-stimulus of modern media, the nervous excitement spawned by commercially inspired and quite unrealisable expectations. Along with the repeated stimuli come the repeated frustrations, and with them the widespread despair and embitterment that express themselves in domestic rupture, in racial strife, in student rebellion, in women's lib; in the growing popularity of weird cults, from drug-tippling to witchcraft—and in a "sex permissiveness" that covers the spectrum from verbal vulgarities, exhibitionist apparel, and erotic advertising at one end, to "educational" sex and pop porn in the middle, to live shows, hard porn and bestiality at the other end; to say nothing of the fashionable promotion of conventional perversions, parading themselves, like "gay liberation", in convivial attire.

The case *against* the prevailing vogue for regarding all such manifestations of "sex permissiveness" as a sort of millennial opening of the gates to uninhibited sexual delights, or as an exhilarating extension of personal liberties, and the case for regarding them, instead, as endangering sexual fulfilment and as incompatible with any legitimate aspiration to the good life, has been argued elsewhere.[1] But though a strong case for increased censorship, at least against sexual obscenity strutting about in the market place, can be made out, its successful implementation requires ultimately a consensus about sexual mores and morals. a consensus that has prevailed in other civilisations reaching back to Antiquity and which, indeed, largely prevailed in the West until about a decade ago. Since then, and under the impact of a commercially sponsored sexual-libertarian assault, the consensus may have begun to disintegrate. Thus, one can no longer feel wholly optimistic about the attempts, by those seeking to preserve the basic values and political structure of the liberal-democratic state, to persuade a consumer-oriented public—too long nourished on the pap of rising expectations—to forgo the promise of immediate excitation that leads only to disillusion and derangement, for the possibility of more enduring gratifications based on the recognition of psychic realities and the social need of taboos. Under the "ideal" conditions presented today by city life in the affluent societies, immoral pornocrats allied with amoral technocrats have been worming their way into the moral substructure of Western civilisation. How far, one cannot say. And though a fierce reaction against the purveyors of pornography, not least among the young, may well be on the way, no clear trend can yet be discerned.

What does society do in the interim? In view of the uncertainty of the extent of any consensus on sexual morals, we might usefully consider a holding operation, one that is guided by the narrower lights of the economist. In his capacity as economist, a man would look upon all erotic or pornographic items and entertainment as market goods—albeit market goods whose consumption may give rise to direct favourable or adverse "spillover effects" on the welfare of others. The advantage of this formal approach is that it is "value-free" in the sense that a social cost-benefit analysis is value-free or, more generally, the concept of economic efficiency is value-free. This implies that no explicit social or moral values are brought to bear on any decision about whether, or how much of, a particular good should be introduced. Only *individual* valuations of the direct effect upon them of "goods" and "bads" are to go into the reckoning.

Suppose then, to start with, we all have the same sexual tastes and the same sexual morals, a problem may still arise, and for the same reason that a noise problem can arise even if we all have the same attitudes toward noise. Noise is appropriately described as unwanted sound, and, if so, the term noise-pollution is redundant. But since the term brings home forcibly the nuisance of having to put up with it when it is not wanted we may continue to use it. You may be a music lover, but if in the middle of solving a problem that required the full power of your concentration, someone were to play, say, Beethoven's *Pastoral*, your favourite symphony, you would resent it. You may be supposed to enjoy sexual activity as much as the next person, and you also may be quite open in this respect to experimentation and innovations. All the same, you do not want it thrust at you when your mind and mood are on other things. You may not want to be sexually stimulated on the way to a hard day's work at the office, any more than you want to hear a joke when you are at a funeral. Sex too has its time and place, and when it slips out of its proper time and place so as to annoy, we can legitimately talk of sex pollution.

Like noise and other forms of pollution, sex pollution has become so ubiquitous that we hardly think to express our annoyance any longer. Men in cities are daily exposed to unwanted stimulus by suggestive and erotic posters, especially in London's Underground railway. They pass windows with daring displays, cinemas dripping sex, and news-stands adorned with startling girlie magazines—distracting on occasions, and embarrassing, if not offensive, if a man is accompanied, say, by a distinguished foreign visitor, or by his wife and children.

In the real world, of course, people have different responses to sexual activity and, today, they are on the way also to having different moral standards. The self-styled advanced thinker loves nothing more than to pontificate on the evils of the state, or of the law, in preventing people choosing what they like. To use Professor Jackson's satirical turn of phrase: "Big Brother wigged and gowned on the judicial bench",[2] interfering with the things *we* want to read and enjoy, is not to be tolerated.

The alleged evil is that of the state imposing its moral values on *others*—these "others" being the producers, the suppliers, or the customers of erotica and pornography. The same "advanced" thinkers, however, appear to have nothing to say of this latter group's imposing *their* standards on the remaining members of the community. The "advanced" thinker would insist that sexual morality is a private matter. And so it is when it goes on behind closed doors. But the permitters are not satisfied with that. They do not want merely the freedom to talk to one another of prurient subjects in the vulgar vernacular, or to watch blue films, or to practise sexual tricks, or to display themselves to one another privately in erotic splendour. This they can already do among like-minded company on private premises. What they want is the public to take notice. They want their books and posters and magazines and displays out on the streets, in the cinemas, in the theatre, and in the mass media.

Thus, when we are explicitly ignoring (as we are here) the broader question of an appropriate moral code for a technological society, and are confining ourselves, instead, simply to the current conflict of interests, we have an instance of what an economist would call "an external diseconomy", or an "adverse spillover effect", inasmuch as in this particular issue the pursuit of pleasure and profits by the pornographic interest inflicts a loss of welfare on the more conservative group.

Consideration of the conflict of interest implied by the concept of spillover poses a difficulty we had better recognise at the start. If we distinguish between a permissive group (which includes also the pornographers and their customers) and a conservative group, we may speculate whether the distress suffered by the conservatives at occasionally being unable to avoid the handiwork of the permitters (or, more precisely, at being unable to avoid it without cost or sacrifice to themselves) is greater than that which is suffered by the permitters if, instead, the public display of their products were prohibited. If there is a point to be made in equity, however, I fancy it should go to the conservatives, since the private activities of the conservatives are of themselves not alleged to give offence to the permitters, while the activities of the permitters do, or, if permitted, would, give offence to the conservatives.

The classical economic approach to such a problem might begin with a demonstration that, if the law were wholly permissive, the unchecked market would produce "too much" sex pollution (in the particular sense that the permitters could *not* afford to bribe the conservatives to accept the last units—however measured—of sex pollution). If, on the other hand, the law was wholly repressive in this regard, there would, on the same sort of argument, be "too little" sex pollution. The conclusion following these formal demonstrations is, clearly, that there is an *optimal* or "ideal" amount of sex pollution, which amount could, in principle, be realised by an excise tax on the polluting activity. It is obvious that quantification in such an instance is not going to be easy, even though the idea of some sort of a tax on an activity offensive to others has some commonsense appeal.

The only purpose served in indicating this familiar economic solution is to stress the affinity of sex pollution with other kinds of environmental pollution, and to draw the same conclusion: that beginning, say, from an unrestricted market situation, *some* reduction of the polluting product or activity would confer a net gain on society (again, in the particular sense that the money worth of the *gain* to the conservative group from some reduction of the polluting activity would exceed the money worth of the *loss* to the permissive group).

Let us therefore turn to another solution to the spillover problem, one which under certain conditions is vastly superior to the "ideal compromise" implied by an *optimal* output of the spillover product, and in this instance decidedly more practical. I refer to a separate-areas solution.

In general, once separate areas are offered to the opposing groups, each within its own chosen area need surrender nothing to the other group: neither group will be subject to the restraint or annoyance of the other. What goes on in one area does not impinge on the senses of a member residing in another area. One may, of course, argue that knowledge, or mere suspicion, that something a person disapproves of is taking place somewhere else can also be a source of annoyance, and there is no need to believe this response to be abnormal. But society can also, on ethical grounds, agree that for all policy purposes such "unreasonable" responses shall be disregarded.

Now *so long as there is no consensus on sexual morality,* so long as there are irreconcilable differences in judgment as to what constitutes erotica, pornography, obscenity, brutality, and so on, and so long as there are differences in opinion as to the proper occasion for the erotic or aphrodisiac, this separate-areas type of solution offers society a far wider accommodation than any tax or compromise solution, and it merits close consideration. What is implied in this instance is simply that there be a place, a known place, for each form of erotica, pornographica, or what-have-you. Indeed, cities sometimes tend to produce such areas, though often they are not fortunately placed. A red-light district in a known suburb of a city is more tolerable than prostitution scattered throughout the centre of the city. Similar remarks apply to nude-shows, and to the misnomered "adult" cinema which has begun to pop up in once "respectable" districts. But whereas, granted the laws are accommodating, there are advantages for both buyer and seller in having a well-organised market in sex gratification (and since the market is not "respectable", relegated to the outskirts of the city), similar incentives cannot be depended upon to produce a local market for aphrodisiac entertainment, since the media for it are already established in the form of bookshops, bookstalls, theatres, cinemas and ultimately television sets, which media serve also, for the present, non-aphrodisiac entertainment.

What is being proposed, therefore, is that in all major cities a large single area, or a number of adjacent districts, be designated in which the most *avant* of *avant-garde* theatres may flourish unmolested; where no literature, drawing, painting, or any work of art will be proscribed, no matter how obscene or shocking, where artists, hippies, and every sort of exotic or adventurous group can congregate and dwell and, if they wish, enact their fantasies, and express and indulge themselves without limit. These areas, which we can refer to as X areas, in order to distinguish them from the "respectable" or U areas of the city, will, however, be well-policed to maintain order and prevent violence. Other than these X areas, which are clearly demarcated for the convenience of the inhabitants and visitors, it would also be possible to locate within U areas a number of licensed *X* bookshops (without window display) offering a full range of books and magazines calculated to titillate the sexual palate.

The question of censorship does not properly arise under these arrangements. The only question for society to determine is whether the work shall appear in the *U* area or in the *X* area. Such decisions could be made, say, by a board of 7 or 9 adults, appointed for their good sense and honesty—though it might become conventional to exclude those with connections in the world of art or publishing. There would be nothing, however, to prevent the board from taking advice from outside specialists if the occasion arose. The criterion it would be guided by, in determining where a place of art should be placed, would obviously *not* turn on whether the work in question "tended to deprave or corrupt", but simply on whether the sexual or sadistic aspects of the works (which term would include all literature, posters, paintings, drawings, sculpture, theatre, cinema, advertisements, and any public displays) *were likely to offend* people if displayed in public in the *U* area. Since the maxim, "when in doubt, throw it out", should prevail, it could be laid down that a one-third vote should suffice to relegate the work to the *X* area. The law is broken, then, only if a work of art is displayed in the *U* area without the express consent of the board. No jury would find its resources taxed in determining the facts in such a case.

Since the purpose of this arrangement is to avoid giving unnecessary offence to members of the public, and to reassure "old-fashioned" parents who are anxious to protect their young against upsetting experiences, the contents of books will, in most cases, be less important than what is depicted on their covers, and the methods used to advertise it. *Playboy*, *Penthouse*, and other magazines specialising in unclad women might qualify to circulate in *U* areas if they appeared in plain covers. On the other hand, a book carrying a title such as *Oral-genital Variations—with illustrations*[3] would certainly be ruled offensive if displayed in public places in the *U* areas.

Daily or weekly newspapers might seem to pose special problems since they would be costly to vet. A likely arrangement would be to permit them to circulate freely in the *U* areas on condition that no nude or semi-nude pictures, nor any picture or report of a sexual nature appeared on their covers; that is, on the front or back pages. However, since the pages of newspapers can be left open in trains and other public places, it is possible that additional rules would restrict the size of print or pictures on sexual subjects. Newspapers which do not wish to conform to these rules would, of course, be permitted to circulate freely in the *X* areas, and citizens anxious to peruse such papers might secure them from such areas or from *X* bookshops in *U* areas. However, the law would require that all papers, books, or works of art bought in these *X* areas or shops, be properly wrapped when carried through a *U* area. Unwrapping, or inadequate wrapping, of such *X* material in a public place in a *U* area would be deemed an infringement of the Act.

Television would come under similar restrictions. All advertising, news, and entertainment turning on sex or sadism would require prior consent. The possibility of having one or more *X* channels, obtainable by turning a special key so as to protect minors, may be mooted, although in view of the plentiful supplies of blue films and other pornographic material in the *X* area there is hardly a case for transmitting it into homes also.

I should not think that, under such arrangements, *U* areas would unduly restrict the range of literature or theatre available. Shakespearean plays would continue to appear unbowdlerised, as indeed would Restoration plays. Scenes that are naughty, or bawdy, or comically seductive, or suggestive, do not generally give offence, and certainly their advertisement outside theatres can hardly offend. Plays of the *Oh! Calcutta!* genre, on the other hand, can, and do, give offence, and would properly be shown in *X* areas.

Under such an institution no adult person need feel himself aggrieved. For not only does each group have the freedom it desires—the permitters to indulge their tastes without restraint, the conservatives to enjoy their outings without fear of being jarred, or embarrassed—but, in addition, any grown person can both have his respectability and, on occasions, discard it. He can be sure of being able to avoid unwanted sexual stimulus without sacrifice of any convenience, and can be equally sure of obtaining it on occasions of his own choosing.[4] In this way sex pollution will be contained, and unnecessary strife and anguish avoided.

Needless to remark, there will be initial difficulties in the implementation of any new scheme. Invariably such difficulties will be blown-up and satirised in the attempt to show that the idea is quite impractical—often enough by "forward-lookers" who love to be seen moving, but are loath to have to change direction. Among the problems that come immediately to mind is the determination of the number, size and location of such X areas—should Soho or Times Square be "cleaned up"? There is also the initial arranging of transfer payments between those people who wish to move into such areas and those who will wish to move out. In addition a number of matters, having to do with buildings, police and traffic, will have to be faced. But it is better to face such problems in a rational spirit, and while there is yet time, than instead to continue to drift on in perplexity, always subject to the risk of our peculiar and unstable civilisation—technologically powerful but morally fragile—slipping into some sort of bedlam beyond the point of no return.

A word by way of Epilogue. The crucial message embedded in my book on *Costs of Economic Growth* is that in a civilisation that is being shaped by the apparently irresistible forces of technology and commerce there are, still, vital options open to society, other than just "forward" or "back", if only we could break away from imaginary pressures to "keep up"; from the temptation to yield to momenta that sweep us along all in one direction. Separate areas, in this and in other contexts, regarded as a means of both preserving variety and reducing conflict— or, put otherwise, as a means of enlarging the area of personal freedom and amenity—is one of these options which are open to a democratic society. And it is one that we ought to start thinking about in all seriousness.

6. Does Immigration Confer Economic Benefits?

The economic aspects of immigration, like those of any other social phenomenon, can be treated as either a *positive* ("behaviourist") or a *normative* ("prescriptive" or "policy-oriented") study. A positive study of immigration may be either historic and descriptive, or else analytic. If the latter, it will concern itself mainly with the impact of migration on resource and product prices. A normative study, on the other hand, will comprehend economic analysis and with its aid seek to appraise the results in terms of "better" or "worse", as does the following study. This it may do within a world context, or else within a regional or national context.

Western economists, whose training begins more often than not with "ideal" or highly simplified models having such features as universally competitive markets, unrestrained mobility of resources *within* countries (though not between countries), unhindered and costless free trade, tend to favour the promotion of such features in the real world. Nor is this predilection entirely unconscious or irrational. Normative studies do appear to endow these "ideal" features with characteristics that are believed to maximise social welfare.

By simple extension of such features, unimpeded migration of all resources might be justified as tending to realise, under familiar conditions, an increase in world economic efficiency—defined as a situation in which the gains (valued at the resultant world prices) exceed the losses; a definition implying that a costless distribution of the gains *could* in practice make everyone in the world better off. The logic that tends to this conclusion is simple to illustrate. If, for example, £1 million of capital which could earn 6% per annum in Western Europe is transferred to somewhere in South-East Asia where, after allowance for additional risk, it earns 15% per annum, its transfer from Western Europe to that area increases world income by 9% of £1 million or £90,000 per annum. Again, if an unskilled worker in Madras earning the equivalent of £3 per week moves to Britain and earns £20 per week, world "real" income rises by £17 per week. In sum, so long as real differentials in the earnings of resources exist between different areas of the world there would appear to be scope for increasing world GNP.

What is true for the whole, however, is not necessarily true for each of the parts comprising it. Just as the doctrine that Free Trade is the best policy was qualified for a single country soon after the turn of the century—a qualification that was the harbinger of the growing interest, in the 1940s and '50s, of "optimal" tariffs—so also must the proposition that unhindered migration raises "real" income be qualified in the case of single countries.

In one respect, however, there is a difference between the free mobility of goods and that of resources. A set of tariffs which raises the welfare of a country as compared with free trade obviously requires the continued existence of some international trade. Indeed such tariffs are consistent with a country increasing its foreign trade over the years. In contrast, the degree of immigration that would maximise the welfare of the host country as compared with unlimited free entry could be zero. It is *possible*, that is, that no immigration at all is the optimum immigration policy, or, for that matter, a policy of net emigration. It is *possible*, then, that any inflow of labour entails a loss of welfare for the *host country*, notwithstanding that *world* welfare is raised by the migration.

Let us now turn to consider the net economic benefits or losses arising from immigration in the host country, with particular reference to Britain. There will be no need to employ sophisticated welfare techniques if we can provide a tentative answer based on widely accepted indices of economic benefit. We can do this for two aspects of the problem:

    i. The effects of immigration alone on aggregate demand, and on the balance of payments, in a relatively inflationary economy over a short period of, say, 10 to 20 years;

ii. The effects of immigration alone on *per capita* real income of the indigenous population and on the distribution of the national product.

In addition, two other aspects may be considered, albeit briefly and informally:

iii. The advantages and disadvantages of meeting particular labour shortages by immigrant labour;

iv. The external effects of immigration, broadly conceived.

Before discussing the first two aspects, i and ii, a few words on the relevance of the approach adopted here.

1. We need hardly pause to reject, in such an appraisal, the pertinence of such magnitudes as the contribution to GNP of the immigrant group, or any other group for that matter, and related magnitudes such as total contribution to the Exchequer, or total demand for goods, total contribution to saving, and so on. We could import working population until at the margin the value it adds to the national product is zero while still adding to such magnitudes. The absolute growth of each of such magnitudes, therefore, is transparently compatible with a continued decline in the welfare of the indigenous population as measured by each and all of the indices suggested above.

2. The analysis of the first two aspects is confined to mass immigration of non-professional labour with little capital other than personal effects, and in the absence of large-scale *emigration* of similar labour. Provided the excess of immigration over emigration is large, the type of analysis used is relevant. On economic grounds alone immigration of a few thousand or so people a year makes too slight a difference for the country at large to be worth bothering about—though it may have noticeable local effects. The only interesting question for economics is whether a fairly large net inflow of this sort of labour, say, about 50,000 a year or more, has advantages or otherwise for the host country.

3. It has been observed from time to time that the economic effects of immigrant labour are comparable with the economic effects of an increase in the indigenous labour force. But even if the effects were identical, restriction of the analysis to immigrant labour alone is warranted on political and administrative grounds. The government cannot as yet directly control the growth of indigenous labour: it can certainly control the entry of immigrant labour. It is to no practical purpose then to argue that importing adult labour is, say, more economical than the domestic production of indigenous labour. They are not, at present, practical alternatives to be decided on efficiency grounds. Total expenditure on children is more aptly regarded as consumption expenditure and, like the annual number of births in this country, can be regarded as determined independently of the immigrant inflow. For the period in question, then, we shall accept the internal population growth as given, the only policy question being whether or not to add to this population growth by immigration, and if so, by how much.

4. Any positive role the government might play in attempts to counter or diminish unwanted economic effects of mass immigration is not here integrated into the analysis. There are, of course, any number of precedents for adopting a method that initially abstracts from government policies. Justification for the method is obvious: until there is more information on the direction and magnitude of the effects *in the absence of* government intervention it is not possible to formulate appropriate government policies.

I. Short-run Effects: Excess Demand & the Balance of Payments
One of the manifestations of an "over-full" employment economy, one subject to creeping inflation, is an apparent over-all shortage of labour. Ministerial remarks in these circumstances that "we need immigrants for the labour they provide" are transparently fallacious.[1] A country with a labour force larger than that of China can generate this over-all "labour shortage" simply by adopting policies that result in excess aggregate demand. Although "over-full" employment, and creeping inflation, may be attributable in the last resort to inept monetary and fiscal management, the question to be answered is whether the import of labour, like the import of goods, acts to curb the inflationary tendencies by reducing excess aggregate domestic demand. Clearly if immigrants subsisted on hope and fresh air the answer would be affirmative.

For they would then add something to the national product and subtract nothing from it. However, they do generate a demand for, as well as a supply of, domestic goods; and not only a demand for consumption goods but a demand for investment goods also.

In the attempt to determine whether the addition to aggregate demand they generate exceeds or falls short of their aggregate contribution to the domestic product—and, over time, by roughly how much—we shall first consider a "unit stream" of immigrants; a rate of entry, that is, of one immigrant family per annum. In particular we shall confine ourselves to the Jamaican data, assuming that in each year one additional average Jamaican family enters the country. If we are interested in rough estimates for, say, a constant annual inflow of 50,000 families, it is necessary only to multiply the unit inflow figures by 50,000.

The magnitude of these aggregates to be traced over this unit time-path are, therefore, quite obviously: *(1)* The value of the annual *output* over time generated by this unit inflow of migrants; *(2)* the value of the annual aggregate domestic *demand* it generates over time; and *(3)* the value of the annual *imports* so generated (all at 1962 prices).[2]

1. We begin with the information that the average household with a Jamaican-born head consisted, in 1962, of 3.4 persons of whom 2.4 were working, with 1.0 economically inactive or unemployed. The pre-tax earnings of such a household work out at about £1,200—incidentally about 10% higher than the earnings of the average British household in that year, owing to there being a larger proportion of earners in the average Jamaican household.[3] Applying to such earnings an average profit of 26%, the addition to the value of output attributable to each Jamaican household comes to £1,512.

2. The time-path of immigrant-generated demand should properly take account not only of the immigrant family's *initial* expenditure but, if on balance it exceeds or falls short of its contribution to the national product, of any subsequent "multiplier" effects on the economy. In a full-employment economy any expanding multiplier effects would take the form of adding to the inflationary impetus, although initially there could be some period during which stocks were depleted and queues lengthened. Information about stock and price responses of industry is much too scanty to warrant speculation about time-lags and the extent of the eventual rise in prices, so we shall confine ourselves to the initial impact or *primary* demand. This restriction on the analysis means simply that *if* there is, on balance, an addition to aggregate demand arising from the unit inflow, the estimate of *primary* aggregate demand alone is obviously an under-estimate of the full potential effect. However, since we are concerned, in the main, with the question whether or not immigration is on balance initially inflationary —something we can answer—we can afford to put up with a minimum estimate of the full effects of any excess aggregate demand induced by the immigrants.

The addition to aggregate demand for domestic output arises from two sources, *current* expenditures and *capital* expenditures. The former can be divided into three items:

    i. *current* expenditures out of immigrants' earnings, which are equal to earnings *after* direct taxes, national insurance, savings, mortgage repayments, and remittances[4] have been deducted;

    ii. *current* expenditures out of profits earned in employing immigrant labour after taxes and savings (amounting, in 1962, to about 77% of profits) have been deducted; and

    iii. *current* expenditure by public authorities for additional health and education services, etc., which expenditure is deemed to vary roughly with the size of population.

From the total expenditure on finished goods obtained by adding the figures for the three items, we subtract the average proportion spent on imports, leaving a total that represents current expenditure on domestic goods alone but at *market* prices. By correcting this total to *factor* prices, the effect of all indirect taxes and subsidies is removed from these immigrant-induced current expenditures which turn out to be equal to about 70% of the average immigrant family's gross earnings— or equal to about 55% of the total value of output generated by the immigrant family.

The other source of aggregate demand is the *capital* expenditure needed to accommodate the immigrants in industry and society. The split between social and capital requirements is somewhat arbitrary, though the division between them is of slight importance as compared with the importance of the composite figure. On the assumption that immigrant households have similar requirements to British households, we can use the average figure in 1962 of £5,300 of capital per household (*excluding* import-content and excise taxes), of which roughly one-third would be industrial capital and two-thirds social capital. We have spaced the output response to these capital requirements over two years, so transforming them into annual investment demands.

3. Since expenditures by and on behalf of the immigrants are assumed to have the same import-content as the rest of the population, rough estimates of immigrant-generated imports can be made by reference to the over-all import-content of consumer's expenditure, the import-content of investment expenditure, and the import-content of current government expenditure, these being respectively 20, 12 and 9%. Finally, we need to make allowance for immigrants' remittances in order to estimate the additional drain on our balance of payments induced by this unit inflow.

Clearly the estimates of both *(2)* and *(3)* above will be critically affected by the expenditures on capital goods since the capital requirements of Jamaican immigrant families are more than four times the value of their annual earnings. The extent to which these capital requirements will result in new investment depends upon the extent of the host country's spare capacity and the distribution of the spare capacity compared, respectively, with the magnitude of the immigrant inflow and its distribution over the country.

If the distribution of the incoming migrants coincided exactly with the distribution of spare capacity, both social and industrial, one could calculate, say, the number of Jamaican immigrant families—roughly 180,000—that would just suffice to use up an amount of spare capacity represented by 1% of the U.K.'s existing capital stock. Such an exercise might suggest that very little excess capacity is needed to accommodate a sizeable influx of immigrants. However, the little spare capacity that exists in the U.K. is badly distributed relative to immigrants' requirements. With respect to social capital, it is to be noticed that, according to the 1961 Census, some three-quarters of Jamaican-born residents settled in the Greater London and West Midlands conurbations where, by standards current in the country, housing accommodation was, and is, scarce.

With regard to the demand for new housing, from the observation that the initial housing requirements of immigrants expend themselves in high rents for over-crowded low-quality accommodation, one cannot infer that immigrants have a small effect on the demand for new housing: only that, initially, there is a shortage of housing relative to immigrant requirements (in a country where there was already a shortage even before the immigrant inflow). If it is believed that the government will not allow housing standards to decline and, indeed, will strive to maintain them, sooner or later provision has to be made for additional social capital of a quality comparable to that enjoyed by the rest of the community.

As for the distribution of immigrant workers in industry, although not perhaps as unsatisfactory as the distribution of families in relation to social capital, what is relevant is not merely the excess capacity of industries attempting to absorb immigrants but also the excess capacity in those industries producing goods to meet the initial expenditures generated by immigrants. Since the limited spare capacity in the U.K. is spread very unevenly over different industries and regions, it is safe to assume that for the relatively large-scale inflow of immigrants—say, 50,000 families per annum or more—by far the larger part of industrial capital requirements, at least within a year or two of the first "batch" of immigrants, would have to be met from new investment.

An impression of the likely effects (in terms of 1962 prices) of a unit inflow of Jamaican immigrants on aggregate domestic demand and on imports is conveyed by Table 1, *(a)* on the assumption that capital requirements are met wholly by new investment, and *(b)* by way of contrast, on the assumption that

capital requirements are met wholly by existing spare capacity
—allowing in both cases for a real growth rate per annum of
$2\frac{1}{2}\%$.

Although it is unlikely that in the first year or two immigrants' capital requirements would be met wholly by new
investment, for a constant immigrant inflow of some 50,000
families or thereabouts the *(a)* assumption is obviously more
plausible for the U.K. in the current economic circumstances
than the *(b)* assumption. Indeed, it is probably more plausible
than any alternative assumption. At all events, if all capital
requirements have to be met by new investment, the excess
aggregate (primary) demand generated for a constant inflow of
Jamaican-type immigrant families is positive until year 10.
Then, and thereafter, a reversal starts, excess aggregate demand
being negative. Although no estimates were made of how a
rising or declining inflow of immigrants would affect this
calculation, it should be obvious that a rising inflow of migrants
would tend to lengthen the period of excess aggregate demand
while a declining inflow would tend to shorten it.

As for the resulting balance-of-payments series, it will be seen
from the Table that whether or not capital requirements are
met by new investment, the figure for imports (which includes
net remittances abroad) will increase year by year, though the
magnitude will clearly be larger the more immigrants' capital
requirements are met by new investment—the *(a)* columns
giving the limiting but more realistic figures for wholly new
investment.

It will be observed in the *(a)* columns that although excess
aggregate demand becomes negative in the 10th year, indicating that then and thereafter the unit immigrant inflow contributes to excess aggregate domestic supply, the excess supply
is more than offset by the magnitude of corresponding excess
imports. This means that the continued immigrant-induced
rise in our international indebtedness, or current excess demand
for foreign goods, exceeds the magnitude of the excess domestic
supply from the 10th year onward—the resultant net imbalance
continuing beyond the 16 years covered by the Table.

TABLE 1

Primary Excess Demand and Import Requirements for an Inflow of one Jamaican Family per Year

	Assuming that all immigrant capital requirements are met from:			
	(a) *New investment*		(b) *Spare capacity in the existing capital stock*	
Year	Primary Excess Demand	Imports	Primary Excess Demand	Imports
	£	£	£	£
1	2,004	687	648	325
2	4,127	1,384	−1,310	645
3	3,598	1,711	−1,985	957
4	3,121	2,035	−2,673	1,259
5	2,623	2,370	−3,375	1,551
6	2,108	2,678	−4,089	1,832
7	1,566	3,000	−4,836	2,126
8	995	3,337	−5,618	2,433
9	395	3,688	−6,436	2,755
10	−236	4,055	−7,291	3,091
11	−899	4,438	−8,185	3,442
12	−1,594	4,838	−9,119	3,809
13	−2,324	5,255	−10,095	4,192
14	−2,089	5,689	−11,113	4,592
15	−3,891	6,142	−12,177	5,009
16	−4,732	6,614	−13,287	5,444

What is the economic significance of this resultant net imbalance over time? If immigrant-induced excess supply in the domestic sector were exactly equalled by immigrant-induced excess demand for imports, the value of domestic resources which could be released from the domestic sector would be *available* for exports (ignoring, provisionally, the import-content of exports), and could therefore prevent further accumulation of foreign debt. Provided the resources released were mobile and substitutible in a high degree and the foreign demand for British goods were infinitely elastic, no more need be said.

Failing these conditions, in particular if the foreign elasticity of demand is less than infinite—and for British goods it is hardly likely to be above 2.5—our export prices must fall relative to foreign prices in order to induce foreigners to take up the available slack in the economy. If export prices do decline, the commodity terms of trade moving against Britain, the real domestic resources needed to maintain international balance will then exceed those made available by the immigrant-induced excess domestic supply. Obviously this is true *a fortiori* if the excess domestic supply falls below the figure for excess imports, as it does during the 16th year and beyond.[5]

Any mistakes in estimating the behaviour characteristics of the Jamaican immigrant group will, of course, be reflected in the figures in Table 1 which serve to convey but a rough impression of the magnitudes to be expected from a constant inflow of such migrants. In so far as a part of the capital requirements are in fact met by existing surplus capacity, and in so far as the investment period exceeds two years, the figures in the *(a)* columns tend to over-estimate the excess (primary) aggregate demand and the excess imports. Yet the critical qualitative results—that over the first decade or so, a constant immigrant inflow will on balance increase aggregate demand in a full-employment economy and add to imports—are hardly open to doubt, for several reasons.

First, since no conceivable errors in the estimate of the immigrants' savings or consumption patterns would alter the *qualitative* results of the Table, such qualitative results could be extended with a fairly high degree of confidence to immigrants from India, Pakistan and other economically-backward countries. We could, for example, double or treble the immigrants' savings propensity, or we could double or halve their receipts of goods and services from the public authorities without being within distance of changing the signs of the figures.

Secondly, we could increase the spread of investment from two years to four or to six years without any alteration of signs and with slight increase in the length of the inflationary period.

Thirdly, although for simplicity as well as realism we have assumed a 100% investment response to immigrants' capital requirements, the shape of the resulting time-path of excess aggregate demand is not so sensitive to error here as may be imagined. Indeed, it can be shown that if only one-fifth of the immigrants' total capital requirements is met by new investment, there will still be some excess aggregate demand until the 10th year. Now one can allow that the proportion of immigrants' capital requirements translated into new investment may be well below 100%, at least in the first year or two. But it is almost inconceivable that—for the size of inflow considered —it will approach a figure below 20%.

Fourthly, after all allowances have been made for possible over-estimates of excess aggregate demand and excess imports we may briefly recall certain limitations of the analysis which tend, in contrast, to under-estimate the immigration effects being considered.

In calculating excess aggregate demand the chief limitation has been the restriction to the primary excess demand induced by immigrants. The multiplier repercussions which are explicitly ignored may well be much more powerful than the primary effects estimated. In so far as these multiplier repercussions raise domestic prices relative to foreign prices they cause a shift in the demand from domestic goods to foreign goods, thereby aggravating the deficit in the balance of payments.

Again, our restriction to estimates of immigrant-induced imports under-estimates the resulting balance-of-payments deficiency. Because of a 19% import-content of exports, only £81 out of every £100 worth of goods exported is made up of domestic resources. Thus for every £100 initially imported we have to export an additional £123. The total exports required would, then, have to be about 23% more than the estimate of excess imports in the Table.

Nor can the absence of any estimate of immigrant-induced exports be properly regarded as an omission. So far as I am aware, no economic model—Keynesian, Marshallian, input-output, or any other—assumes any direct relationship between national income, or domestic labour supply, and aggregate exports. Exports of the home country, say *B*, feature simply as the imports of the other trading countries in the model, which imports—like those of country *B*—are positively related to their national incomes. And the magnitudes of the national incomes of these other trading countries are only remotely connected with the number of immigrants entering country *B*.[6]

Notwithstanding these arguments, there remain two features of the model used which might raise objections: *(1)* the continued application over time of an unaltered capital-labour ratio in industry; and *(2)* the assumption of continued neutrality by the government.

Justification for the first, as an approximation, depends upon the length of period in question. Yet even if the real costs of meeting current housing standards, or the standards themselves, fall by as much as a half over the decade the immigrant aggregate demand trends would only be reduced, not reversed. Similar remarks apply to industrial capital.

As for the possible substitution of labour for capital if (in response to the immigrant growth of labour) the wage level tends to fall relative to profits for a period as short as, say, 10 years or so, it is unlikely that the order of magnitude of the fall in relative wages will be such as to encourage the adoption of industrial techniques that are noticeably more labour-using. Be that as it may, the relevance of such an effect in the context of the model, one prone to persistent creeping inflation, and one in which the exchange rate is fixed, is questionable. Wages relative to profits *may* be declining over the period in consequence of the additional immigrant labour, notwithstanding which the initial inflationary impact, which is of major concern here, will continue unabated. Indeed, it is *via* the mechanism of inflation —in which profits rise faster than money wage-rates—that the decline in wages relative to profits is in practice brought about.

The justification for the second feature, the neutrality of the government, has already been indicated. The government can —and in the event of a large and continuous inflow of migrants, should—intervene in any of a combination of ways if (as we may suppose) it wishes to combat the resulting inflationary pressures arising from the immigrant-induced excess demand. But whether the response of the government takes the form of larger budget surpluses or tighter money or both, success is achieved only by effectively increasing domestic saving in the economy, over the decade, sufficiently to offset the excess of aggregate demand that would otherwise arise. It should, however, be evident that such additional domestic saving brought about by government intervention could, in the absence of immigration, add to the social and industrial capital of the indigenous population.

In a fully employed economy, such as that of the U.K., in which spare capacity is negligible, a constant stream of relatively unskilled immigrant families has an adverse balance-of-payments effect and, if the stream is large, almost certainly has an inflationary impact on the economy for about a decade (longer if the inflow rises over time, smaller if it falls over time). Thereafter, unless the resulting inflation takes on a momentum of its own, there is apparently an excess aggregate domestic supply. If we could then transfer all the available domestic resources to producing for export, they would not suffice for another decade or so to prevent continued growth of immigrant-induced international indebtedness.

A very rough impression of the order of magnitudes to be expected is indicated by the estimates made for a unit inflow of Jamaican families at 1962 prices, but for reasons given less reliance can be placed on the figures than on their signs. No policy implications follow from this, or any other, analysis. But if the country does choose to add to its growing population by immigration of this sort, it must be prepared for additional pressure on its balance-of-payments and, ultimately, for less favourable terms of trade. The inflationary impact can always be combated by fiscal and monetary policies designed to extract additional saving from the economy—at least, if we ignore possible political difficulties in any further raising of taxes or interest rates.

II. Long-run Effects on Per Capita Real Income & Its Distribution
Over a long period, measured in decades, we may disregard the initial inflationary effects of large-scale net immigration and transform the inevitable adverse balance-of-payments effects resulting from net immigration into adverse terms-of-trade effects—on the assumption that the country seeks over a long

period to maintain international balance through a reduction in domestic prices relative to foreign prices. We are thereby enabled to turn our attention to these underlying "real" effects, from which we can select two indices of economic gain or loss. Over time we trace the impact upon them of large-scale immigration.

Thus A will stand for a measure of the impact of immigration on the *distribution* of the national product, in particular that between labour and capital, and B will measure the impact of immigration on "real" *per capita* income of the *indigenous* population in the host country. A third index, "real" *per capita* income of the composite population (indigenous plus immigrant), though of general interest in itself, cannot provide a measure of gain or loss to the indigenous population alone. Because of its prominence in policy discussion, however, we shall include it as the C index.

A simple static picture of the economy suggests the sort of answers to expect. Imagine a competitive open economy with fixed amounts of land, capital, and labour. An influx of labour alone *(a)* will reduce wages relative to profits[7]—the A index falls, the distributional change being "regressive"; *(b)* unless there are sufficiently increasing returns to scale, real income *per capita* of the population as a whole declines—the C index falls; and *(c)* the real income *per capita* of the indigenous population rises provided there are no terms-of-trade effects[8]—in that case the B index rises and a gain is registered for the indigenous population. Once we take account of the adverse terms-of-trade movement required to maintain external balance, however, no clear qualitative result emerges. Estimates have to be made to determine the outcome of the two opposing forces.

The only certain effect emerging from this simple model is the regressive distributional effect, or decline in the A index. For B, and—once scale effects are introduced—also for C there can be off-setting tendencies which cannot be resolved without some idea of the relative magnitudes involved. Estimates of the magnitudes are necessary for another obvious reason: even if the indices are clearly favourable, or clearly adverse, the importance of the contribution economics can make to any immigration policy will depend upon the estimated *magnitude* of the changes induced by immigration.

A somewhat more elaborate model is required, one which traces effects over time in response to a continued inflow of migrants. We shall suppose that a full-employment level of output of the host country is determined, at any point of time, by the existing technical knowledge and by the endowment of labour and capital. Over time, technical knowledge improves steadily—adding, we shall suppose, $1\frac{1}{2}\%$ per annum to national product for any *unchanged* capital-labour endowment. In the absence of all migration we could estimate the growth in the stock of both capital and labour by extrapolating, respectively, existing net saving and net reproduction rates. This information, along with the allowance of $1\frac{1}{2}\%$ per annum for improved technology, enables us to trace over time the path of real national income and, therefore, real income *per capita* (index C).

With a little more analysis, this time-path will also yield information on distribution (index A) and on indigenous *per capita* real income (index B). We could then start all over again and trace another such time-path, this time allowing a net inflow of immigrants of, say, 500,000 each year. Observing year by year the differences between the relevant estimates along the two time-paths, we come up with our indices A, B and C.

Even in so aggregated a model, however, a good deal more information is required than is readily available, or reliable, and the consequent limitations of the method of analysis had better be made explicit before examining the results.

National income for the U.K. in 1962 was roughly £23,000 million produced with a labour force of about $25\frac{1}{2}$ million— about one worker for every two persons. A rough estimate of average net saving gives it as about 11% of net income. Using a familiar form of the relation between labour, capital, and the resulting aggregate product, to which is added *(a)* the built-in technological improvement of $1\frac{1}{2}\%$ per annum,[9] and *(b)* a 1% increase in the indigenous population over time, we are able to generate a full-employment non-immigration time-path of aggregate real income from which the three indices can all be derived.

Turning to the analogous immigrant time-path we have, arbitrarily, chosen to introduce a constant annual inflow of 500,000 immigrants, *without* additional outside capital, the labour from which is taken to be freely substitutible for indigenous labour. Indeed, for a long-period analysis the assumption is made that, in respect of the average ratio of dependents to earners, the net propensity to reproduce, and the propensities to consume, to import and to pay taxes, the immigrant population is no different from the population as a whole.

In addition to the above assumptions and estimates, there are three critical features of such a model for which dependable estimates are not currently available. The first, σ, is the so-called *elasticity of substitution* between labour and capital, and is a measure of the degree to which labour can be substituted for capital. The more elastic is the substitution between capital and labour, the more can labour be used in lieu of capital and the less, therefore, will additional labour tend to depress wages relative to rentals. This elasticity is most frequently taken to be equal to one, which is obviously a convenient figure to work with. Since the results could be sensitive to this value, however, we have made calculations for an elasticity of less than one and more than one. It transpires, however, that the differences made to the indices B and C by changes in this elasticity are not very important.

The second coefficient to which the results might be sensitive is the elasticity of demand in foreign trade, which we need to know in order to calculate the adverse terms-of-trade effect which enters as a negative component into the B and C index. The higher is E_2, the degree of foreigners' response to a reduction of our prices relative to theirs, and the higher is E_1, the degree of our response to a rise in foreign prices relative to our domestic prices, the smaller will be the adverse movements of the terms of trade—brought about, say, by a decline in the value of the pound relative to foreign currencies—necessary to restore international balance.[10] In taking two alternative values for each of these Es of 1.5 and 2.5, we are almost certainly erring on the high side and, therefore, almost certainly underestimating the adverse terms of trade.

M

The third coefficient to which the results could be sensitive—and indeed to which the B and C indices turn out to be highly sensitive—is V which measures the economies of scale. If when the amounts of both labour and capital are increased by, say, 10%, output is increased by exactly 10%, V is equal to one and we talk of constant returns to scale. If V were 1.2, a 10% increase of both labour and capital would increase output by a little more than 12%. Few economists take V to be much less than 1 notwithstanding that for the country as a whole the amount of land is fixed, but fewer still would adopt a figure for V as high as 1.2. The more common value attributed to V in empirical studies is, not surprisingly, unity, and this is the value adopted here. We do, however, make the necessary calculations for a V of 1.2 in order to indicate the substantial difference made to the results by employing such a value.

The results are tabulated below for selected years from $t=0$ (1962) to $t=30$ (1992) for three possible cases, each case being a combination of the three sensitive variables mentioned above. Case *(1)*, with the more conservative values of these variables, has estimates of the A, B, C indices for six-yearly intervals, the remaining two cases having estimates only for the first and last years.

Before glancing down the Table the indices will be carefully defined: A, the index of distribution, is defined as the immigrant rental-wage ratio at any point of time as a percentage of the non-immigrant rental-wage ratio. The more this index exceeds unity the more regressive is the immigrant distribution at that point of time compared with the non-immigrant distribution.

B is the increase (positive or negative) of the *per capita* real income of the indigenous population as a whole as a result of the immigrant inflow up to that year over the *per capita* real income of the indigenous population in the absence of immigration.

C is the increase (positive or negative) of *per capita* real income for the total population, including immigrants, at any point of time compared with the non-immigrant *per capita* real income. A positive £ figure implies an immigrant-induced differential rise in *per capita* real income; a negative £ figure, an immigrant-induced differential fall in *per capita* real income.

The three cases mentioned above embody the following three alternative combinations of the sensitive coefficients:

Case (*1*), for $\sigma = 1.0$, $E_1 = E_2 = 1.5$, and $V = 1.0$.
Case (*2*), for $\sigma = 1.0$, $E_1 = E_2 = 2.5$, and $V = 1.0$.
Case (*3*), for $\sigma = 1.0$, $E_1 = E_2 = 2.5$, and $V = 1.2$.

In response to a constant 500,000 net immigration per annum over 30 years the indices *A*, *B* and *C* are as shown in Table 2.

A σ above one, indicating greater substitutibility between capital and labour, reduces the positive value of *A* in all cases and reduces also the negative values of *B* and *C* in cases (*1*) and (*2*), while increasing the positive values of *B* and *C* in case (*3*). The reverse is true for a σ below one. The only serious difference to the order of magnitudes conveyed by Table 2, however, is in the *A* index. Thus for a σ of 2 the *A* index becomes 111 or so for all three cases in the year 30, while for a σ of 0.5 it becomes about 150 for all three cases.

TABLE 2

Indices of Distribution and Increase in Real Income with Net Immigration of 500,000 per year for 30 years

	Year (0 = 1962)	A (in %)	B (in £ at 1962 prices)	C (in £ at 1962 prices)
Case (1)	0	101	−0.83	− 1.5
	6	109	−10.42	−14.0
	12	116	−18.50	−24.5
	18	120	−24.76	−35.5
	24	124	−29.33	−47.0
	30	126	−32.30	−54.5
Case (2)	0	101	−0.40	−1.0
	—	—	—	—
	—	—	—	—
	30	126	−11.33	−42.5
Case (3)	0	101	0.90	0·5
	—	—	—	—
	—	—	—	—
	30	123	61.75	17.5

In view of the somewhat arbitrary, though not implausible, assumptions made, and the parameters adopted as constant over time (such as a constant ratio of earners to population, a constant propensity to save and to import, a fixed net reproduction rate and fixed rate of technological growth), it is unnecessary to stress the tentative nature of the estimates made in Table 2. Nonetheless, despite possible errors in the estimate of these particular parameters, the figures shown are not likely to convey a misleading impression for the simple reason that— although large departures from any, or several, of the above assumptions could result in rather different time-paths than those traced in the Table—it is the *differences* between immigrant and non-immigrant time-paths that enter into our indices *A*, *B* and *C*. An alteration in any of the above parameters would, that is, affect *both* time-paths in much the same way, so that the difference between the resulting immigrant and non-immigrant time-paths is not likely to vary markedly from the magnitudes conveyed by the Table.

There are, on the other hand, the three coefficients mentioned, *V* (the scale effect), the *E*s (the elasticities of both foreign and import demand) and to a lesser extent *σ* (the elasticity of substitution), which do bear more directly on the difference between the immigrant time-path and the non-immigrant time-path. Because of the greater sensitivity of the results to these three coefficients, one must take the precaution of experimenting with a range of values for each of them, as indeed has been done in our calculations.

The figure of 500,000 immigrants per annum over a 30-year period may appear high to some people even if it were supposed that the U.K. resumed its traditional "open-door" policy at least for Commonwealth immigrants. But the figure in itself is of no importance. The only reason for choosing it is to ensure that the changes wrought in our indices *A*, *B* and *C* are all large enough to be perceptible. The assumption of a rate of inflow below 500,000 per annum would imply figures (roughly) proportionally smaller than those in the Table, and vice versa.

At all events, the estimates for *B* and *C* shown in Table 2 are significant only inasmuch as they are surprisingly small. Those who maintain that immigration imposes large economic losses on the country cannot derive much support from this sort of analysis—not unless they anticipate immigration on a scale very much larger than the 500,000 per annum assumed here. As for those who anticipate economic advantages from net immigration, a case could be made out in terms of the B and C indices only if evidence could be produced of large economies of scale for the country as a whole—that is, of a V larger than 1.2. If, however, the conventional view is allowed to prevail, and for the economy as a whole constant returns to scale are assumed, one must anticipate some decline in over-all real income *per capita* (indigenous plus immigrant), and some *per capita* net loss for the indigenous population alone. As suggested above, however, neither is large when taken as a proportion of income *per capita* or of aggregate income respectively. For an annual migrant inflow of 500,000, for instance, the decline in *per capita* real income, B or C, does not exceed 6% after 30 years in any of the three cases. This limited decline in *per capita* real income, B or C, can be attributed in the main to the built-in neutral technological progress that is a feature of our model.

Only for A, the index of distribution, does the outcome look somewhat more sombre. In all three cases immigration makes the resulting income-distribution distinctly more regressive. All three cases, however, assume a σ of unity. If the σ instead were equal to 2, the consequent rise of the A index by 11% over the 30-year period—rentals rising 11% more than wages compared with the position in the absence of net immigration—could be borne with, since real wages would in any case be rising at an average annual rate of about 2%. *Per contra*, if σ were 0.5, there would be a more than 50% rise in the A index over that period which, for the same immigrant numbers, could effectively prevent real wages rising over time, or very nearly.

Is a value of 0.5 for σ at all realistic? There is a tendency today to be impressed with the fixity of proportions in any given state of technology, so that such a value would not be thought implausible. But even if we accept that the proportion of labour and capital is relatively impervious to changes in the prices of labour and capital, we could invoke the opportunities for product-substitution to impart flexibility and limit the relative decline in wages.[11] As suggested above, however, we know practically nothing of the actual size of the consumption effects to be anticipated, and we have no option but to conclude, rather lamely, that the regressive distributional effects of a σ of 0.5 cannot be ruled out on grounds of plausibility.

Summary

In a long-run aggregate model of the economy in which we ignore all "temporary" dislocations, all inflationary effects and all external diseconomies, we may plot a movement of three indices, A, B and C, over a 30-year period by comparing an immigrant with a non-immigrant time-path using a number of arbitrary but plausible assumptions for the relatively insensitive parameters while experimenting with the more sensitive ones. Attributing fairly conventional values to the sensitive parameters as in Cases *(1)* and *(2)*—σ of 1, V of 1, and Es of 1.5 or 2.5—Table 2 reveals a fairly pronounced regressive distributional effect over time, a *decline* in the B index of *per capita* income over 30 years of less than £33[12] per annum, and a *decline* in the C index of *per capita* income of less than £55 in the 30th year. A large enough increase in the economies of scale for the country as a whole—a V of 1.2 or more—would, however, raise both the B and C index of *per capita* income to about £62 and £18 per annum respectively. But a value of 1.2 for V would not be regarded by economists as realistic for the country as a whole, and pending evidence contrary to the prevailing belief one may conclude tentatively that an economic case for large-scale immigration, at least one based on indices which would be widely acceptable, is not proven. On the other hand, on the basis of the same indices, the economic case *against* immigration —except on a scale much larger than that conceived in the analysis—is not compelling save perhaps in respect of distributional effects.[13]

III. Immigration & "Essential" Services

The popular belief that Commonwealth immigration has helped to overcome shortages in particular service industries may now be examined in an informal way.

It is not always certain, however, that Commonwealth immigrants' entry to an industry suffering from a labour shortage invariably acts to reduce the shortage. If there is among some of the indigenous workers a dislike of working with some kinds of immigrants, or if some stigma comes to be attached to occupations that employ a large proportion of coloured workers, the entry of coloured workers into an occupation can prolong or aggravate the initial shortage of labour in so far as it causes some of the existing workers to leave and in so far as it deters those of the indigenous population who might otherwise have entered. In such circumstances the effectiveness of Commonwealth immigrants in remedying a shortage is reduced and could indeed be negative. The observation of a large proportion of immigrant workers in occupations most easily accessible to them is consistent on this hypothesis with very little increase in total numbers and possibly with a continuation of the shortage. Public transport and nursing are occupations that might well belong to this category.

Allowing, however, that on balance immigrant labour is eventually effective in relieving an initial shortage, is there any clear advantage in following a policy of admitting foreign labour into occupations that are short of labour for the time being rather than adopting the alternative policy of meeting the shortage from existing domestic resources?[14]

Consider first the allocative aspect. To a passenger depending upon a bus or train service, its maintenance at the same fare is understandably preferred to its withdrawal or to its continuance at a higher fare. But this is clearly a partial view only. In the absence of immigrant labour, which may realise this outcome, this sectoral shortage would be remedied in part by a differential rise of wages in public transport. All intra-marginal workers in such an occupation would gain, and this gain must be set against the loss to passengers. A transfer of "real" income from indigenous passengers in favour of indigenous (intra-marginal) workers is the apparent outcome of the non-immigrant solution to the shortage.

But what of the allocative effect? If the shortage in any industry is remedied as effectually by an inflow of labour from abroad as by a release of labour from domestic sources, and if in either case labour moves until the value of its marginal social product is the same in all occupations, then there would be nothing to choose as between the immigrant and the non-immigrant solutions except for two things, one in favour, one against: (i) the non-immigrant solution may take longer, so prolonging the loss to the consumers of the service, and (ii) the immigrant solution may imply a lower level of welfare for the indigenous population as a whole as measured by the indices in Part II—though, as also indicated, such losses as a proportion of the relevant magnitudes are not large. Since these two considerations are opposed in their effects on the indigenous population, quantitative estimates would be necessary to determine the net result.[15]

Let us turn next to the long-run consequences of accepting a policy of admitting foreign labour to industries claiming to suffer from a labour shortage. In an advanced and fully-employed economy subject to continual fluctuations in the conditions of demand and supply, shortages in some sectors are sure to appear from time to time matched by surpluses in other sectors. The duration of such shortages, and surpluses, will depend *inter alia* on institutional factors (trade union influences and demarcation rules) and also on the active policies pursued by governments which bear on unemployment pay, retraining facilities, incentives to geographical and occupational mobility, monetary and fiscal management, and so on. A policy of encouraging immigration whenever a sectional shortage of labour occurs would, because of its manifest asymmetry,[16] issue in a continued net inflow of foreign labour into the country having the broad effects discussed in Part II.[17] However, any rule that sanctioned the admission of immigrant labour into any industry after the persistence of an unfilled vacancy beyond some agreed time-period might well lead to increasing friction between management and labour. For such a rule would clearly act to discourage any employer from negotiating wage increases and from providing facilities calculated to attract domestic labour if, by waiting a little longer, he can meet his requirements by immigrant labour at existing wages.

Finally, there is the broad question of the so-called "optimal" size of population—sometimes identified by economists with a population for which (within a static framework) average product per worker, or *per capita*, is highest. As indicated in Part I, however, there can be no "economic need" of a larger population or, more precisely, there are no clear economic advantages in Britain either in the short or the long run of a larger population—though landlords and businessmen favour a continued growth both for its immediate market-expanding effects and for the long-term distributional effects in their favour. If a population larger than that which would result from the growth of the existing domestic population is believed to be desirable on "non-economic" grounds—or desirable subject to some restriction on the rate of net immigration—in full awareness of the initially inflationary effects and the long-term regressive distributional effects, then the economist has little to add.

Certainly the so-called optimal population is not an un-ambiguous economic concept: it can be defined in a number of ways, such as the population yielding the highest *per capita* income, or the population enjoying the highest over-all level of welfare per family, or that suffering the fewest adverse neigh-bourhood effects. If an optimum population has any affinity with the latter sort of definition then it is certainly relevant to observe that population per acre in Britain is one of the highest in the world. In particular, the area of England and Wales is today more densely packed with people than either Japan or Belgium. It has about twice the population density of Italy and four times that of France. India, Jamaica and Pakistan, from where the bulk of the post-war immigrants have arrived, have each less than half the number of people per acre than England and Wales. Holland alone can boast a country more densely populated than ours.

In an era as conscious as is our own of the impending "population explosion,"[18] any proposals for augmenting the already dense and growing population of this country by an influx of people from other lands can no longer count on ready acceptance.

IV. External Effects

Some consequences of large-scale immigration do not lend themselves so easily to measurement as those considered in Parts I and II, but they may be at least as important and a good deal more noticeable. A number of these effects are readily classified as external diseconomies. In the short run immigrants tend not only to settle in the existing conurbations but, within them, to concentrate their numbers in popular areas or districts, so manifestly aggravating an existing housing shortage and imposing additional burdens on the social services and possibly also on the public transport systems. Inevitably they reduce, for some years, the amenity of the neighbourhoods they settle in.

One can, of course, dismiss such external effects as teething troubles necessarily associated with the process of settling down. Keynes' dictum, that in the long run we are all dead, is relevant in this connection; for it is during the short period in which we live that the discomforts have to be borne with. Such net disutilities as are suffered by segments of the indigenous population are unambigiously a part of the cost of absorbing numbers of immigrants and wherever possible they should, as Pigou put it, be "brought into relation with the measuring rod of money".

External effects, however, can be broadly or narrowly defined. On a broad definition any response, positive or negative, of any inhabitant of the host country to the entry of any or each of the immigrants qualifies as an external effect. On such a definition it is not necessary that the economist be able to identify any benefit or damage to an inhabitant arising from the entry of immigrants. The effect can be solely subjective—"pure prejudice", if we like. Without ever meeting a single immigrant the mere knowledge that immigrants, or immigrants of a certain type, are entering the country can add to or subtract from the satisfaction of any member of the host country. On the so-called *Net Benefit criterion* (which is the foundation of all allocative propositions in economics), unless the gains from immigration can be so distributed as to make every person included in the host population better off, the host country is not to be regarded as better off.

On this criterion, then, an economic improvement would require that, irrespective of his prejudices, the sums needed to compensate each member of the indigenous population suffering any discomfort whether "real" or "imaginary" from the entry of immigrants could be more than covered by the gains made by other members of the indigenous population *plus* the gains made by the immigrants.

A narrower definition of external effects, one I favour, would exclude all those responses to others' behaviour that cannot count on an almost unaminous approval from the society in question. Thus evidence of direct damage to a man's property, or health, or physical environment, or peace and quiet would in Britain, I think, be almost universally regarded as relevant to the issue. Dissatisfaction arising solely from private principles or prejudices would, however, not qualify as agenda on this narrower view.

If we accept the narrower definition of external effects, the ideal experiment is then to determine for each locality into which immigrants enter, or affect by the repercussions they generate, the minimum sum (reckoned either as a capital sum or annual payments) which, if received by the affected members of the indigenous population on condition of admitting into the localities in question a known number and type of immigrants, would in practice make the members indifferent as between receiving the immigrants and maintaining the *status quo*.

Needless to remark, no one has yet attempted to estimate the magnitude of these compensatory payments, and while this is no reason for failing to mention them, or for failing to dwell on them,[19] it must be admitted that there is no firm basis even for a guess at the social costs involved.[20] For the present, then, no more can be done than explicitly to acknowledge their incidence and potential significance, and to offer the obvious generalisation that they are likely to increase with the number of immigrants, their rate of arrival, their initial level of poverty and lack of sophistication, and with the degree of their concentration within already densely populated areas.

In conclusion one may hazard a prediction. With the inevitable extension of communications there will follow, among the economically under-privileged, an acute awareness of the increasing disparity between their standards of living and those of the ordinary workers in economically advanced countries. In the *absence* of government checks to immigration, the growing temptation to migrate to the few prosperous countries open to them would be strengthened by private shipping and airline companies which would find it profitable to encourage mass migration by offering cheap passenger rates and credit facilities. As it is, and even in the presence of government controls, one can reasonably anticipate a growth in the numbers of illegal immigrants into the wealthier countries, in particular into Britain and North America.

We are not, however, precluded by the above observation from making attempts to ameliorate the economic conditions of the poorer countries if we conceive it to be part of our moral duty to do so. Though some proponents of liberal dogma appear reluctant to concede the possibility, an economic policy may yet be acceptable to the nation without necessarily redounding to its material advantage. If, therefore, on moral grounds we wish to make some contribution to the well-being of the poorer countries we could make our contribution the more effective by undertaking a careful examination of the various methods of affording economic relief (such as removing trade barriers to their sales of products in this country) and by giving direct aid as an alternative to the policy of transferring some part of their growing populations to these already crowded islands.

Considerations of distributional justice would seem to favour exporting capital rather than importing populations. We should hardly regard it as fair to earmark the additional capital sent abroad—which would be an alternative to using it to equip immigrants entering Britain—to be distributed among those families that might otherwise have entered this country. Rather we should want our aid distributed within the poorer country according to some more acceptable principle of social priorities. As an alternative to the export of capital, the import into Britain of a small proportion of their populations is, then, a highly unsatisfactory method of distributing economic relief to poor countries. As a means of promoting economic advance in such countries this alternative is also less efficient on allocative grounds.

A Postscript on Commonwealth Immigration and Race Relations
Concerning the connection between immigration and race relations there are a number of elementary facts that can bear some brief emphasis.

First, parallels drawn by politicians between post-war Commonwealth immigration and immigration in the past of Huguenots, Jews, and Irishmen provide no guidance whatever to immigration policy today. The fact that particular immigrant groups entered this country in the past proves no more than that, notwithstanding the event, the country has survived. There is no evidence to suggest that in each and every instance the consequences for the host country were wholly, or on balance, beneficial. Certainly there is no foundation for the belief that under all circumstances immigration of any peoples in any numbers confers immediate or subsequent benefits on the host country. The conclusion seems unavoidable: granted that the interests of the host country are one of the considerations in determining immigration policy, the question of whether and which immigrants should be admitted is a legitimate subject for public debate.

Second, governments at least should be familiar with the historical observation that the reception accorded to foreigners settling in the host country varies, *inter alia*, with their numbers. Such is the imperfect state of man that there is apparently a limit to the number of immigrants entering a country beyond which any initial cordiality of the native population turns to resentment. That this tolerance limit for any given country depends upon a variety of factors is also indisputable. The more obvious of these are the wealth, the education, the independence and skills of the migrants, their ability to speak the language, their readiness to acclimatise themselves to their new social environment, and the degree of their dispersion over the country. Not the least in importance, alas, are their colour and physical characteristics, which may be alleged to operate on the popular mind at an irrational level.

If our enlightened rulers were aware of these facts, they must have thought it proper and decent to ignore them. For it is apparent now that we must have passed this tolerance limit at some time in the '50s.

Third, the transformation of Britain during the 1950s from a relatively stable and homogeneous nation to a multi-racial concern was not historically inevitable. Nor is it, in the increasingly race-conscious world of today, a manifestly desirable consummation. At all events the British public was not given the opportunity to debate the question. Through a tacit understanding between the leaders of our three parties to act like "enlightened" liberals and to put off for as long as possible any measures of control that might be construed as "racialist", and through the connivance of the Press, the country has simply floundered into a multi-racial society.

Fourth, it is not surprising that the people whose inaction was responsible for this gratuitous social transformation should now seek to persuade us of its inevitability, and of its desirability, and to soothe our apprehensions of the dangers we are courting by recourse to the language of "challenge". It is no more surprising that a large part of the public, belatedly discovering the transformation, feel that somehow they have been "taken for a ride" by the intellectuals. At no time can they recall being presented with a clear choice of whether or not to transform their country into a multi-racial, or multi-coloured, society. On an issue having momentous consequences for their way of life, their opinions were never sought and their wishes never consulted. Indeed, as indicated, the question was never explicitly formulated, and the range of economic and social implications of embarking on this venture was never openly debated.

It ought therefore to be put on record that the ordinary people of this country were, in this instance as in others, the hapless victims of liberal dogma and complacency. It may be "enlightened" or "humane" dogma, but it is dogma just the same. And if there is a lesson to be drawn from the sorry history of such events, it is that men today whose political instincts are guided by such dogma, and not by ruthless pragmatism and forethought, are unfit to grapple with problems in a world erupting with new forms of social strife, the consequence of over-swollen populations and of rising tides, everywhere, of unrealisable expectations.

Fifth, if we discount the hope of raising sums sufficiently large to tempt the large majority of Commonwealth citizens to return to their homelands, we shall have to resign ourselves to the fact that Britain is now, and will henceforth remain, a multi-racial society. Indeed, an effective population policy will be that much more difficult for the country to agree upon since there is an obvious inducement for non-white residents to increase their population faster than the indigenous inhabitants in order to increase their political leverage.

There is, then, everything to be said for our going to considerable expense and trouble to prevent the virus of American race conflict from infecting our shores. At the same time we can only hope that anxieties over racial issues will not, as they have done in the United States, reach such dimensions as to distract the public's attention from the complex of urgent social problems created by rapid urban and economic growth.

Sixth, the measures that are now being taken in good faith have disadvantages that can bear thinking about. The establishment of a Race Relations Board and the enactment of special race legislation may, perhaps, seem justified in the immediate circumstances. But they also act continuously to remind us that there are elements of society in our midst for which the ordinary laws and institutions of the country do not suffice. What is more, such machinery as is put together will not be easy to dismantle. Owing to the self-justifying propensities innate in bureaucracies, we may inadvertently have initiated another "growth industry" whose chief beneficiaries will be (perhaps otherwise unemployable) social scientists.

Press coverage of race incidents and alleged discrimination is unavoidable. But informing the public without inflaming any part of it is the ideal to be pursued. What is of equal concern is the recent flood of newspaper articles and television features calculated to shame the native population into better treatment of the newcomers.

It is doubtful whether this policy acts to promote racial harmony. Not only can it become a frightful bore: the repeated presentation of immigrants as innocent underdogs, whose plight is almost wholly attributable to callous treatment by the indigenous population, is worse than doing nothing. For it creates a hyper-consciousness about coloured people, an excessive caution in their presence, an over-considerateness and artificial humour in dealing with them that is productive only of repressed irritation on both sides. Even the most liberal White begins to jib at the endless tweaking of his conscience by journalists eager to find a vocation in exposing racial disharmonies. Such consequences are subversive of progress toward an easier and more open relationship which is a precondition of racial harmony.

It is not impossible, then, that less pressure from above, less condescension, less publicity, less musing and moralising by all of us, will—granted that the immigration phase is really at an end—better enable the new races to come together with the existing population and in time, and in their own way, discover their common humanity.

7. *On Making the Future Safe for Mankind*

A close study of history might yet uncover periods over which there was no less day-to-day trepidation, no less obsessive soul-searching, and no less persistent reappraisal of contemporary manners and institutions. There may too have been times like our own in which people looked back with cynicism and nostalgia and looked forward with exhilaration and apprehension. But I doubt whether the prevailing anxiety has ever spread so wide, or whether the sense of something awry, of "something rotten in the state of Denmark", has ever before reached so far down into all strata of society and agitated it at every level.

The phenomenon need cause no wonder if we bear in mind that humanity stands not at the edge of one crisis but at a confluence of three crises, technological, ecological and social, all obviously related and all engrossing our attention over the last decade. For the development of mass media ensures that, whatever the specific forebodings are, no segment of society can be deprived of its due share in the general alarum.

The pace of technological advance is primary and is itself responsible for the other two crises: an ecological crisis currently dramatised by the phrase "the Population Explosion", but whose chief visible manifestation is the spread of industrial pollutants over land, sea and air; and, arising largely from the mounting frustrations of urban life, a social crisis, a seemingly chronic restlessness and discontent marked by such familiar symptoms as the growth of drug-addiction, of wantonness, obscenity, and incipient violence. Add to these sources of apprehension the emerging vision of an automated, computerised, highly programmed, and centrally controlled society on the one hand, and, on the other, the existing "balance of terror" between the great powers, each searching relentlessly

N

for new weapons of yet more incredible destructiveness, and it becomes evident that the phrase "living on the brink of annihilation" is today no idle hyperbole. The crisis, or the conjuncture of crises, is all too real, all too fearful, and quite unprecedented.

The task I set myself may also seem unprecedented by reason of its ambition. For I would convert you to the opinion that the continued pursuit of economic growth by the "advanced" nations is itself almost wholly responsible for the crisis. The general acceptance of such a view by society, I need hardly remark, would have far-reaching implications for the conduct of our economic policies. Once convinced of the close connections that exist between economic growth and the less amiable features of our civilisation we could no longer anticipate an eventual improvement in our condition by the simple expedient of moving with greater or less momentum along the expansion path.

Let me assure you that I am woefully aware of my temerity in undertaking so ambitious an enterprise. No less a figure than Arthur Koestler has pointed up the follies committed by specialists who stop specialising and start generalising. But until such time as the universities produce trained generalisers, we are faced with a dilemma. Put crudely, the maintenance of high standards of scholarship today by increased specialisation acts to constrict the area of relevance covered by any one scholar. On the other hand, a primary commitment to social relevance imposes scientific disabilities. For one can hardly address oneself to these larger questions without receding from fastidious methodological standards and advancing towards bolder speculation based on general reading, casual observation, intuition and reflection. There is an obvious danger of depending too closely on historic imagination and premonition; a danger therefore of slipping into charlatanism. One is caught then between Scylla and Charybdis. Facing the worst outcomes, one has the choice of being relevant but wrong, or of being meticulous but irrelevant.

We may now wind ourselves into the subject by asking an apparently naïve question. If it is true that society finds itself at the confluence of these crises, why is it that we have been so tardy in recognising it? Two closely connected reasons suggest themselves: the first concerns the entrenchment in our over-sized societies of existing institutions, political, economic, technological, and the apparently irresistible momenta they set up towards further economic and technological developments (a phenomenon I shall return to). The second reason, which I take up immediately, covers those aspects of the ideology of perpetual progress which, on the basis of confused thinking, lend themselves to complacency—to the belief that there is really nothing to be alarmed about after all. This complacency expresses itself in two main forms, the historical and the scientific, and I deal with them in that order.

Those exuding the first historical form of complacency use ridicule, most of which turns rather monotonously on such epithets as "Doomsday prophets", "Modern Jeremiahs", and "latter-day Cassandras"—forgetting, perhaps, that Cassandra was invariably right. More important, however, is their use of history as a means of dispelling concern. Talk of unprecedented happenings and they will immediately quote you some historical parallel. *Plus ça change plus c'est la même chose* is the refrain, at once cynical and comforting.

For at least two centuries, they will point out, men have distrusted machines. But, I would add, they were not always wrong. The first half of the 19th century was, in Britain, a time of acute distress, suffering, and degradation for the labouring classes, men, women and children. Whether such an epoch, with its evocation of the Black Country and the "dark satanic mills", was a necessary condition for the material advance of later generations is doubtful. But whether or not, it can be justified only on the immoral premise that the ends justify the means. What is more pertinent, however, the "industrial revolution" that began in the 18th century or earlier, far from abating, is gathering force and, propelled by the boundless ambitions of technocrats, is expanding over the earth on a scale that has begun to fissure the physical environment and to produce complex chains of ecological disruption. The forebodings of the past may after all soon be vindicated.

The complacent historian may also observe that for at least four centuries men have looked back wistfully to an earlier age and deplored the growing materialism and irreligion, the unnecessary bustle and change—from which observation one may deduce a number of things, but *not* that the present age is no more materialistic, no more irreligious, or no more rapidly changing than any other period in history.

Indeed, one can go back further. Since the age of Chaucer historians have been delighted to discover—in poems, essays, sermons, plays, diaries and novels—a recurring nostalgia for the times when nature was more abundant, communities more intimate, and life more wholesome. In particular, they will find a recurring dismay at the disappearance of the green forests and of the irreplaceable beauty of the English countryside. And if today conservationists inherit this mood of concern and deplore the rapid erosion, since the war, of coastline, of meadow, dale and woodland—much, that is, of our remaining scenic heritage—one may legitimately infer that the concern of some people at the destruction of the rare and the beautiful is one of the abiding characteristics of humanity. One *cannot* infer, however, that things have not changed, and have not changed for the worse in this respect. One cannot deny, moreover, that the remaining area of accessible natural beauty is but a tiny fraction of what it was during, say, the 18th century—when the population, incidentally, was less than a fifth of the present population and the size of the towns such that wherever a man dwelt or worked, he could be in the open country within a few minutes.

Again, the belief that the end of the world was drawing nigh has been widely held at different times in human history. But from this historic fact there is no consolation to be had. Only since the last World War have men succeeded finally in prising open Pandora's box and among other exciting things which flew out was the secret of instant annihilation of all living things. Time, measured only in short years, will disseminate this sort of knowledge among smaller, poorer and less stable nations, some of which are ruled by adventurers or fanatics. From this prospect alone one may conclude that the chance of human life surviving the end of the century is not strong. To annihilation from irresponsibility, from military mischance or bluff carried too far, must be added the chances of extinction of our species from uncontrollable epidemics caused by the deadlier organisms that have evolved in response to widespread application of new "miracle" drugs, or from some ecological calamity caused by our inadvertent destruction of those forms of animal and insect life that once preyed on the pests that consumed men's harvests. In sum, doomsday fears of yesterday had no rational basis. Those of today have plenty.

The second form which complacency takes is one that is most congenial to the forward-looking scientific spirit, one that implies a view of man's destiny best summarised by Arnold Toynbee's thesis of "challenge and response", a view that is strengthened by the belief in the infinite adaptability of man.

As an instance of this spirit I quote some remarks from Sir Peter Medawar's address to the British Association in 1969, during the course of which he assured his audience that

> the deterioration of the environment produced by technology is a technological problem for which technology has found, is finding and will continue to find solutions.

While admitting the difficulties technology would have to overcome, Sir Peter ended with an affirmation of faith in the beneficent potentialities of science and dismissed the faint-hearted and the doubting Thomases as follows: "To deride the hope of progress is the ultimate fatuity, the last word in poverty of spirit and meanness of mind." Splendid language—though it smacks more of hubris than of faith: faith speaks in a humbler key.

But however we rate his peroration, the question is surely whether we are to be guided by faith at all. Never in history did we need faith less and agnosticism more, an agnosticism that must encompass also the scientific attitude and the implicit judgments of science. Indeed, irreverence must go further if we are at all in earnest. Not even the pursuit of knowledge for its own sake can qualify as of right in the agenda of a sane society. Unless such activity is motivated and constrained by decent and humane ends it must remain suspect. Contrary, then, to the prevailing ethos, a vaunted thirst for knowledge is no more laudable than a greed for possessions. They are in fact closely related responses. The devotees of each are impelled by an insatiable desire; whatever is realised serves to whet the appetite more. To change the metaphor, they follow blindly whithersoever the trail leads.

Again, men in unchecked pursuit of wealth or of knowledge are prone to vindicate their impulse by invoking the same serviceable euphemisms about "challenge" and "thrust" and "dynamism" and, in the last resort, by invoking the concept of a widening horizon of opportunities—the accumulation of wealth adding to man's estate and the accumulation of knowledge to his control over nature.

If we are to be heretical enough to reject all propositions based on faith, and to respect only the power of reason and the evidence of our own senses, we should have to bring into judgment the pursuit of knowledge itself. On the authority of the Bible we have it that "He that increaseth knowledge increaseth sorrow". And if I demur, it is only to qualify the judgment to the extent that in particular historical circumstances the revival of learning and the pursuit of knowledge can indeed make life more interesting and pleasant. Yet it can also outreach its usefulness and become an obsessive activity, gathering pace and extension irrespective of its effects on society. A more forthright statement is that the growth of scientific knowledge over the last four centuries, channelled into a thousand specialisms, and translated into technology by market forces or state power, has become subversive of civilised living.

Having said this much, let me return in a less accommodating mood to this invitation from a renowned scientist to repose our hopes for a better future in the further advances of science, and to believe that technology will itself solve the problems bequeathed to us by its widespread application—problems such as burgeoning populations, atmospheric pollution, traffic-choked cities, oil-fouled beaches, aircraft noise, and so on. The first thought which should occur to us is that such problems can also be solved by the use of less technology, not more. By reducing the production and the use of certain kinds of technological hardware, say the automobile and the aeroplane, we can certainly diminish atmospheric pollution, tourist blight, and traffic congestion. It may be conceded that there is nothing very clever about solving the problem in this way, and it goes without saying that science and technology would much prefer opportunities for further research with the aim of discovering ways that will enable us to absorb yet more of these technological all-sorts while limiting the extent of their unwanted overspill.

There remains, however, the substantive issue about which is the better way of relieving humanity of any one of the currently unpleasant by-products of applied science. Even if it could be ascertained in advance that science *does* have a contribution to make in solving *some* of the problems it has inadvertently brought into being, the relevant considerations in any political decision to finance the required research ought to be, first, the time over which humanity, hanging grimly on to its hardware, has to suffer before substantial relief is at hand and, secondly, the degree of risk incurred in any technological solution to specific problems—and, for that matter, the degree of risk incurred also in providing us with new technological opportunities—of accidentally releasing on our heads a plague of new ecological or other spillover effects. In the light of the experience of the last fifty years—in view, particularly, of the marked tendency of technological innovation to put at the disposal of every person, sane or sick, moral or immoral, powerful means of (inadvertently) annoying or threatening the health or lives of others—the alternative of seeking an improvement in our living conditions by using *less* technology rather than more *has* to be taken seriously.

I might add for good measure that there are also some consequences of applied science that cannot be undone. I am thinking not only of the post-War holocaust of natural beauty that has taken place over the last two decades, a consequence chiefly of the phenomenal rise in mass tourism, but also of the risks from rising levels of radioactive pollutants lodged in the air, under the earth, and beneath the seas. Science is unlikely to be able to reduce this risk in our lifetime, a risk that grows with the proliferation of nuclear power generators. And what of the irrevocable damage perpetrated in the name of scientific advance? Can science restore to Thalidomide babies the limbs it has shrivelled? Does technology plan to restore the lives of the 130,000 people killed each year in car accidents? The man who makes his discoveries available to an imperfect society, a society known to be suffused with ignorance, impatience, avarice and corruption, may not disown the responsibility for the outcomes. In particular, he should not overlook the fact that the existing balance of terror is a direct product of applied science. For without the advance of science, the power for destroying all life on earth many times over (and in a variety of increasingly hideous ways), a power possessed already by several countries, would just not have been possible.[1]

Let us not, then, be too easily soothed by the assurances of those whose bright vision of the future—comprehending as it does a cornucopia crammed with research grants—remains undimmed by those follies of the past and present that could not have been perpetrated without "technological progress".

As for the adaptability-of-man thesis on which the technocrats also place so much store, two questions arise: can man adapt, and should he?

Man as a distinct species has not changed for 100,000 years. Mentally and physically he is the same mammal that ran through primeval forests in search of prey. Until scientists induce mutations so as to transform him into a different being, man can adapt only within limits. It is altogether possible that many features of our new technology-based civilisation move strongly against the grain of man's instinctual needs. Such a civilisation might then be unstable inasmuch as it imposes on ordinary people increasingly intolerable strains giving rise to such familiar symptoms as a break-up of families, a growing incidence of sex perversions, and increasing recourse to drug-taking, destruction, dropping out, freak cults, and violent forms of protest, self-assertion and defiance. Let us say simply that recent findings in medicine, in zoology, and psychology are not at variance with the hypothesis that the spread of technology is pushing men beyond the elastic limits of their adaptability.

But even if, at some cost and with the aid of some providential new drugs, man *could* be made to adapt, *should* he be made to adapt? To hold that man ought to adapt himself—in order "to meet the challenge of the future", as our technocrats so quaintly put it—is surely an inversion of ends and means. A moment's reflection on the theme of the good life suggests that we seek first within ourselves to discover what is good and satisfying for man, and then adapt technology to that end; not the other way round. The fact that problems will arise in reaching accord about the essential ingredients of the good society does not weaken the force of this dictum. For the alternative idea of continually altering man's way of living so as to fit into a world shaped increasingly by the intoxicating visions of technocrats, the mere idea of society as a sort of residuum, as a by-product of perpetual technological innovation, ought surely to be repugnant to us.

As a footnote I would add that this crucial question of adaptability to technology and free choice is imperfectly understood by many who continue to regard the competitive market as offering to men a wide range of choices. I shall therefore return to it in a later context.

Having, I hope, cleared away some of the undergrowth of complacency that clings to the current debate on these large questions, I shall now propound my thesis that the chief cause in the West of society's present crisis is to be found in the economic growth that our leaders are so anxious to achieve. Put less provocatively, my contribution to the debate will consist of examining in an informal way the effects on our well-being of the products and processes of economic growth in technically advanced countries. [2]

As a matter of intellectual curiosity some of you may be wondering innocently if in fact economists can do very much in the way of controlling a country's economic growth. In a short reply one has to resist the temptation to be cynical. For if the economist does indeed know the secret of rapid growth he must, in Britain and America at least, be guarding the secret pretty closely. The post-War period has unleashed a riot of growth models of increasing mathematical complexity, though ostensibly for the purpose of studying the conditions (in terms of selected variables) for stable or balanced growth. The policy implications of these impressive models are however neither novel nor potent. Institutional factors, education, autonomous technical innovations, climate, stages of development, and other less controllable factors offer more plausible explanations of secular *differences* in over-all growth rates as between periods and countries. And though one cannot rule out *a priori* the possibility that economists may yet extract some catalytic ingredient from these esoteric models—some "economist's stone" that transmutes our erratic progress into a "golden age" of everlasting and harmonious growth—I shall continue to remain sceptical.

To return to the main thesis, let me admit at the start that a doubt that economic growth is a good thing may seem to some a piece of gross impertinence: it certainly would have seemed so a couple of decades ago. After all, the effect of economic growth, it is commonly asserted, is simply that of making available to men alternatives they could not hitherto afford. Provided they are always free to choose what they wish, how can anyone with a liberal conscience allege that they are *not* better off?

Now it so happens that the economist himself is best equipped to sow the seeds of doubt and distrust about the value of economic growth. And though I speak for myself only, and make no pretence at being strictly detached from the enquiry, I shall initially be making use—proper use I hope—of some familiar bits of economic thought. Moreover, I shall separate the environmental problems arising from economic growth, which to some extent can be remedied, from the social problems of economic growth that seem to be more intractable, and discuss the former group of problems first.

We can do this by touching upon some elementary but by no means trivial propositions; for instance *(i)* that the production costs to a business concern may be greater than or (more often) less than the costs borne by the economy as a whole; or *(ii)* that from the fact that people demand a particular good one cannot justify its production inasmuch as people choose subject to constraints that are *institutionally* determined. For example, to explain why there are in the United States a hundred million vehicles on the roads we should remind ourselves *(a)* that they are all priced *far* below their social costs; *(b)* the physical environment created in response to the automobile can make it all but impossible to survive without one; and *(c)* that the public has no living experience of an alternative and viable non-automobile environment.

In this connection the economist's concept of a spillover effect is crucial. If what I wear or use or produce *directly* alters the well-being of other people—and not *indirectly*, through price changes—I can be said to generate spillover effects. Clearly spillover effects abound in society and range from the trivial (say, Mrs Smith's envy of Mrs Jones's new ear-rings) to the tragic (say, death of parents through a traffic accident). The current application of this concept, however, to all forms of environmental pollution introduces difficult problems of equity and allocation.

In so far as the spillover effect in question is fairly simple, and in principle measurable, the economist would tend to favour excise taxes on the polluting products or else a scheme of incentives to use preventive techniques or purification plants, rather than outright prohibition or direct controls. But though the economic literature of spillovers, both of the theory and the applied work, is fascinating and indeed central to the problems of universal pollution which, rightly, have begun to agitate society, I will not discuss it here—save to point out that there are clear instances of the widespread adoption of industrial products which generate effects so elusive and intricate, or so prolific and interconnected, that the *idea* of research designed to measure them all, or to deal with them adequately by any of the conventional methods, is chimerical.

Two examples will illustrate this important thesis—the automobile and television.

I once wrote that the invention of the automobile was one of the greatest disasters to have befallen mankind.[3] I have had time since to reflect on this statement and to revise my judgment to the effect that the automobile is *the* greatest disaster to have befallen mankind. For sheer irresistible destructive power nothing—except perhaps the air-liner—can compete with it. Almost every principle of architectural harmony has been perverted in the vain struggle to keep the mounting volume of motorised traffic moving through our cities, towns, resorts, hamlets and, of course, through our rapidly expanding suburbs. Clamour, dust, fume, congestion, and visual distraction are the predominant features in all built-up areas. Even where styles of architectures differ as between cities—and they differ less from year to year—these traffic features impinge so blatantly and so persistently on the senses as to submerge any other impressions. Whether we are in Paris, Chicago, Tokyo, Düsseldorf, or Milan, it is the choking din and the endless movement of motorised traffic that dominate the scene.

I need hardly dwell on our psychological dependence on the automobile. It is the very staple of automobile advertisements to depict it as a thing with sex appeal, to depict it as a status symbol or as a virility symbol. And, over the decades, as the automobile population has grown, along with vast industrial empires that produce and cater to it, the annual sales of new cars have become a separate indicator of the "prosperity" of the economy. We have, that is, mesmerised ourselves also into the belief that we are economically dependent upon the automobile.

Our physical or environmental dependence upon this vehicle is, however, in fact the direct result of its adoption. Our cities and suburbs have, in consequence, expanded without pause for the last quarter-of-a-century and promoted a demand for massive road-building projects that encourage the flow of traffic which in turn further promotes the demand for traffic projects. Since the motorist wants to see everything worth while from his motor car, the choicest bits of the countryside tend to be built over. The motorist wishes to "get away from it all", and the highway-builders in the attempt to provide him with the means to do so succeed ultimately in ensuring that it is virtually impossible to get away at all.

And, believe me, people *do* need to get away. The one economic activity showing *really* impressive post-War growth is the creation of places we all want to get *away* from. Speeding along the multi-laned highways in the United States, the isolated motorist sees nothing but other cars, vast hoardings, garages, motels, and outsize "drive-ins"—all the commercial paraphernalia of an uprooted society, restless, ever in transit.

One could go on, for the extent of its subversive influence is unlimited. Robbery, crime, violence today all depend heavily on the fast get-away car. Motorists kill off other people at the rate of 130,000 a year (55,000 a year in the United States alone), and permanently maim over a million. Through the emission annually of millions of tons of foul gases the automobile's contribution to sickness and death from cancer and from bronchial and other disorders is just beginning to be understood. What, in contrast, is already fully understood—but about which, for commercial reasons, nothing at all is being done—is the connection between air and automobile travel and the greatest holocaust of natural beauty since the beginning of history.

And not only have the physical environment and the economic structure of each Western country been transmogrified to accommodate this infernal machine but inevitably also our whole style of life: the sort of food we eat, the clothes we wear, the way we court, the forms of entertainment; all bear its stamp. Indeed, our speech, our manners, our health, and our character have been moulded, cramped, distorted, in order to maintain the momentum of an industry whose chief visible achievement has been to transform a society of men into a teeming swarm of motorised locusts that have already eaten the heart out of their towns and cities, and now scurry hungrily over the captive earth along bands of concrete spreading in all directions. The better life we overtly aspire to—and the ease, space, leisure, beauty and intimacy that are conceived as essential features of such a life—can never be realised in the automobile economy.

In view of their far-reaching and interrelated influences on modern society, a proposal to evaluate the full range of the spillover effects of the automobile cannot be seriously contemplated—nor can the application of the notion of optimality. A large political decision is called for: either to continue to build roads and automobiles until something gives (we shan't have to wait long), or in some degree to de-escalate; that is, to promote a changeover from private to public transport and to direct the resources released from automobile production and maintenance to the rehabilitation of our cities, suburbs, towns and villages; as a beginning to promote the creation of larger pedestrian precincts within cities and the creation of viable non-motorised residential areas outside the cities.

I now turn to my other example of an intractable spillover problem.

Communications media, in particular television, produce effects on society that are not easy to evaluate. This is so not only because they are pervasive and intangible, but also because, even if they lent themselves to measurement, the relevant comparison is between those habitually exposed and those not exposed to these media—effectively then a comparison between present and past generations of the same age group in a hypothetically unchanged economic and cultural milieu. Such an experiment cannot in the nature of things be undertaken, and we are therefore thrown back on informed conjecture—in this instance about three sorts of effects, those on language, on personality, and on the family.

1. Since mass media dispose daily of torrents of words and images, the image-creating resources of a Shakespeare could not hope to meet their insatiable demands. The repeated attempts to compel attention on matters large and small issue in near frenzy. Words are misused, abused, over-used, broken up, incongruously combined. And the sheer volume and interminable repetition themselves are destructive of the beauty of language. Words of delicate sentiment begin to lose their fragrance. Phrases once rare or solemn, poignant or poetic, to be uncovered only on particular occasions, get dragged about in the dust of sales campaigns, rolled in with crude imperatives, until they become stale, misshapen, and shorn of the joys of evocation. Even obscene utterances, once reserved for special circumstances, have become so common in use as to lose their power to shock or amuse us. Along with the general degradation of language goes the degradation of our response to it.

Moreover, mass media being themselves large-scale manufacturers of popular jargon, verbal fashions sweep the country. Half-consciously people grope their way toward some voguish cliché, at once to avoid the effort of thought and to produce evidence of being *au courant*. But for every piece of jargon adopted, for every "in" word, a score of fine distinctions are discarded. The rich resources of language fall into desuetude. The aim once associated with a classical education, that of giving precision to one's thoughts, of imparting dignity and beauty to the flow of one's discourse, is perhaps obsolete for a high-pressure technological civilisation—in which, apparently, time becomes scarcer in proportion as labour-saving devices become abundant.[4]

It is hard to believe that a consequent frustration of this nature—the growing inability, and the awareness of that inability, to express oneself fluently and persuasively—has no significant effects on people's character and behaviour. Is there no connection between this media-induced frustration and the modern accent on the "image", on the action rather than the word, on "doing one's thing" rather than on expressing one's thoughts?

2. Television is commonly spoken of as an "educative force of immense potential". Without troubling ourselves to evaluate this rhetoric, we may accept the fact that today panels of eminent personages and a diversity of specialists use the medium to address themselves to politics, science, economics, crime, sex, history, literature, housing, health, art, music, ethics, bringing up the children, and the education of parents. Neither need we enumerate the alleged advantages of these programmes; how, for instance, they enable people to perceive all sides of an issue and to acquire tolerance, if not scepticism. We need touch only on two consequences. First, that this daily parade of expert opinion on every aspect of knowledge must certainly act to inhibit the range of educated men's speculation and discourse. A century or two ago, the civilised man would hold forth boldly and joyfully on any subject under the sun. Today his spirit is muted in deference to the authority of the expert. Apprehending something of the incredible reach and complexity

of modern knowledge, he is left abashed and helpless by the extent of his virtual exclusion.

Secondly, the sort of tolerance a man acquires from being witness to continual re-examination of fundamental questions about religion, politics, psychology, manners and morals, is the product of uncertainty rather than of enlightenment. The distinctions between good and bad, truth and falsehood, vice and virtue, sickness and health, are blurred and reblurred by an unending succession of specialists, victims themselves of the current erosion of the moral, aesthetic, and intellectual consensus on which a civilisation is raised. Inevitably then the confidence of both educated and ordinary people in their own judgment and sense of right begins to ebb. The tolerance that emerges is the result largely of moral paralysis.

3. Finally, and contrary to superficial opinion, television, regarded as an institution, must be accounted a potent factor contributing to increased isolation. Allow the programmes to be ever so enlightened, the charge still remains. For it acts to displace our dependence on other people for amusement and affection and to transfer this dependence to the meretricious flicker of the television screen. It saps the authority of parents, and interposes itself between members of the family—maintaining the peace only by disrupting the flow of feeling between them.

It is to be noticed, in particular, that the claims made for this as for other technical innovations relate primarily to efficiency: television seen as a universal purveyor of entertainment and instruction. The associated social losses are in terms of less tangible but more fundamental things; in terms that is of a total response to life. They include a stunting of our emotional life, a thinness in our relationships, a lack of awareness and of the vividness of the here and now.

I confess that I cannot see sociologists, psychologists, or economists agreeing on methods of computing these sorts of gains and losses, or coming up with an ideal tax to reduce their ownership or use. Though a political decision is conceivable, I cannot believe that, within the ethos of the existing consumer society, prudent regard to any later consequences of unchecked indulgence in technological knick-knacks would carry much political weight.

In respect of spillover effects in general, therefore, we may conclude as follows. The economist's concept does surely have heuristic value: it does contribute to organised thinking about complex social problems, and it does act as a check to the mood of indiscriminate abuse against "the System". Moreover, under restricted conditions, the skilled economist can integrate the concept into practical programmes for making worthwhile improvements. There remain, however, a number of flagrant instances in which the resulting spillover effects are too pervasive, intangible, or complex for the economic calculus to cope with effectually. Remedial action, if any, in such cases must depend ultimately upon political initiative.

Before turning our attention to social problems, however, let me digress for a while in order to appraise the validity of the perennially popular contention that economic growth, whatever its defects, is yet necessary if we are to have sufficient resources available to solve these urgent environmental problems.

Growthmanship

"The appeal to necessity", according to the younger Pitt, is the excuse for every infringement of liberty. Be that as it may, "*economic* necessity" has become the maxim through which critical choices are denied the citizen. A government spokesman can assert (fallaciously, I may add) that only a higher rate of growth will enable the country to improve its balance of payments or check its current inflation. He may also assert—and this sounds more commendable—that it will enable us to help the poor and underprivileged at home and abroad. Mention the slums, mention the shortage of hospitals and staff—mention the schools, mention the plight of the orphans and the aged—and the pat answer is "more economic growth". Talk about the congestion in the cities, the spread of suburbia, the growth in diseases of heart and lungs—talk about the pollution of air and water, the ecological breakdown—and what does the growthman reply? Why, more economic growth of course! By way of

o

illustration let me quote a passage from Mr Anthony Crosland's recent Fabian tract. "Even if we stopped all further growth tomorrow we should need to spend huge additional sums on coping with pollution: it will, for example, cost hundreds of millions of pounds to clean our rivers of their present pollution." (He omitted to remark, however, that the present pollution of our rivers is just one of the many adverse by-products of the post-War economic growth.) But to continue with the quotation:

> We have no chance of finding these huge sums from a near static GNP any more than we could find the extra sums we want for health or education or any of our other goods. Only rapid growth will give us any possibility.

There is something almost exhilarating about the uninhibited opportunism of our growthmen. If, dimly and belatedly, they have begun to perceive an environmental problem they make use of it on the spot to update the relevance of the historic growth dogma. All facts become grist to the growth mill. For wherever economic growth appears to have improved living conditions, we surely have evidence of the benefits of economic growth. *Per contra*, wherever it appears to have made living conditions pretty hideous, why again (as Mr Crosland has so cogently argued) there is a clear case for economic growth in order to remove the hideous features!

Quite apart from the two-headed-penny character of growthmen's arguments, the call today for faster economic growth in order to tackle our environmental ills is fallacious for at least five reasons.

First, over the last twenty years the prevalent type of industrial growth, in particular the growth of chemical products, plastics, automobiles, and air travel, has generated incomparably more pollution than is eliminated by private and public expenditures. What is more, economists anticipate much the same sort of industrial growth over the next ten years or so.

Secondly, as a slight acquaintance with economic concepts makes clear, a successful reduction of any specific form of pollution uses up less in the value of resources than it confers in benefits. "Real" GNP, that is, becomes larger, not smaller. Indeed, the movement for an abatement of pollution and a reduction in polluting activities depends for its economic justification on the cutting down of *excess* social loss. Any contrary impression is the consequence of too literal an interpretation of official statistics that, at present, attaches positive values only to man-made goods and ignores altogether the losses arising from the man-made "bads".

I might add, in this connection, that certain "radical" writers who, in the name of social justice, attack the gathering concern with environmental quality as purely a middle-class value—a gratuitous insult to the working man—in the belief that it retards economic growth are guilty of a compound confusion. Not only do appropriate anti-pollution measures add on balance to "real" income (under conventional economic criteria): not only does investment in more attractive and more variegated environments provide the vital choices that can make an invaluable contribution to social welfare; but the *distributional* effects of such environmental improvements are decidedly progressive. For it is the rich alone, at present, who are able to opt out of any environment that is sinking in the scale of amenity: not the working man, and certainly not the poor who have no choice at all.

Thirdly, if in recognition of the social dividend to be gained from pollution-reducing expenditures a government were indeed to commit itself to use a large proportion of the annual *increment* of GNP to combat existing forms of pollution, the argument for pressing on with economic growth might take on a semblance of plausibility. But the bulk of the annual increment of GNP is at present spent on the usual technological hardware and software. In the United States, for instance, the annual growth in GNP ranges between \$25 billion and \$50 billion.[5] Of this massive increment, what proportion is directed by the Government into *additional* expenditure on anti-pollution activities? No one has yet come up with a reliable figure. But I should be surprised if at present it exceeds one-tenth of 1% of the annual increment. And my guess is that the proportion for Britain is no higher than that in the United States.

As another aside, I might add that a glance at the United Nations statistics is enough to dismiss also the alleged need for economic growth in order to help the poorer countries. The annual direct contributions of the United States and the United Kingdom to poor countries do not exceed one-half of 1% of their GNPs.

It is therefore up to those who persistently invoke this argument to state the proportion of the increment of GNP that will be directed to attack pollution problems—or the public will continue to suspect that future expenditures on "cleaning up the environment" will continue to fall far short of the damage caused by growing GNP.

Fourthly, the "need" for more GNP in order to do good in this and other ways is pure fantasy. True, economists have not yet been so bold as to produce from the available statistics that proportion of GNP which in reality only goes to making life more costly, or to estimate those proportions of GNP that could reasonably be classified under such broad categories as "expendables", "luxuries", "near-garbage", "regrettables"[6] and "positively inimical", but the trend toward larger proportions of such items is unmistakable. Granted that the average American was materially very comfortable about 1950 (producing then more *per capita* than is produced in Britain today), we should hardly feel unjustified in imputing a goodly proportion of this *per capita* increment of "real" income over the past two decades to expenditures on these unprepossessing categories, with much of the remainder being spent in ways that only make life more costly, frantic and wearing. Consider for instance, the post-War expenditures on the fantastic build-up of urban and suburban areas all over America along with the accompanying fume and din, the longer hours commuting, the increase in tensions, frustration and conflict, and the consequent additional expenditures on tranquillisers, drugs and medicines, on police, prisons and sanatoria, and on research into the growth of violence, delinquency and nervous diseases.

To talk then of the *need* for more resources before pollution problems can be effectively tackled is manifest nonsense. It is true only in the trivial sense which accepts as unalterable data all existing institutions, mechanisms and political programmes —among other things accepting as a datum the annual expenditure in the United States of a score of billion dollars on the task of endlessly persuading consumers to buy more of a virtually unlimited assortment of goods that presses hard against the consumers' capacity to absorb them, an assortment ranging from plastic gew-gaws to private planes, from liquor to extra automobiles, from electric boot-brushes to pornographic literature and entertainment.

Fifthly, and perhaps most relevant of all, very little increase in public expenditure is called for. What is called for is effective legislation that puts the burden of curbing further pollution squarely on the shoulders of the pollutors. The outcome of such legislation would be a re-allocation of resources away from pollutant-creating goods and toward investment in research for more economical pollutant-preventive techniques.[7]

But if further economic growth is not necessary, perhaps it is desirable. So I end the digression and return to the latter part of my thesis.

Growth & Well-being

Having, then, urged upon you the wisdom of not prejudging the issue in favour of continued scientific and economic growth either by reason of faith or complacency, and having reminded you of some of their more blatant defects, we now face the crucial question. What grounds are there for disbelieving that economic growth—once we are well above subsistence levels—can add to our well-being? Although this appears to be a broad quasi-philosophical question, I can muster some specific reasons first for doubting it, and second for believing that on balance continued economic growth in the West will act to reduce well-being.

Let us look first at the doubts from an economic perspective and consider three propositions.

First, the oft-quoted "widening horizon of choices" happens to refer only to the range of manufactured products and services. Ignoring wholly the man-made "bads"—ignoring that is, our inability to escape unscathed from the pervasive and damaging by-products of the manufacture and use of many so-called goods—which I have touched on, the horizon of choices has nothing along its expanse corresponding to the conditions of work. I do not propose to argue that every change in these conditions of work has been for the worse. One can easily think of periods of history over which improvements, say, in factory conditions were enjoyed by many groups in the working force. I remark only that there is precious little social choice operating at this end of the market; the pattern of production alters continuously so as to meet the changing pattern of the public in its capacity of consumers. In addition, the specific methods by which goods are produced are not chosen by the workers but simply follow the pattern of technological advance.

Thus, from one period to the next, workers at all levels may find their work more rewarding or else more boring and frustrating. But such responses in an "efficiency-oriented" economy have virtually no influence on the resulting pattern of production or on the techniques employed. All we can say in general is that the idea of work as a source of legitimate pride in craftsmanship, as a form of communication with nature, as a source of gratification and spiritual sustenance, as a good in itself, forms no part of the ethos of an industrial civilisation and has no influence whatsoever on the direction it takes. Yet who can deny that, like the environment in which we are immersed, the sort of work that men do and their attitude towards their work are among the chief components of human welfare!

The second proposition is one that is touched upon in every good economic textbook: to the effect that the consumer who is observed to reject the customary batch of goods still available to him in favour of a new batch can be regarded as better off only if his tastes remain unchanged. When economists address themselves to broad policy questions, however, they tend to overlook this critical proviso or to make the convenient assumption that tastes do not change very much. For really poor countries we might let that go. But for really rich ones, the given tastes assumption is untenable. To conclude as much, we need not belabour the distinction between "natural" and "artificial" tastes, or that between "spontaneous" and "induced" changes in demand. We know that the difference between the sort of goods our forbears made use of and those we make use of is not simply a quantitative one, nor simply a qualitative one in a narrow sense. From the mere fact that we can indeed buy a horse today but instead choose to buy a car, we cannot infer that we are today better off. A hundred years of product innovation has changed the world we live in out of all recognition, and has thereby changed the social context in which choices are made. A real choice would be that of alternative *social contexts*—between, for example, a more leisurely pre-industrial world of small towns, wood fires, mansions and cottages, a close-knit society of privileges and obligations, and, on the other hand, a highly competitive post-industrial world of congested highways, unquiet skies, metropolitan overspill, of increasing pace and pressure, of corrosive envy, and of endless jockeying for status. But in the nature of things such choices cannot be offered to us.

No less pertinent is it that the tastes we acquire are them-selves the products of a changing social context and of the institutions it gives rise to. We all recognise that in the mixed economies of the West substantial resources are employed, not in order to satisfy the current pattern of wants, but in order to change them. Resources, that is, are used not to satisfy wants (as the earlier textbooks would have it) but expressly to create dissatisfaction with what we have. Again, there is no need to enter the debate on the efficacy of commercial advertising in moulding people's tastes.[8] Speaking only of the broad social repercussions of commercial advertising, it can hardly be denied that it does appear to have succeeded wonderfully in one of its aims: that of making people discontented with what they already own. Indeed it is hard to imagine anything that would initially throw the American economy into greater disarray than a religious conversion that overnight made the bulk of the American people perfectly contented with their material lot.

The third proposition bears on what economists sometimes call "consumer interdependence". Once subsistence levels are behind us, the satisfaction we derive from a good depends not only on the amount of it we ourselves buy, but also directly on our observation of, or on our beliefs about, what others buy—this being no more than a formal statement of the notion conveyed by the phrase "keeping up with the Joneses". But the potency of this "Jones effect" in reducing the satisfaction to be had from a steady rise in *per capita* "real" income, or in productive power, should not be underestimated.

It is doubtless very grand to own two cars when most people around you have not even one. A lot of this satisfaction however evaporates when almost everybody in the neighbourhood also has two cars or more. Again, quite apart from the utility of a refrigerator, or an air-conditioning unit, or a colour television set, the satisfaction it affords a person tends to diminish as the ownership of these things spreads throughout the community.

Indeed, a distinguished economist by the name of James Dusenberry took the argument to its logical conclusion in 1950 and formulated a "relative income hypothesis" which states simply that what matters to a person in a high consumption economy is not so much his "real" income as his position in the over-all structure of incomes. In its strongest form, the hypothesis would imply that, given the choice, the affluent citizen would choose say a 5% increase in his income alone to the alternative of participating in a 25% all-round increase of incomes. The evidence in favour of the hypothesis in its strongest form, though plausible, is not conclusive. But in a modified form it is hardly to be controverted. The more truth there is in it, however, the more futile as a means of raising welfare is the official policy of promoting economic growth.

Along with the "Jones effect" operating to dissipate the pleasures of rising real purchasing power, there are within a country other factors that cannot be presumed to be beneficial. Without distinguishing them at this juncture we may provisionally assess their potency by reference to common impressions. For instance *per capita* "real" income in the United States in 1946 was about half that in 1970. If such an index has any welfare content there should be no doubt whatever that, on balance, life in America today is more enjoyable. But there is plenty of doubt about this among Americans themselves. For that matter, to take a more extreme instance, the average *per capita* real consumption in America today is about five times as high as it was in the Britain of 1950. But, despite the rationing, my recollection is that life was far more comfortable and pleasant in the Britain of 1950. For this was before the automobile and the developer had made hideous our cities and suburbs, before television held people in a semi-bovine state for up to six hours a day, before the commercial cult of youth and the growth of exhibitionist attire, and before hippydom, drugs, gay liberations, and bowdlerised pornography began to spread over the land. The skies in those innocent days were not rent by shrieking aircraft, nor was the air thick with auto fumes. People could stroll along the streets and converse without screaming at each other; they could mingle in the parks and squares; they could linger in the cafés or walk through the city at night without fear of molestation. If not gay and carefree, at least people were comfortable and secure. They did not stare hard through peep-holes before cautiously opening their front doors. Compared with the figures in America today, suicide, drug-addiction, theft and thuggery were negligible.

From such considerations alone we may dismiss as naïve the notion of sustained economic growth as a historical process that, over time, removes obstacles to human well-being. The process is rather that of a sequence of over-all life-styles as between which there can be no choice. And along with them go irrevocable changes in the quality of the pleasures and pains that people experience. Such changes in quality demand our closest attention.

It is one thing if society is so ordered that its pleasures spring in the main from a spirit of contentedness and acceptance; from friendship and kinship, from an abiding sense of home and family; from surrender and worship, from sacrifice, passion, and creation, from a closeness to nature's breath and pulse. It is quite another if men's primary sources of pleasure are to be found in self-seeking, in self-display, in vindictiveness, in triumphs over others, in listless indulgences and futile titillations.

So also with humanity's woes, with "the slings and arrows of outrageous fortune". It matters crucially whether the pains that we suffer are physical or spiritual, and whether they are sorrowful and perceptive or petty and plaintive. Our suffering, that is, can be dignified and ennobling, or else it can be coarse and degrading.

Looking ahead, then, should we not wonder whether the pleasures of living will become more intimate, keen, and resonant, or will instead become more passive, dull, and oafish? It is surely not a matter of indifference if, in the era we are moving into, the kinds of pleasure we shall come to seek and the kinds of pains we shall come to endure act on balance to humanise our lives or else act on balance to dehumanise them.

Alas, in this vital regard, the forces exerted by technology and commerce are (as we shall see) neither benevolent nor neutral.

Growth & the Positively Inimical

Having, with the aid of some familiar economic ideas, given reasons merely for doubting the existence of a positive relation between economic growth and social welfare, at least in wealthy economies, I turn now to the second part of my task: to distinguish some of the features inherent in the very nature and process of technological advance that appear positively inimical to society's welfare. Systematic study at this level of enquiry is virtually non-existent. Perforce I move into this area of conjecture with less assurance.

I confine myself here to three consequences of scientific and technical progress on the shape of society.

Consider first the impact on religion and morality, on custom and tradition, of the progress of science and technology. If men ever want to believe in a personal God; if there is in men an instinct for worship; if ever they would be God's creatures, they must henceforth be denied. For the myths by which men live cannot survive the relentless scrutiny of science. There is no mystery, no source of exaltation, no beatific vision, through which men may hope to communicate with God that science cannot turn to ashes. There is nothing preternatural or remarkable that it cannot explain in terms of atmospheric effects and chemical processes.[9]

Humanists have declared for a morality founded on an enlightened consensus rather than on Biblical injunction. Their aspirations stem from the belief in the perfectibility of men. But there is no evidence that the human race is drawing closer to moral perfection or that a new enlightened consensus is emerging to fill the present vacuum. As traditional moral codes crumble before the tide of scientific advance, what is there left in a commercial society to moderate the scramble for material status or to curb the frenzy of self-seeking—attitudes that are at once the outcome and the pre-condition of sustained economic growth in the West?

Indeed, not only is morality involved, but every norm that guides society in its choices. For the Western growth economy requires a consuming public whose tastes are severed from traditional notions of excellence, a public whose acquisitive impulses are unrestrained by any standards of propriety. Once disjoined from tradition, tastes become the slave of fashion, and fashion the creature of profits. And if such an "ideal" consuming public—uprooted, free-floating, volatile, infinitely mouldable— is conveniently coming into being at a time when, under the existing dispensation, the greatest threat to the growth economy is the flagging momentum of consumers' expenditure, thanks are due not only to the hard-working ad-men but due also to the technocrats who trumpet forth the exciting idea that perpetual and accelerating change is the very essence of the civilisation we are about to enter; a civilisation, that is, in which social norms are to have no time to form and in which therefore concepts of good and evil, of right and wrong, can only be functional and ephemeral.

There is, of course, a disarming frankness about this vision. For we are not being misled for a moment into the belief that, *given the choice*, men would really opt for this somewhat convulsive form of living as being by far the most gratifying to man's instinctual nature as it has evolved over hundreds of thousands of years. Such a helter-skelter life—call it (as you wish) exciting, hectic, frenzied, or neurotic—is after all simply a residuum, the sort of life that men will have to bear with or perish if technology continues to be given its head.

Turn next to the perennial question of machines displacing men. I am not one of those who believe that the original Luddites were wholly wrong. Whatever our judgments are on this sorry episode of history, the unfolding of events imparts a new twist to the argument. We know that scientists and technologists busy themselves today producing improved translating machines, machines that can play chess, or that can *learn* to play chess, or any other game, machines that can write poetry or compose music, machines that can make complex decisions, evolve hypotheses, and produce mathematical proofs. Of course, we should all be very proud. Is not man truly wonderful! But the exclamations of pride do not dispose of the resulting problem. For ignoring the possibility of genetical innovations that will produce for us a race of superbrains, how is the ordinary man and woman to respond in the future, knowing that in one accomplishment after another they can be outdone by contraptions of wire and batteries? For almost everything a man can do there will be a machine that can do it as well or better, and infinitely faster. Such an aim at least provides one of the great steering lights of technological innovation, an aim, apparently, that technology has little difficulty in realising.

Adapting his mode of living to the technology of industry and to the flow of gadgets on the market, every year that passes sees the man in the street more of a bewildered spectator of what goes on about him. True, his leisure may increase over time and there may be goodies a plenty in the supermarkets—a robot and a computer in every home, information unlimited, three-dimensional television, round-the-clock synthetic entertainment, trips to the moon and to the bottom of the ocean. But what of his self-respect? For scientists, technocrats, and professional men there will still be opportunities for distinguishing themselves—though the pace of obsolescence of knowledge is sure to place them, too, under increasing stress. The plight of the ordinary mortal however, is seemingly inescapable. If his muscular and mental exertions, if his manual skills, come to have no value in a world of increasingly sophisticated computers and elaborate control mechanisms, how can he not feel himself to be expendable? How can he hold his head up when it is plain beyond doubt that as a producer he does not rate; that nobody depends on him for anything; that he is but a drone in a world become a buzzing hive of technology?

We now come to the third consequence of scientific and technological progress on the texture of society. There can be many reasons why a new product commends itself to the buying public. It may promise a novel experience (as does a private plane or a bugging device) or a new form of home entertainment (as does television) or increased leisure (as does a washing machine or an electric knife-sharpener). Once it becomes universally adopted, however, social consequences emerge which cannot be undone by any single person acting on his own.

One fairly obvious outcome is worthy only of ironic comment. No people more than the Americans are addicted to labour-saving devices, and no people are more concerned with their weight and general physical condition. Theirs is an irresistible compulsion to buy anything that saves muscular effort. At the same time, no other country is so lavishly endowed with gymnasia and weight-reducing sanatoria. No country sells so much home-exercising equipment and slimming contraptions.

Far more serious, however, is the consequence of technological innovation on the relationships between people. If we accept the view that (above subsistence standards at least) the chief sources of men's satisfactions reside not in the goods they buy, but in such enduring things as love, friendship, tranquillity, and the perception of beauty, the question arises: do the innovations produced by the technology of a growing economy act to promote or to thwart these prime sources of satisfaction? I do not think there can be two answers.

Increased mobility is not a force making for increased friendship, least of all when one is for the most part incapsulated in one's automobile. A person can extend the number of his acquaintances indefinitely without really caring for any of them. A week in a mountain hotel, a package tour in the Mediterranean, or seeing ten countries in seven days may have their moments of elation—though the border-line between elation and anxiety is sometimes difficult to define. But there is time enough only to throw postures, to go through the conventional motions of revelry, and hope that something or somebody will turn up. The flurry of emotions, the stylised infatuations that such opportunities offer to the young (and the would-be young) do not however have any affinity with that serenity of spirit with which I am concerned. As Somerset Maugham once observed, "We never know when we are happy; we know only when we *were* happy." And part of the reason is simply that (*pace* the American Constitution) the pursuit of happiness is a fruitless enterprise. For the state of happiness is one that cannot be directly realised, least of all by trying. It appears, to quote the late Aldous Huxley, "only as a by-product of good living". And good living, in this context, means neither fleshpots nor sanctity, but something akin to Plato's ideal of harmonious living. It presupposes a dependable institutional and moral framework held together by myth and taboo; one that establishes an external order that does no violence to man's internal order; one which permits his instincts to range without hurt to himself or others. In particular, a society congenial to man is one that strengthens his roots in the earth and makes him a part again of that eternal rhythm of nature in which there is time enough for things to grow slowly; in which there is time enough for trust between people to form; in which there is time to learn to care, and time to wonder and to perceive beauty.

If there is any truth in these reflections, it should be apparent that further economic growth predicated on accelerating technical change can only take us farther from the good life. Can one reasonably hope for an easy, open-hearted relationship with one's fellows in a highly competitive and mobile society, where work has become an endless struggle for material rewards and status? The indispensable ingredient of such a relationship is mutual trust, a quality nurtured in the pre-industrial small-scale society that was held together by overt mutual dependence. The resulting intimacy arising from this close personal interdependence, an inescapable feature of pre-industrial communities, is the first casualty of technological growth. For in the unending search for greater efficiency technology seeks expressly to emancipate men from direct forms of dependence on one another. Machines come to mediate between them, and they come to depend ultimately for their wants, not on the care of others, but on a row of buttons and switches.

Unavoidably, then, technological progress provides men increasingly with the elegant instruments of their mutual estrangement, and thus constricts further the direct flow of understanding and sympathy between them.

What Is to Be Done?

It is time to stand back and take our bearings in order to determine what, if anything, can be done.

If I may caricature economic ideologies, though not excessively, the 19th century was one that eulogised thrift. The good citizen was something of a miser. The second half of the 20th century has reversed those economic ideals. The good citizen is now something of a glutton. For the declared objectives of increasing material prosperity and expanding industrial output can be maintained only by the vigilant cultivation of virtually insatiable appetites. The distributional injustices associated with the system in no way detract from this conclusion. Whatever the distribution of the national product—be it perfectly egalitarian—the continued growth of the economy would still require insatiable appetites of its citizens.

To be blunt, economic growth in the West is in fact institutionalised greed. We go on as we do from acquired habit, and from institutional momentum (much of it taking course from the design, research, investment and sales departments of giant corporations, and from the propensity of modern governments to engage in vast technical projects and to invest heavily in research) and because we really don't know how to stop. We fear to jettison our growth ideology, along with our hope of salvation by science, because we can see nothing to replace it; because there is no road back. So we drift on making a virtue of necessity, calling out for more speed, and soothing our apprehensions with technological fantasies, and our consciences with repeated promises to do good works as we become richer. If I may say so without disrespect, President Johnson's "Great Society" amounted to little more than this.

Where, then, can we turn for guidance? To the desperate expedient of perpetual guerrilla warfare directed against the Establishment? Though I have the greatest sympathy with those actively disliking many of the features of this emerging civilisation, I cannot agree that it is *repressive* in any familiar libertarian sense. I can agree, however, that we experience today far greater *frustration* than, say, fifty years ago. This is so not only because (as I have indicated above) the demands of a highly technical civilisation and the intuitive needs of ordinary men are beginning to pull in opposite directions, but also for simple political reasons.

With the unprecedented growth in technology and population over the past 200 years, political power has continued to gravitate toward the centre. Yet it is just because of the extending power and compass of modern technology that centrally-determined policies have such far-reaching repercussions on every aspect of a man's private and working life. The tentacles of government reach into every nook and cranny. Unfortunately as the political constraints on our freedom of action grow, so also do our personal desires to influence events at home and abroad. For it is today the devoted task of an army of ambitious newsmen and commentators to impress us with a sense of urgency and involvement in events both far and near. But even when account is taken of the political effectiveness of organised lobbies, the influence the ordinary citizen can hope to exert on national issues is all but negligible. The vast populations, and the diversity of interests and beliefs in the large countries of the affluent West go far to ensure that much of the resulting legislation will be a compromise that pleases few and irritates many.

The sense of helplessness is perhaps particularly keen among the young and impetuous. Yet attempts by extreme groups to sabotage the "System" by direct acts of violence are as ill-conceived as they are immoral. If such violence does spread so as to pose a threat to society, the response will of necessity be repressive. For security comes before liberty; indeed, it is the precondition of liberty. And if perchance the violence cannot be contained, the resulting anarchy will pave the way not for a Utopia but for a despotism, a despotism which, by wielding the immense power of modern technology, can be made all the more onerous and totalitarian.

Turning to more traditional sources, has the political philosophy of Edmund Burke anything to offer us? I think not. His reflections are apt enough for a society in which technology has limited impact. Under conditions of slow technological change one can indeed argue a presumption in favour of existing political and social institutions, and defend a reluctance to introduce any radical alteration without much forethought and debate. But in a society shorn of its myths, bereft of any guiding ethic, a society that is in the throes of a technological upheaval, the experience of the recent past has little to contribute.

For much the same reason the works of Karl Marx cannot provide us with clues. However his interpretation of history is appraised, as a guide to the future it must be discounted. For in the last resort it is not the capitalist class that is the villain we have to fear. The villain, as I have tried to make clear, is technology itself irrespective of the economic system. Moreover, the historical determinism of Marx—the belief that choice is but an illusion; that it is futile to attempt to control or even deflect the pre-ordained movement of history—serves to promote either a resigned or a dogmatic spirit comparable to that which sustains the momentum of economic growth. If ever we hope to create a society more congruous with man's nature, the mediating spirit must be the reverse of dogmatic or resigned: it must be pragmatic, reflective, and deeply concerned.

Finally, what of the young? Among those of them who have not yet been sucked into the vortex of the new industrial society, a significant number during the last decade have begun to reject the relevance of the Protestant ethic, as popularly understood. Rejected also by many of the young—in particular the middle-class young—are the alleged economic virtues of the "consumer society" as well as a variety of features associated with what is loosely called "the System". Many other young people, though perhaps less articulate, are none the less sensitive to the physical ugliness about them and have ambivalent feelings about the approach of the automated society.

But while these youngsters have let it be known, with varying degrees of politeness, that they do not like the "System", I doubt whether their ebullience or impulse will deliver us from bondage and transport us to the promised land.

The more innocent among them—and these tend to be the more vociferous—are impatient of the facts and, indeed, of the evidence of their senses. Being impatient they are prone to take a Jekyll-and-Hyde view of the problem, a view that is common to both evangelical and revolutionary movements. They want to slay the wicked Mr Hyde—the "System" and its minions; the conspiring capitalists, the vainglorious technocrats, and the corrupt politicians or government officials—and let good Dr Jekyll live forever in pure love and sunshine. But for better or worse, Jekyll and Hyde are indissolubly wed in a single being that is man; and it is for just such mortals that society, the good society we aspire to, has to be fashioned.

It follows that if inhibitions are needed to keep wicked Mr Hyde in check in order that good Dr Jekyll can breathe more freely, such inhibitions must be firmly rooted in the unquestioned taboos of society. The search for unchecked release of all instincts, a part of the dream world of the dissatisfied young (and the not-too-young) throughout the ages, leads not to "some white tremendous daybreak", but only to disenchantment and despair.

Be that as it may, from infantile visions of being borne forever on the crest of an orgasmic wave no values can be salvaged. Today's unheroic protest movements, hippies, yippies, and others "sore given to revel and ungodly glee" (to quote from Byron) offer no viable alternative to the present dispensation. Their social significance derives only from their being one of the symptoms of the crisis of the West. Hippy colonies, for instance, are not new self-sustaining growths, but parasitic ones—barnacles clinging to the underside of the affluent society.

I see little hope for us either in the current trend of what is euphemistically called "permissiveness". Where some affect to perceive increased tolerance, I confess I see little more than a disintegration of sensibility, a failure to distinguish between propriety and impropriety, between decency and indecency, between moral and immoral—one of the unhappier consequences of half-a-century of unprecedented technological change in the West. Nor surprisingly in a commercial society, the sexual aspects of this "permissiveness" have become the most promi-

nent. Year after weary year we are being persistently emanci-
pated from those outrageously repressed Victorians—a figment,
if there ever was one—and being persistently urged to escape
our sorrows by gorging our eyes on erotic images and lascivious
display. The transparent result of these gratuitous acts of
liberation is to expose the protesting citizen to increasing dos-
ages of sordid sexual pollution. The blazoning of highly
salacious entertainment by cinemas and theatres, the city
centres in which rows of shops are given over to the sale of
pornographic literature or gadgetry are sights not likely to
promote patriotism, civic pride, or an admiration for the
character of one's countrymen. To urge that they "meet a need"
is, indeed, a pathetic confession, a virtual condemnation of society.

I could continue to entertain you or to bore you by comments
on doctrines, movement, and fashions that will appear, on a
brief examination, to have little bearing on the problems that
face humanity in the latter part of the 20th century. But time
is running out and some of you may be impatient to discover
what, if anything, I have to offer in the way of practical advice.
Prepare then to be disappointed while I blithely reiterate that I
undertook only to reveal connections between the mounting
discontent and disorder and the economic and technological
growth we continue to pursue. Nevertheless, there is one thing
that may be said with some confidence: that if we are ever to
find a way out of the crisis we must first wrench ourselves free
from the dominating ideology of growth. Instead we must start
thinking about the future in an utterly uncompromising and
agnostic way. Whatever conclusions we are led to, they will
have to be predicated on three propositions, each one a
judgment of fact.

First, that the earth, seen today as a tiny planet warmed by a
dwarf star whirling along in a cold, dark and inhospitable
universe, is man's only refuge. In consequence the notion of a
unique and finite globe having limited resources of earth, air
and water to sustain the complex ecology of life has to supplant
in men's consciousness the older idea of an endless frontier of
opportunities for systematic plunder.

Secondly, whatever civilisation we choose to adopt, its continuance is not compatible with anything like the current rate of destruction of natural resources by the West or with the current rate of growth of human population.

Thirdly, and as a corollary of the first two propositions, we must persuade ourselves anew that, despite the expanding forces of technology and commerce, the future is *not* pre-empted. Though we all know this to be literally true, and though we are ready enough to accept the belief in free will—at least we act in our day-to-day affairs as if we can choose between alternative courses of action open to us—the temptation to project trends when visualising the future is strong in any society that habitually thinks of its history in terms of technological progress. Futuristic studies, of which that by Kahn and Wiener is a prototype, appear for the most part an exercise in extrapolating scientific and technological trends and then in speculating upon their social consequences. Given, say, specific scientific discoveries between the years 1980 and 2000, or the adoption of specific sorts of technology, the question they ask is: what impact will this make on our way of living? In direct contrast, the new way of thinking predicates itself on free will to the extent of reversing this logical sequence. We are to ask, that is, first what sort of a society do we *wish* to establish, after which the consequences for science and technology are to be determined.

This proposition about free will and its social implications is then no platitude. Such a way of thinking about the future runs counter to that which the West has wholeheartedly espoused since the 18th century. Inasmuch as vast material and intellectual interests in science, technology and modern industry are deeply entrenched, it will be something of a miracle if this new agnosticism comes to prevail in the counsels of men.

Whatever the prospects, I cannot envisage any decent way of life without a wholesale reversal of the powerful trends—technological, ideological, economic—that began in the 18th century. The phenomenal expansion of human population, the secular trend toward centralisation, the hectic pace of obsolescence, the spread of automobilisation and air travel, the growth in mass media, the increasing mobility and uniformity: all such forces will have to go into reverse if such commonly voiced aspirations as variety, order, intimacy, conservation, care, margin, space, ease and openness, are ever to be realised.

I conclude from these reflections that the race that is critical to humanity's future is not the conventional growth race: not the pitting of the growth indices of one rich country against those of other rich countries until doomsday. Rather it is the race within each country or within the West as a whole between, on the one hand, the existing momentum towards yet faster consumption of the earth's limited resources, and on the other, the slow-gathering forces of sanity and understanding.

8. Futurism and the Worse that is Yet to Come

Until the close of World War II active speculation about the technological features of the future was restricted in the main to the literature of science fiction, regarded until then as an exhilarating avenue of escape from the humdrum of the all-too-solid present. Secure in the here-and-how, and undeterred by premonitions, the reader's imagination could soar freely through time and space. He might even smile at the incidental reassurance provided by some of the tales of such pioneers of the genre as Jules Verne and H. G. Wells, in which contemporary society continued to move soporifically along its customary grooves undeflected by the cataclysmic discoveries of some scientific maniac. And what could be cosier than a Wellsian time-machine that, following a fearsome trip into the far future, could be depended upon to return the author to the present in good time for tea around the parlour fire?

It is this once-powerful sense of the here-and-now that has begun to recede since the War. Much that was only yesterday relegated airily to the realm of science fiction is now recognised as sober scientific fact. And there is virtually nothing in today's science fiction that is thought of as "impossible" tomorrow. The increasing pace of technological and social change in the post-War world is actively dissolving the familiar signposts of our civilisation before our media-soaked eyes. Willingly or reluctantly we are impelled to give more and more of our attention to the shape of things to come.

Just now we are obsessed with the pattern of life over the next ten, twenty, or thirty years. Private and government organisations both in Europe and America have begun to busy themselves in this fantastic new field of futuristic research, interpreting the present, extrapolating the future, issuing bulletins of "prevision" from time to time—as yet manifestly uncertain whether their task is to mould the future or to make provision for it. The problems that are beginning to exercise us, however, are not those of science *per se* but the problems posed by the impact on society of the products and by-products of scientific and technological progress of which the so-called population explosion is one of the more topical instances.

A recent example of the growing concern with the more immediate future was a series of articles which appeared in the London *Times* (October 1969) each written by a well-known figure in the social or physical sciences. With the exception of Arthur Koestler's distinguished contribution, the over-all impression conveyed was one of qualified optimism. Admittedly there were some sticky issues we should have to grapple with. But one was not to worry. Man's powers, we were assured, are growing all the time and doubtless he will meet the challenge when he has to. A decorous concern was admissible, but there was no cause for alarm.

But perhaps there is just a little cause for alarm. For the scientist's vision of the future is apt to be biased by the conventional myth through which he rationalises his unending probings into the universe, a myth in which he sees himself as directing mankind toward a widening horizon of technological opportunities from which men may freely choose their style of life. Any serious scepticism about the ultimate benefits to be conferred on humanity by the onward march of science tends, therefore, to be interpreted as an attack on scientific achievement in the past, or as an attack on the scientific method, or as a lapse into intellectual Ludditism.

Scepticism of this sort can in fact be perfectly rational. The efficacy of the scientific method may be readily conceded. Nor need one deny that a goodly number of scientific discoveries appear to have made the lot of mankind physically more comfortable. At the same time it is perfectly reasonable to debate the question whether a particular scientific development has been or is likely to be worthwhile. It is no less reasonable to pose the question whether future developments in any one, several, or all fields of scientific endeavour are likely on balance to make the bulk of humanity *more* contented or *less*.

These are not questions the scientist cares much to answer. They are large questions, elusive, in the last resort perhaps unanswerable. But they are surely the relevant questions and deserve widespread and prolonged debate. When confronted with them, in fact, the scientist has a propensity to wander towards the inevitability thesis or the neutrality thesis, or both. As to the first, the essence of it is that man's irresistible curiosity, regarded as the supreme virtue of *homo sapiens*, enshrined today in vast temples of scientific research, can never be satisfied. *Ergo* scientific progress cannot be halted. The question of social benefit may be relevant, but in the light of an inevitable historic process it is of academic interest only.

As to the second, the scientist cannot be held responsible for the outcome of his discoveries since science itself is neutral. It provides men with the means of power over the universe. But it is up to men themselves to make use of that power for good or evil.

There is, of course, a sense in which science is neutral, and that is the trivial sense in which a gun is said to be neutral: it cannot harm anyone unless someone pulls the trigger. The accumulation over time of scientific and technological information does not activate itself. Men consciously make use of the new knowledge that is vouchsafed to them. And what happens to the world depends upon how they use it. So much is obvious, and tells neither for nor against science.

But there is a pertinent sense in which science cannot be neutral—even though every scientist were to pledge himself never to make a political statement. Given the condition of society as we know it, given the momenta arising from existing economic and political institutions, and given also the incidence among mankind of impatience, ignorance, ambition, folly, avarice, and corruption, some outcomes—some ranges of outcomes—of the possible fruits of any particular branch of scientific research are more likely than others. If then something goes amiss, or some unexpected mischief is wrought, the scientist may admit to bad judgment: to having attached more weight to the chance of social gain than to the risk of hurt. In the last resort he may plead ignorance of the sort of world he lives in. But in a world where scientific knowledge is continually being put to use by imperfect beings in an imperfect society, the scientist cannot evade responsibility.

Turning to another familiar controversy, whether we can solve the problems that arise in the last resort from the widespread application of science—problems such as ecological airplane, we can certainly diminish atmospheric pollution, traffic-clogged cities, exploding suburbias—without further application of science,[1] there is in this case a non-trivial sense in which the answer can be *yes*. By reducing the production and use of certain kinds of hardware, say the automobile and the airplane, we can certainly diminish atmospheric pollution, tourist blight, and traffic congestion. Since such a policy is technically quite feasible we may properly infer that we can solve some very pressing problems by using less technology, not more.

Removing this strand of truth from the controversy, there remains the substantive and probably unanswerable issue about which is the better way of relieving humanity of any of the currently unwanted products of applied science. For even if it could be determined in advance that science would be able to contribute solutions to some of the problems its applications have brought into being, the pertinent considerations in any decision to finance the necessary research are, first, the *time* over which we might have to continue to suffer before any perceptible relief would be experienced and, secondly, the *risks* inevitably associated with technological solutions, indeed with technological opportunities also, of creating new and possibly unmanageable social and ecological problems. In the world of the 1970's, the alternative of seeking immediate improvements by using less of the existing technology has to be taken seriously.

The experience on which a reliable assessment of humanity's prospects can be based is obviously too short, for it is only during the last century that science has begun to be applied on a universal scale. Perhaps the least controversial judgment would be to regard the widespread use of science as a mixed blessing, with possibly an edge of advantage if the choice ever comes to all or nothing—at least for the condition in which the application of science has left humanity today. But such judgments are not of topical interest. What is of topical interest is the question whether the apparently unabating advance of science over, say, the next half-century will improve the human condition or whether it will cause it to degenerate. Again, this is a large question and one which cannot be resolved on the basis of empirical knowledge, though it is one on which some light may be shed by informed conjecture. My own conjectures, I need hardly add, run counter to much of the prevailing complacency which is apparently founded on a faith that Man, being infinitely resourceful, will ultimately meet the Challenge of the Future.

The word "ultimately" is obviously equivocal, but even if we suppose that man will somehow perpetuate his race in the universe for all time—the ultimate triumph—I find little consolation in the vision. For there is a vital distinction we are wont to overlook whenever we utter these heroic sentiments, one which, when established, will enable us properly to take the measure of what matters. The distinction is between *man* and *men*. It is man, seen as Prometheus Unchained, who is the real hero of science, as indeed he is of Science Fiction. But man is an abstraction, an embodiment of the ingenuity of social institutions, the singular inheritor of the knowledge produced by an array of scientific disciplines manned by armies of specialists. Men, on the other hand, are but ordinary mortals: vain, foolish, weak and vulnerable. Measured against the sum of modern knowledge, each one of them is infinitely ignorant. Man is a paragon, an undivided intelligence, a god. Men are a multitude of creatures spread over the earth, for the most part living in daily struggle and frustration: their feet in the mud, their heads in the stars; beset with doubts and fears; worshipping, hating, loving and sorrowing; victims of endless turmoil within and without.

But, in all that matters, it is *men* who are the substance, and *man* that is the shadow.

The good society for a mortal man is one which, somehow,

manages to bring him into harmony with himself, and so with others. It is one that manages to establish an external order that does no violence to his internal order; a society evolved or devised to allow his instincts to range without malice to others or hurt to himself. In order to endure, it must not only cater to the aspirations of an *élite*, it must make ample provision for the needs of ordinary men and women. The features of the new era, however, one that began with the post-War affluence, impress me as being least likely to promote such a society. I would not for a moment deny the more obvious products of economic growth, which include a bewildering assortment of automobiles, television sets, vacuum cleaners, refrigerators, washing machines, electric tooth-brushes, electric back-scratchers, all advertised to make life more pleasant for us—and, in order to beguile the time, a growing range of plastic baubles and a profusion of inane gadgets that mock the power of hallucination to invent.

But, of course, we are not to ignore either some of the more salient features of our post-War civilisation that arise from the widespread use of these products of applied science—the irresistible spread of steel and concrete, or the growing plague of motorised traffic (on the ground and in the air) plus the accompanying din, stench, pollution. Notwithstanding the potential contribution toward their solution of further technological innovations, there appear each year fewer avenues of escape.

I might add, however, that such unprepossessing features are not privileged to enter directly the grand GNP computation, being entirely negative in value and obstinately resistant to quantification. For all that, some of their social consequences manage to gate-crash into the index; for a growing proportion of GNP is, in fact, everywhere being devoted to increased expenditures on law-enforcement in the attempt to curb the mounting delinquency, the sporadic violence, and the organised "American-style" crime—to say nothing of the vast expenditures on perverted forms of urban construction designed to keep the rising streams of traffic moving through our polluted cities.

Since life has become increasingly complex, frustrating, frantic and wearing, any statement that, "on balance", we are better off than we were, say, twenty years ago, is purely a declaration of faith.

Some other consequences of being born into an era graced by widespread application of science can bear a little emphasis. Whatever our occupation or our prospects, we all suffer from the accelerated erosion of the environment in a wider sense: *i.e.*, from the increasing pace of obsolescence, and from a harrowing degree of specialisation that cuts us off from the largeness of nature and from the ease of intercourse with our fellow men. The scientist or academic, though his work subjects him to the most gruelling pace, believes he has some compensations—recognition of published work, intellectual communication with others in his field, occasional mention by the Press. I believe that he, too, is under illusions that will not weather the future. But we shall let that pass, and turn instead to the greater part of humanity. For it is the ordinary men and women who are destined to become the victims of the future.

There will be the obvious economic problem of providing them with employment in a world where automation can reproduce any routine skill and where computers can undertake any routine calculation or other mental tasks. But if the bulk of what we today call the working force is to become unemployable, the problem will not simply be one of providing men with means of "organising their leisure". This is the sort of "challenge" that is viewed with equanimity by scientists, since it is generally associated with research grants, and viewed with particular relish by social workers, who also are anxious to advance their uncertain and tenuous status. But they have entirely overlooked the far more important human problem; that of providing for the self-respect of the ordinary mortal. And, frankly, I see no way of providing for it in the indescribably complex technological civilisation we are about to enter.

As the ordinary man moves further into the age of automation, and perforce is freed from mental and muscular efforts, all the syrupy sounds of the television ads, all the gadgetry and paraphernalia of soft living, all the tranquillisers and eupeptic drugs in creation will not suffice to conceal from him the nakedness of his predicament. Social workers may teach him to play games for his health, and suggest recreations to soothe his thwarted instincts. But as an ordinary human being he will have nothing really to offer society. He may be regaled with goods and privileges. But nobody needs him. He will live by the grace of the Scientific Establishment, earmarked as a drone, protected for a while longer by social institutions and the remnants of a moral tradition; yet transparently expendable, like some ten thousand million others, heaped like ants over the earth.

One way of circumventing this ignoble destiny was envisaged, though more as satire than idea, by the late Aldous Huxley: a *Brave New World* in which specific types of humans were raised in test tubes to fill the occupations they were later to follow. There were, "happily", no sex-taboos, and any vestigial anxieties were invariably calmed by a euphoric tablet, *Soma*. Indeed, since man and social environment had been so designed to fit perfectly, Huxley's Brave New World might well be regarded as the Nemesis of today's fashionable and fuzzy-minded "progressive", with his touching faith in salvation by science, his impatience to explore the limits of physical pleasure, and his outraged rejection of the notion of sin, or of the value of human suffering. For in this beautifully adjusted civilisation, presided over by a complacent and benevolent dictator, the concepts of good and evil were indeed obsolete. There was neither vice nor virtue, morality nor immorality. The behaviour of a man was to be judged by reference to only two categories, health and sickness—these being clearly related to efficiency and inefficiency.

And what are the consequences for humanity of having achieved so perfect a state? Imagine a potential Romeo, in this Brave New World, stumbling for the first time across a potential Juliet. The first flicker of incipient desire would be extinguished by instant fornication. And if, for some perverse reason, Romeo vacillated, Juliet could be counted on to console herself at once with a couple of *Soma* tablets. In a world without frustrations, in a world of instant gratification, there can be no sublimation and, therefore, there can be no romantic love. In such a world, there can be no conflict, and therefore there can be no drama. There can be no passion, and therefore no poetry. There can be no suffering, and therefore no tragedy. And there can be no self-sacrifice, and therefore no heroism. The irony of it all is that only in Huxley's comically colourless and unheroic society have the dreams of countless reformers been realised, and the long search to free men from the frictions and frustrations of this world been brought to a successful conclusion.

As a parable, I find the story is well worth pondering on. But as a portent of things to come, it is not to be taken too seriously. Not because it is technically unfeasible—but simply because it runs counter to the dynamic of modern science. Brave New World, though perfectly conceived, is essentially a static society, stranded in time, bereft of aspiration.

In contrast, the prevailing Establishment has become fascinated with the idea of change: of perpetual change; of change as a norm of society; of change as an end in itself. And this Establishment is all the time transforming itself. If it is thought of, at present, simply as a conglomerate of dominant groups in government, business, and the professions, the situation must also be seen as one of interregnum. For the prevailing Establishment is well on the way to becoming a *Scientific* Establishment.

The growing investment in higher education and the increasing number of young people today passing through the universities do not alter this fateful prospect. First the overwhelming proportion of students are not specialising in the physical sciences. The bulk of today's students are to be found in the humanities, in the social sciences, or training for the professions.

Secondly, in view of the size of the student population—currently running to eight millions in the United States—it is not surprising to remark that standards of accomplishment are on the decline, save perhaps for a handful of universities. More *does*, after all, tend to mean worse. Since the War, the bachelor's degree has been virtually worthless. Today, even the Ph.D. has lost its power to evoke respect in the community, and can no longer be depended upon to launch the successful candidate toward the upper echelons in government or business. If present trends in mass education continue, there is every likelihood of millions of dissatisfied ex-students milling about American cities, their frail expertise unwanted (how many sociologists can the nation employ?), unable or unwilling to fit into the uninspiring niches provided by industry and government, and inevitably forming a sort of intellectual *lumpenproletariat* that will go far to aggravate the general unrest, dissent, and desperation.

Turn now to those graduating in the physical sciences (where the prospects are brighter). In view of the rapidity of advance of modern knowledge, one observes that most of them are thankful to have mastered some of the basic theorems and techniques —well enough, at least, to enable them to engage in routine research. Few, very few, are capable of making original and substantial contributions to the subject. High up in the pecking order, increasingly recognised by industry and governments, as well as by their peers, are a few thousand of the elect. These few, the paladins, do get around. They know one another personally or through their publications. They form a grand international fraternity, and one increasingly impatient of the constraints of national states, increasingly contemptuous of administrators and of the manoeuvres of big business.

Thus the question of whether power can safely be vested in an *élite* of any sort, or whether, after all, it had better be entrusted to the common man—a question also raised in Tolkien's *Lord of the Rings*—may, though it seems to be of perennial interest, soon be of academic interest only. The fact is that power— political power—is gravitating surely, and not so slowly either, toward the scientists and technocrats, the high priests of the new ecumenical faith.

The implications of this transformation are radical in the extreme. We are prone to think of scientific research simply as an adjunct of government and industry. Indeed, we have yet among us the traditional socialists committed by doctrine to think in terms of a propensity of private enterprise to subvert the potential of science for its own nefarious ends. But, over the last two decades, the prestige of science, its hold over the popular imagination, and its influence over the young have grown irresistibly. A few more decades at most, and industry will be the adjunct, and government the agent, of science; economic activity will become subservient to the purposes of global scientific and technological research—the reverse of the relationship we are accustomed to think of.

As this state of affairs is realised, and unquestioning deference is paid to the principle of scientific research for its own sake, the question will inevitably arise: what is the Scientific Establishment to do about the masses of ordinary human beings?

Even if, by some miracle, the world population is stabilised at four or five billion souls, an all-powerful scientific establishment clearly has no need of some thousand millions of now useless mortals moving about the globe and cluttering up the limited space of the planet-laboratory. The prospect of diverting resources to provide them indefinitely with goodies and to ply them with entertainment and medicines will not be attractive. The temptation to be rid of them will grow stronger. Moral objections may no longer prevail: and political expediency can hardly act as a check once power has shifted irrevocably to the controllers of the Scientific Establishment. Of course, the means may not be cruel. Water supplies, for instance, could easily be doctored so as to make human reproduction physically impossible—at least without special medical intervention. Within a couple of generations, only the chosen few—a select group of a few thousand beings, part-men, part-computers—would be left to inherit the planet earth. The story of mankind will have drawn to a close. And the era of pure science will have begun.

True, the earth may not survive that long. We may yet be engulfed in the Malthusian nightmare. As a result of some scientific mischief or miscalculation, we may all go up in smoke. If we do not perish in a nuclear or biological holocaust, we may be the victims of some ecological disaster, and if, physically, we remain intact, the psychological strains and stresses of living in an automated society, with human activities increasingly programmed and regulated, may prove to be greater than the bulk of humanity can bear. The outbreaks of violence and hysteria we have begun to feel uneasy about (since they are manifestly unrelated to poverty or deprivation) may grow to such proportions as to break through the thin skin of civilisation. We may find ourselves, once more, in Sodom and Gomorrah—

frantic and frustrated, with gloated eyes, and shrunken gullets. None of these possibilities is unlikely. But if, perchance, we survive this gauntlet of hazards, the destiny that awaits us, the ultimate triumph of science, will be one that ends forever the human drama.

Is one still permitted to end an essay or a book on a pessimistic note? Perhaps an epilogue is called for. Let me then say this: the reins of power, though slackly held, are still in the hands of the people. The options are still open. True, men are the products of history. But not the passive products, or history would never change. And, if we believe in free will (and I do), it is at least as true that history is the product of men's choices.

There is, then, nothing in the physical state of the universe to prevent men making the transition from an economic system that, in the West at least, appears to depend for its survival on its capacity to mesmerise already wealthy populations[2] to continue to ransack the world's limited resources on an unprecedented and growing scale while spreading their wastes so indiscriminately as to foul their commonly shared environment; nothing to prevent their making the transition to a saner dispensation, one adopting as its priorities quiet skies, clean air, pure water, traffic-free towns, smaller populations, an easing of tempo, and extension of space, an enlarging of life, and the cultivation of an attitude of loving care to our tiny and unique planet. This latter option is technically quite feasible. Strange though it must sound to modern ears, and notwithstanding the banality of endless government exhortation to material ends, society can survive comfortably, indeed more comfortably, by moving off the exponential growth path. If men so willed it they could—incredible though it may seem—call a halt to the broad advance of technology and confine its impetus to a limited number of humane projects directly connected with the relief of suffering.

The standard "respectable" defence of indiscriminate economic growth employed from about 1850 onwards is that it provides the wherewithal to relieve the poor and heal the sick and do good works generally. The continued popularity of this defence resides, paradoxically, in the fact that the ailing and needy appear ever to remain with us. For economic growth of itself is not a force making for greater equality any more than it is a force making for greater contentment. If a nation such as the United States, with an average family income today of some $16,000, a nation consuming more near-rubbish *per capita* and disposing of more garbage *per capita* than any other nation, does not perceptibly improve the economic state of its indigent citizens it is simply a consequence of its overt political priorities—priorities that are themselves fashioned by the growth ideology that powers the existing system.

And talking of the reckless rate of consumption of natural resources required to keep the system from floundering, one can say more. In whatever ways its aggregate income were to be divided among the population, the system would still be geared to persuading people to absorb more GNP-stuff each year than the year before. The cities would still be clogged with traffic, homes would be still strewn with frippery gew-gaws and technical knick knacks. It is naïve to pretend that economic growth is a deliberate policy directed toward worthy ends. It is simply an institutional compulsion.

But we should have to give up our toys! A hundred thousand academics would have to abandon their hopes of status and recognition. A million executives and bureaucrats would have to watch their little empires dwindle. Research laboratories would go to rust. Stackfuls of learned journals would cease to appear. The ambitions of technocrats would be thwarted. And what of the multitude, fretted with discontent, impatient to enter the city of the future, and made gullible by promises of new excitements, of miracle drugs, perennial youth, and undiluted pleasures? How are they to be disabused, and their fevered spirits calmed?

So, pushing on in imagination, we perceive the crux of the problem, arising as it does from the fact that we have lived too long in a civilisation dominated by avarice, eulogised as "ambition". Greed pulses through our psyche as naturally as blood through our veins. Whether it is the public man for office, the private man for money, the scientist for status, or the hippie for pleasure, our greed is unbridled, and we push on ruthlessly in quest of gratification. An element in man's nature has become swollen out of all proportion; and there is no harmony within him. How, then, can wisdom prevail in the counsels of men?

Try as I might, then, it appears that I am destined to end on a pessimistic note after all. To the effect, in sum, that in their despair or greed, or both, men have come to place their faith in research, what they reverently call "*scientific* research". For deliverance they turn from Mammon to Science. And when the time comes, Science, in its turn, will consign them to oblivion.

NOTES

Chapter 1. *Some Heretical Thoughts on University Reform*

[1] In 1971–72 it rose to £333 million (capital expenditure of £72 million plus current expenditure of £261 million).

[2] These figures represent the total number in full-time higher education. Of the 180,000 in 1960, 117,000 were in universities proper (including former Colleges of Advanced Technology), the remainder being divided between 42,000 in colleges of education and 21,000 in technical colleges. The figures for 1968 were 210,000 in the universities, 110,000 in colleges of education, the remainder being in technical colleges.

[3] See, for instance, the article by Colin Clark, "An Unorthodox Proposal", in *Encounter*, May 1968.

[4] The economist is invited to substitute the words full cost *marginal* pricing for this more familiar but less accurate average concept. For long-run costs, and thinking in terms of 100 more or 100 fewer students at any given institute, there may be little difference between marginal full cost and average full cost.

[5] The average figure for 1966/67 was about £970 per annum, having risen by about £50 over the previous year. For the calculations, see R. Layard, J. King, and C. Moser, *The Impact of Robbins: Expansion in Higher Education* (Penguin). I am indebted to Mr Layard for advice in calculating these figures.

[6] This figure of £930 is used to simplify the argument. The per student contribution by the Treasury works out at roughly £750, leaving £180 or so to be accounted for by specific grants from government and private sources. Endowment revenue is negligible.

[7] It has been briefly suggested that with the ultimate source of fees vested in the state "Parliament would require still more inquisition into the nature of the fare provided" (*cf.* Lord Robbins, *The University in the Modern World*, Macmillan, 1966, p. 31). This was said in 1964, about three years before the Public Accounts Committee acquired powers to investigate the universities' books.

But if, as an act of political wisdom, the government were to agree to a proposal calculated to restore the independence of the universities at no extra cost to the taxpayer, it cannot surely be envisaged that at the same time it would deliberately make a mockery of the gesture by arrogating to itself yet greater powers of "inquisition". At all events, such a "deal" is no part of the above proposal, which would depend upon competition between free institutions to keep costs under control.

[8] Once the Government abandons its practice of allocating student places as between universities on the basis of its grants to them, the competition for student fees would act to prevent universities from raising their fees for any particular course much above those of other institutes of equal standing.

Nevertheless, the Government could at any time limit its financial liability in respect of fees by switching to a voucher scheme. The student would then retain the option of applying to any university, paying, if accepted, the difference (if any) between the fees and the voucher value.

⁹ As has been pointed out by Sir John Hicks in his monograph *After the Boom* (Institute of Economic Affairs, 1966).

¹⁰ The exhilarating vision of a rapidly expanding university system to which both democrat and technocrat appear to be wedded has been ridiculed by a few "lone voices" including that of Kingsley Amis in his famous *Encounter* essay (July 1960). I am not sure that "More" will always "Mean Worse", but some of the changes that have accompanied the increase in student numbers have been anything but reassuring. The idea of a university as a sanctuary from worldly affairs or as a forum for rational debate and dispassionate inquiry has, today, a distinctly nostalgic flavour. Indeed, owing to increasing student intolerance, the universities have become today (1969) one of the few places in Britain where free speech and open political debate are no longer assured!

¹¹ The conditions under which their results are identical are spelled out in my "Proposed Normalisation Procedure for Public Investment Criteria", *Economic Journal*, December 1967.

¹² See Mark Blaug's "Private and Social Returns on Investment in Education", *Journal of Human Resources*, Summer 1967, which estimates an average internal rate of return on education beyond the age of 18 of $6\frac{1}{2}\%$. A less representative sample gives a rate of return between 3% and 6% for first degree graduates. (No allowance, however, appears to have been made for the effect of economic growth on the future differential earnings of graduates.) In contrast, the rate of return on equities between 1948 and 1962 averages 12% in real terms before tax.

¹³ The calculations do, however, attribute the whole of the universities' current expenditures to the costs of student education. By attributing less than the whole, the rate of return could be raised somewhat, though it would still be lower than the return to industrial investment.

¹⁴ This is something we cannot allege at present as the bulk of teachers' salaries are determined by government regulation. Having, in effect, nationalised higher education for pretty much the same confused reasons that it nationalised medicine (see Arthur Seldon, "Crisis in the Welfare State", *Encounter*, December 1967), the Government has a continuing short-sighted interest in *holding down* salaries of secondary school and university teachers in ostensibly righteous endeavours to economise on public expenditure. Free vocational training plus relatively depressed pay afterwards may appear to offer a rough form of social justice if we ignore all quantitative aspects.

But so long as North America offers real salaries at least twice those in Britain, the option of *both a free education and good pay* is still open to British graduates willing to leave home. The consequent shortages of native-born teachers and physicians in the U.K. are not likely to be overcome, despite any extension of training facilities, so long as this tempting option is left open. The government has the choice of prohibiting emigration, which is politically impossible, or allowing earnings in medicine and teaching to rise in real terms —which, in the short run, means at the expense of the rest of the community.

¹⁵ We may include in this category the views of those who conceive of

higher education as a sort of "infant industry" (see Lord Robbins, *The University in the Modern World*, p. 30). But the opposition to the infant industry argument arises not so much because of the indiscriminate allegation of such cases in international trade, but because of the standard device used to foster the growth of even a genuine infant industry—import tariffs. Governments prefer tariff protection of the infant industry rather than paying subsidies to it, for in the former case they collect revenue rather than disburse it. Thus, it partly conceals from the public the loss to be endured—which loss tends to become permanent, for under tariff protection the infant "never grows up".

I do not think the infant industry analogy is apt. Is it being assumed that the real returns to higher education will grow over time with the scale of education? No, the assumption is either that education has widespread benefits (as above) or that potential students underestimate its benefits—in which case there is everything to be said for providing better information. But whatever the case for intervening in order to correct the market solution, it should (for the reasons I have given) take the form of direct and overt subsidies to the graduates in question. A person who believes that such overt subsidies are "politically unrealistic" is confessing to a doubt whether the arguments he could present for the subsidy would command a consensus in the country.

[16] For example, having satisfactorily defined a working-class or "poor" family, if the number of working-class or "poor" students falls below the desired $x\%$ in one year by (say) 1,000, the following year a competitive examination would select the top 1,000 working-class or "poor" candidates for scholarships. This initial figure of 1,000 would be revised over time so as to make up the desired social aim of maintaining $x\%$ working-class students.

[17] For example, A. R. Prest, *Financing University Education* (Institute of Economic Affairs, 1966). More recently the arguments have been re-stated by H. Glennerster, S. Merrett and G. Wilson in the Autumn 1968 issue of *Higher Education Review*. A similar proposal has been made by Irving Kristol in the course of a lively attack on American Universities (*New York Times Magazine*, 8 December 1968), now reprinted in his *On the Democratic Idea in America* (1972).

Apart from the question of political feasibility, the chief argument of the graduate tax proponents is that the full-cost loan repayment would place an "intolerable" burden of debt on the student. The scheme therefore envisages that the student repay only a portion of the full cost of his higher education. I need hardly point out that "intolerable" burden is emotive terminology which blurs the critical point at issue. For the rationale of allocative mechanisms is to select only those students who believe that investment in their education will pay for itself: not to encourage those who don't.

[18] I am not suggesting for one moment that the full-cost loans scheme will not be resisted by students, potential students, their parents, and many others whose direct interests are served by the existing scheme. No group passively abandons such exceptional privileges. But if the public is ultimately convinced of the injustice, and the inefficacy, of the present system the opposition of even a powerful minority interest will not prevail.

Be that as it may, I am concerned above with the consequences of the loans scheme once it is in operation. The simple proposition I put forward is that the larger are university fees relative to the resources of the student and his family the smaller is his temptation to engage in any action that is likely to disrupt his studies.

The notorious events at Berkeley in California, and at Columbia University in New York, cannot be regarded as evidence to the contrary. Higher education is, in any case, heavily subsidised in both these universities. Fees are nominal, particularly at Berkeley. In New York, grants covering about one-third of the fees are available in addition to loans at 3% (less than one-third of the rate of return on good industrial investment). Federal loans at 3% are also available, with the option of having to repay only one-half of the loan if the graduate enters special occupations such as teaching or university lecturing. For the greater number of American students and their families tuition fees and maintenance are no great burden.

In contrast, a sum of £5,000 or more over a three-year period is substantial enough in Britain to ensure that only a small proportion of British students will receive the whole sum as a gift from their families.

[19] In particular, I am indebted to Mr Nigel Lawson, Professor Alan Prest of Manchester, Mr Colin Clark of Oxford, and Mr Tyrrell Burgess of the London School of Economics. Though they pointed out the deficiencies of the logic at certain points, none are to be implicated in my attempts to remove them.

[20] In economic parlance it is more accurate to say (notwithstanding that some published work is generally expected of university teachers) that the salary paid is the supply price of teaching only, with intra-marginal staff members enjoying a "surplus" or economic rent.

Chapter 2. *The Spillover Enemy*

[1] I disregard here a veritable wilderness of ecological consequences of man's short-sighted interference with nature—many of them ably discussed by Peter Laurie in the *Sunday Times Magazine* (London) of 17 November 1968, and also by John Davy in *The Observer*, 10 and 17 November. This is not because they are less important than the spillover effects treated above; nor because they fall outside the economist's purview. Indeed they can, and should, be brought into the economic calculus. There are rational and systematic ways of dealing with half-knowledge, probabilities, likelihoods, uncertainty and ignorance. Whatever their imperfections they yield far more justifiable solutions than the present method of excluding consideration of all consequences save those pertinent to commercial gain or technological triumph. However, I confine my attack here to those tangible and familiar spillovers that are becoming increasingly intolerable.

[2] Though I concentrate largely on "bad" or unfavourable spillovers to the exclusion of "good" spillovers, this would bias the argument in the text only if it could be supposed that good spillovers are somehow to be offset against bad spillovers—much as the good features of an age might be offset against the bad ones before a judgment is reached.

But this notion is erroneous. The larger the number of spillovers—whether all good, all bad, or equally mixed—the greater the scope there is for allocative improvement. Within a competitive setting, the greatest improvements are made by first tackling the more outstanding environmental spillovers.

I might add in passing that on a broad definition of the term there is apparently no limit to the number of relatively trivial spillover effects one can think up, such as person *A*'s envy of *B*'s new car or *B*'s new wife, his disgust at *C*'s body odour, his pleasure at *D*'s promotion or demotion. These spillovers are ignored by economists either *(1)* because the cost (in terms of time, effort, and money) of correcting them exceeds the potential gain from doing so; or *(2)* because the satisfaction or dissatisfaction experienced in this connection is regarded by society at large as ethically unjustifiable. *A*'s envy of *B*'s status or *A*'s sadistic pleasure at *B*'s suffering is not at present allowed for by the economist in framing economic policy, though in a future society they may well enter into the calculus.

³ "A new 'dimension' of hazard is given also by the fact that while man now can—and does—create radioactive elements, there is nothing he can do to reduce their radioactivity once he has created them. No chemical reaction, no physical interference, only the passage of time reduces the intensity of radiation once it has been set going. . . .

"Wherever there is life, radioactive substances are absorbed into the biological cycle. Within hours of depositing [radioactive waste products created by nuclear reactors] in water, the great bulk of them can be found in living organisms. Plankton, algae, and many sea animals have the power of concentrating these substances by a factor of 1,000 and in some cases even a million. As one organism feeds on another, the radioactive materials climb up the ladder of life and find their way back to man. . . .

"The point is that very serious hazards have already been created by the 'peaceful uses of atomic energy', affecting not merely people alive today but all future generations although so far nuclear energy is being used on a statistically insignificant scale. The real development is yet to come, on a scale which few people are capable of imagining." (E. F. Schumacher, "Clean Air and Future Energy", *Des Voeux Memorial Lecture*, October 1967.)

⁴ According to a *Newsweek* report (8 January 1968), Professor L. C. Cole of Cornell University (in a paper delivered at the 134th annual meeting of the American Association for the Advancement of Science) asks whether man is not destroying the earth's natural supply of oxygen. He points out *(1)* that the increasing combustion of fossil fuels has greatly accelerated the formation of carbon dioxide in the atmosphere; and *(2)* that, in the United States alone, some one million acres of suburbanised forest and grassland each year lose their ability to regenerate the oxygen supply through photosynthesis.

⁵ The interested reader is referred to Chapter 6 of my book *Welfare Economics: An Assessment* (North Holland Publishing Co., 1969).

⁶ He who will not concede this much may yet allow that the suffering of the more sensitive citizens could be relieved without undue expense, even under existing laws, by the Government making provision for viable separate areas not too far from towns and cities, areas in which complete protection against all aircraft and traffic noise was assured.

Chapter 3. *A Modest Proposal to Transfigure the Environment*

¹ Though reduced by less than it would be in the absence of such mutual agreements.

[2] The dichotomy is functional only since a person can be both pollutor and polluted. The air-line passenger pays for a noise-polluting service and also, when not in flight, suffers from it. The car driver both adds to and suffers from traffic congestion.

Such facts do not require modification of the above arguments, however. Mutually beneficial agreements, for instance to reduce the amount of traffic, are in principle possible: if, say, a hundred motorists were banned from driving their vehicles through the city during certain hours, the gain (reckoned as a willingness to pay for the extra room by the remaining motorists) could be more than enough to compensate the hundred for their inconvenience. One could go on making such calculations by withdrawing motorists by the hundred, by tens, or singly, until gains were no longer greater than the necessary compensatory payments. The reduced traffic resulting from this sort of experiment is what economists would call an *optimal* flow of traffic—at least in respect of this one spillover, congestion.

[3] Assuming population remained unchanged, what natural goods would have been lost would be more than offset by the benefits of man's industry. The unchecked increase in population that requires an expansion of industry, and can directly reduce amenity, is not so easily dealt with in economics. What the enforcement of pollutant-repressive law implies, as population increases—and all that *optimality* really implies in this circumstance—is making the best of a bad job.

The continued rise of population in a world where resources are finite does eventually cause scarcity. The economist points out that this takes the form of rising prices. And the fact that prices rise "optimally"—that is, according to some relevant *marginal* principle—is not so consoling a thought (even when it is true) as some economists seem to believe.

[4] One can, of course, be sophistical here also. The *prevention* of suffering can be conceived as a good and so, also, as a "pleasure" of sorts. The *deprivation* of opportunity to pursue pleasures that have become popular in richer countries can be conceived of as a "bad" and, therefore, as a form of "suffering".

But these philosophical symmetries, useful for classification and clarification in abstract argumentation, should not be allowed to cloud the issue where particular contexts are in mind. When one is aware of what is at stake, the profits of a corporation or, say, the interests of air travellers, on the one hand, and, on the other, the disturbance to the peace of a neighbourhood, the effect on a man's health and his enjoyment of life from continual aerial disturbance, the dictum is neither ambiguous nor inappropriate.

[5] This allegation lends itself to more than one interpretation. It may mean that the rich really care more about clean air and a healthy environment than do the poor. Or it may mean that although the rich care no more about the environment than other groups, being richer they are prepared to pay more for the same good. I would favour the latter interpretation.

[6] True, a developer can—and in the U.S. he frequently does—buy up a choice bit of land and furnish it with ultra-modern homes and garages, and with popular recreational facilities such as tennis courts, golf courses, swimming pools, saunas and possibly a lake for fishing, or sailing, or water-skiing.

But these expensive and patently exclusive pre-fabricated resorts, equipped with all the chic activities sought after by the *nouveau riche*, often protected by private police, have no relation to the separate amenity areas that I am discussing. Such advertised "paradises" are obviously not for the family of modest means, and certainly not for the sensitive family seeking a retreat from the assault of the internal combustion engine.

[7] The proposal also has an international aspect. The "package" tourist trade, apparently in a competitive scramble to uncover all places of once-quiet repose to the money-flushed multitude, is literally and, in effect, irrevocably destroying them. The famed resorts around the coastline of the Mediterranean are being transmogrified into so many traffic-congested Coney Islands. Without a thought to the desolation of the future and the deprivation of their grandchildren, the post-War generation has abandoned itself to wholesale destruction of the earth's most precious and irreplaceable heritage of natural beauty.

One limited solution, technically and politically feasible, is international agreement to set aside a number of select mountain, lake, coastal and island resorts scattered about the globe to which all means of swift travel are removed. Such areas would be set aside for the true lover of nature who is prepared to make his pilgrimage by boat, arrange for his accommodation among the local population, and is willing to explore islands, valleys, and woodlands on foot.

[8] Once the political decision to introduce such areas is taken, there will of course be some debate also on the *number* of areas to be introduced. However, as argued above, the number should be allowed to grow over time in response to the demand for them.

[9] Local opposition, frequently led by small shopkeepers who fear (often mistakenly) some loss of custom from prohibiting traffic, is apt to be more vociferous than powerful. In the event that losses continue to be incurred by some shops or firms as a direct result of banning traffic, considerations of equity would require that they be compensated, or given financial assistance if they elect to move elsewhere. However, a trial period will usually convince shop-owners that the absence of motorised vehicles from their streets does not necessarily reduce the amount of shopping, and is more likely to increase sales than to reduce them.

[10] I should be pleasantly surprised to discover that I was wrong in this surmise, and that the lower-income groups responded to the innovation with no less enthusiasm.

[11] Possibly some modifications of the full rigour of the law may be contemplated where the disturbance arises from some youthful prank. But the responsibility falls mainly on the parent for allowing importation into the area of the means of disturbance.

[12] As I indicated in my book, *The Costs of Economic Growth*, I have no objection whatever to setting aside, on the same principle, separate areas suitably equipped with metalled highways and racing tracks for those who appear to derive keen enjoyment from roaring along in racing cars and motor bikes, so enabling them to disport themselves to their hearts' content.

It is however just possible to suspect that some portion of the enjoyment of roaring along on a motor cycle depends upon being able to startle and annoy others. But no reasonable person would want to make provision for one group to derive their pleasure by directly annoying others.

Chapter 4. *Making the World Safe for Pornography*

[1] Along with other terms having about them a penumbra of doubt or irony, I put the term "permissive" in quotes. As has been remarked by a number of people, the apparent growth of sex permissiveness is a poor consolation prize for the mounting frustrations of individuals in the modern industrial welfare state. Indeed, Quintin Hogg once observed that, sex aside, modern society with its increasing number of regulations and controls (all for our own good, of course) has become the antithesis of permissive.

[2] Academic colleagues have agreed with me that we, of the older generation, are wanting perhaps in that "maturity" which would enable us to regard these scantily clad nubile figures with the detached complacency proper to an art form. It may well be the case—though the young people I have spoken with deny the fact—that a new generation is emerging which is able to regard highly erotic attire without any sexual interest. Whether true or not, I confess that I should feel just a little alarmed if I discovered that the sight of bouncing bosoms and buttocks no longer stirred my lusts a little—from which declaration the reader is *not* to infer that I approve of current fashions.

Sex stimulation arising from the sight of erotically clad females has its place and its function. But sexual stimulation as an all-pervasive phenomenon is as much an abuse of liberty as it is a perversion of taste. To put it mildly, it is a nuisance for an ordinary healthy man to be exposed to sexually-inviting attire on the way to work, on the streets, in buses, in trains and in offices; sexuality forcing itself continually on the privacy of his thoughts and feelings. There is in fact a good liberal case against "sex pollution" too. I shall touch on this aspect in the following chapter.

[3] The quoted phrases are from a brochure issued in 1970 by a firm under the name of John Amslow & Associates (Culver City, California), a business concern offering the "adult public" an "advanced sexual techniques kit" consisting of 8-mm. movie films plus seven photographically illustrated manuals.

[4] To choose a fairly recent impression by Ludovic Kennedy in an article, "New York Revisited" (*Spectator*, 7 March 1971): "Times Square was a shock too, despite friends' warnings. In one window, a still life of dildos in a mug, like toothbrushes, all shapes for all seasons, and beside them blown-up rubber girlies, man-size, pink and brown, brunette and blonde, to keep one warm in bed. In another window a picture of two rhinos on the job. . . .

"*Screw* and *Ban*, *Orgy* and *Pleasure* are the depressing pornographic broadsheets available at any kerbside paper-stall. . . . The stories cover the usual porno ground from bestiality to analingus, but the ads are almost unbelievable. 'Sincere, hairy guy, white, 32, with enviable 8 x 6 wishes to meet sympathetic AC/DC couples, any color, for groovy threesomes. My specialities French and Greek cultures, also watersports and S and M. Discretion assured. Photos please'. . . ."

[5] Although there is an affinity between these developments, it is understood that pornography need not use obscene language and that obscene language may have nothing to do with pornography. The frequent recourse to quotation marks in the course of this essay is to be interpreted by the reader as affirming that little purpose is served by the use of more precise terminology at that point in the argument.

⁶ In regions where even the skilled psychiatrist is as yet unsure of his footing, "progressive" teachers can be found giving pat advice to young people about sexual behaviour much as if they were coaxing tots to eat more buns at a tea party. "If you are attached to a member of your own sex, and if you both want to give physical expression to your feelings, then do so," advise Messrs M. Hill and M. Lloyd Jones in their booklet *Sex Education*, put out by the National Secular Society (London, 1970).

⁷ According to *The Times* (18 December 1971), the Working Party's Report presented to the Birmingham Educational Committee "felt that many children were not receiving the sex education they needed". (It would perhaps be nearer the mark to say that the children were not receiving as much sex education as some of the teachers were anxious to offer.) With the results in mind of a questionnaire of three-quarters of the city's schools revealing a recent increase in children's sex inquisitiveness, the Report alleged that "teachers were becoming aware that children of this age had a *natural and healthy* curiosity (about sex), and it was urged that this should be dealt with simply and truthfully." (My italics). Why "natural and healthy"? Why not—in view of the mass media's current obsession with erotica—simply *infectious curiosity?*

In the same issue of *The Times* there happens to be a letter from Lord Elton on the debate about the standards of the BBC in the 1970s: "Let it be recorded before this correspondence closes down that the Corporation contrived to include an attempted rape into (of all books!) *Tom Brown's Schooldays*."

Perhaps, after all, we shall not have to wait long for some enterprising pornocrat to make a "modern" film version of Dickens' *Old Curiosity Shop*, with Little Nell cast in the role of a juvenile nymphomaniac.

⁸ *New York Times*, 1 April 1969. The editorial is more fully quoted by Walter Berns in an excellent article, "Pornography versus Democracy: A Case Study for Censorship," *The Public Interest* (Winter, 1971). As Berns points out, to the regular readers of the *New York Times* literary and drama reviews, the editorial must have appeared as something of a *volte face.*

⁹ *The Sunday Telegraph*, 29 August 1971.

¹⁰ Walter Berns, in *The Public Interest*. (According to *Life Magazine* this film cost $160,000 to make and, up to 1970, had made $5 million in the United States alone.)

¹¹ W. C. Williams, writing in *The Public Interest* (Winter, 1971), offers the following comment on Berns' proposal for legal censorship on pornography: "In one area, censorship would be both safe and possibly helpful: the censorship of one's self. Artists, scientists, philosophers and intellectuals generally owe themselves and their fellow citizens the duty of gauging their utterances, works and writings in terms of their likely impact on the life of men."

¹² Such books and films would, presumably, also be available in libraries to psychologists, pathologists, and other interested scholars.

¹³ Their findings appeared in a book, *The Obscenity Laws: A Report by the Working Party set up by a Conference convened by the Chairman of the Arts Council of Great Britain*, published in 1969 by André Deutsch, London, with a Foreword by John Montgomerie. With the exception of Professor Frank Kermode and John Mortimer, Q.C., the sixteen members of the Working

Party were writers, booksellers, publishers, or in societies promoting (or defending) literature and art.

[14] It has recently been alleged by Michael Foot in *The Times* that D. H. Lawrence once declared that the most pornographic novel of the nineteenth century was Charlotte Brontë's *Jane Eyre*. It does not matter much in this case that Lawrence had highly idiosyncratic opinions, or that he used words in unconventional ways to give expression to his approval or disapproval, or that he would hardly have given his blessing to the current flood of smutty writing to be found in bookshops and corner book stalls. If Michael Foot's point is simply that standards of obscenity change over time then it follows only that the law, as an expression of public opinion, should also change over time.

The question of whether censorship, legal or conventional, can be justified in any period of history by other than contemporary values or sentiments is, again, a separate issue.

[15] Just because of such habits it was hardly surprising that John Mortimer, Q.C., who apparently sees connections everywhere and distinctions nowhere, should remind the jury, in his defence of the *Oz* editors, that Socrates was condemned to death for seeking the truth on the alleged grounds that he was thereby corrupting the morals of the people.

As Keith Botsford aptly remarked at the beginning of his fascinating piece on "The Innocence of Oz" (*Encounter*, November 1971), such a parallel "is offensive to history, to due proportion, and to plain fact".

[16] *Report* of the Arts Council's Working Party, p. 55. Barker later hazards the remarkable view that "it is the puritanical pressure groups in this country that cause pornography to flourish. If this pressure ceased then the problem would fall into quite a different perspective" (p. 57).

Presumably the same puritanical pressure groups have begun their nefarious activities in America also, for pornography there flourishes more than it does as yet in Britain. And what of Denmark where it flourishes most? Presumably we are to infer that these puritanical pressure groups gained enormously in strength during the later 1960s and were at their weakest during the mid-Victorian era.

[17] Both quotations are from an article, "Obscenity and Maturity", which by any standards is a model of vacuity, ambiguity and inconclusiveness, written by Dr John Robinson (formerly Bishop of Woolwich) which appeared in *The Sunday Times* (14 December 1969).

Dr Robinson contrives a distinction between the erotic, which he enjoys, and the obscene, which he does not—apparently because the latter does not involve "human relationships". One wonders casually just what human relationships were involved in his declared enjoyment of the photographs of "Paula Kelly dancing completely in the nude, pubic hair and all. Nothing could be more beautiful and entrancing." (The construction of the sentences does, I'm afraid, leave one a trifle uncertain whether the prelate's enjoyment arose from the contemplation of Paula's dancing in the nude or from his contemplation of her "pubic hair and all".)

Dr Robinson's solution to the problem of pornography, needless to say, does not include penal legislation. It is simply that of "encouraging values and relationships which will make people *not want* to do dirt on sex or anything else". It is a solution, apparently, that would not withhold licence from anyone in search of profits to produce films or entertainment in which actors would indeed "do dirt on sex".

[18] *Report*, pp. 33–4. This is as good a place as any to remind the reader that the terms "permissiveness" and the "permissive society", even where they are restricted to sexual aspects, are misleading. The "permissiveness" being debated is that which, if extended, initially offers the public increased opportunities for excitation, *not* for gratification. For nobody in authority is challenging any person's right to engage in sexual activity with other persons in any way he wishes, as often as he wishes, with willing adult partners.

Permission to indulge and enjoy is not the issue at all. The permissiveness that is in issue is whether complete licence should be extended to writers, impresarios, actors and film producers to depict sexual activity of any variety in public places, and permission for the public to pay and stare.

[19] I cannot pretend that I have had as much experience of nudist colonies as the members of the Working Party, but I should have thought that the degree of erotic experience would vary with the age, shape, posture and activities of the nude colonists.

[20] The fashionable protests and violence of the young have been explained (*inter alia* by Robert Nisbet in his *Encounter* article, "Who Killed The Student Revolution?", February 1970) in terms of *too little* repression. Middle-class liberals, having imbibed Freudian tid-bits from hack journalists, and eager to rear the ideal uninhibited child-prodigy, mistook the master's message, and more often than not found themselves the harassed parents of a litter of snarling pups.

The absence of conscience, the absence of a sense of guilt even, can be regarded as a psychological defect. The propensity of some of today's students to protest at any imagined deprivation, to rant and rampage at the slightest grievance, real or imaginary, can plausibly be interpreted as a vengeful search for the strong father-figure they were denied in their infancy.

[21] Some of the starved inmates of Nazi concentration camps were so far obsessed with visions of food that, when rescued and offered food, they would not eat it. They either gazed at it rapturously or sought to hoard it. The parallel with orgasmic starvation may be thought forced, but not by all psychiatrists.

[22] "A Reply to Pamela Hansford Johnson," *Encounter*, April 1970. (I say "*if* it is true" because the statement also lends itself to a tautological interpretation: to wit, a person who wants to be violent about anything will feel frustrated unless he is being violent.)

[23] The relevant passage from Mr Halloran's testimony is as follows: "The evidence from American studies offers little support for the catharsis argument. However, there is slight support from one or two Italian studies, and some Australian work suggests the possibility of a double effect. In general the evidence from these laboratory studies is usually taken as indicating that heavy exposure to media violence increases the possibility of violent behaviour in the post-exposure situation." (*Report*, p. 69.)

This statement (made presumably in 1968) applies to media portrayal of violence and aggression, not to pornography as such. Since that time, however, further experiments conducted in this country and in the United States have tended to confirm the commonsense view that repeated exposure to scenes of violence increases the likelihood of violent reactions in the viewer.

For recent comment on these experiments see the chapter by Professor H. J. Eysenck, "The Use and Abuse of Pornography", in his book *Psychology Is About People* (1972).

[24] Apart from its disregard of the ultimate consequences on the character of *society*, those supporting the abolition of all censorship mistake the consequences for *literature* itself. Irving Kristol (*New York Times Magazine*, 28 March 1971) puts the question: how much has literature lost from the fact that practically anything can be published today in America? He argues that in a free market "Gresham's Law can work for books or theatre as efficiently as it does for coinage—driving out the good, establishing the debased. The cultural market in the United States today is being pre-empted by dirty books, dirty movies, dirty theatre. A pornographic novel has a far better chance of being published today than a non-pornographic one, and quite a few pretty good novels are not being published at all simply because they are not pornographic, and are therefore less likely to sell. Our cultural condition has not improved as a result of the new freedom."

[25] Irving Kristol rightly points out that whereas the doctrinaire libertarians tell us not to take pornography seriously, the nihilists and those dedicated to challenging the existing social order—people like Herbert Marcuse, Susan Sontag, Norman Brown, even Jerry Rubin—take pornography and obscenity very seriously indeed.

[26] I am not, however, denying for a moment the existence of homosexual conventions in ancient Greece or Rome, nor the occurrence of private orgies, private lascivious displays, or other obscene activities not only in the ancient world but in other civilisations. We are not comparing private practices, or sexual conventions, throughout the ages. The issue is the prevalence of wanton sexual performances as a legitimate form of *public* entertainment.

[27] A perhaps idiosyncratic view, though not an implausible one, of the consequences of the abandoning of all sexual taboos may be touched on in passing which, although not unrelated to the main stream of conjecture, could only be treated adequately by a more thorough-going anthropological and psychological approach. The existence of sexual proprieties and taboos enables and requires a man to hug his sex fantasies to himself—to have and to hold, for his private anxieties and delectation, a world within himself of the outlandish and licentious. The emergence of the pornographic society would dissolve the illusion of the peculiarity and power of these sub-surface desires. All potent sources of excitation that lurk like furtive monsters in the dark recesses of his imagination would dissipate and melt away in the glare of public pornography.

For the ordinary man, such a loss could be irreplaceable: the last refuge of his inner world, the guarded sanctuary of his lusts, broken open and all its contents dragged into the market place, there to be made the common stuff of mass entertainment. True, the opportunities for overt sexual titillation become multiplied. But with the loss of each man's secret refuge he might feel much like an animal that has been deprived of its own peculiar odour and identity.

[28] In order to avoid turning the question into a semantic issue, it could be re-phrased more precisely as follows: does abstracting from sentiment *vis-à-vis* the sexual partner strengthen the physical sensations of pleasure or does it weaken them?

[29] See his review of the books written by Dr Viktor Frankl, *The Doctor and the Soul* and *Psychotherapy and Existentialism*, and that written by Dr Rollo May, *Love and the Will* (*The Times*, 20 March 1971).

[30] It should be unnecessary to remark that such feelings have, of themselves, nothing to do with xenophobia. They are in fact wholly consistent with a love of racial diversity, a respect for the achievements of other peoples, and a sympathetic understanding and, possibly, admiration for their institutions.

Chapter 5. *The Economics of Sex Pollution*

[1] In the chapter entitled "Making the World Safe for Pornography".

[2] *The Obscenity Laws* (A Report by the Working Party set up by a Conference convened by the Chairman of the Arts Council of Great Britain). André Deutsch, London, 1969.

[3] Volumes carrying just such titles can be bought (1971) on New York City's 42nd Street (between 6th and 7th Avenues), in any of a rash of small shops which appeared in the late 1960s. They are now facing heavy competition from West Coast mail-order firms, and several have either closed down or moved to less expensive premises in the last couple of years.

[4] Though I do not envisage any restraints on pornography as such, it would be wise to keep an eye on developments in the depiction of *sadistic brutality*. If the brutality of the scenes increased, if their popularity grew, and such scenes were known to be a potent factor in the incidence of lawless violence, restraints on such art and literature may have to be imposed even in the *X* areas. The warrant for such restraints is that any resulting increase in crimes of violence is itself a spillover effect of the *X* area which cannot, however, be confined within the *X* area.

Chapter 6. *Does Immigration Confer Economic Benefits?*

[1] Lord Butler, in replying to the debate on the control of Commonwealth immigration at the Conservative Party Conference of 1961, asserted that we needed Commonwealth immigrants for the labour they provided. The claim has been repeated since by others in high places.

[2] The economic effects of a unit stream of *emigration* are not, however, symmetrical over time with those of a unit stream of immigration. For one thing, the rate at which capital capacity can be released is limited by the rate of amortisation of the existing capital stock. Thus the rate of additional saving made available by the net outflow of labour differs in general from the rate of additional investment required for a net inflow of labour.

[3] The data are based on a survey of seven London boroughs by R. B. Davison (*Black British*, Oxford University Press, 1966. See in particular his Table 46).

[4] An average of between 10% and 12% of Jamaican earnings goes in income tax, national insurance, and personal saving. Remittances to relatives in Jamaica initially account for between 10% and 15% of earnings, though these taper off over time. (Davison, *Black British*).

[5] Full details of the sources of data, the calculations made, plus a specification of the model constructed for the purpose, can be found in E. J. Mishan

and L. Needleman, "Immigration, Excess Aggregate Demand and the Balance of Payments," *Economica*, May 1966.

⁶ True, if there happens to be some foreign demand for our exports that cannot be met by increasing their output (or raising their prices) because of a sectoral shortage of specialised labour then, provided immigrant labour is able to offer the necessary skills, it can make some temporary contribution to exports. The one industry for which exports could have been increased during the 1960s if the appropriate type of labour could have been recruited was the machine-tool industry. But immigrant labour does not appear to have been used there in any discernible numbers.

⁷ More accurately, "rentals", being the market price for the services of capital assets (which could, here, include land), rise relative to the price of unskilled labour.

The returns to skilled or professional labour in the long run partake of the returns to capital—at least in so far as the capital market is such that funds for investment in "human capital" are available as an alternative to investment in physical capital, or claims thereto.

⁸ To be more explicit, the influx of labour causes *wages* (equal to marginal product of labour) to fall more than the average product of labour, and this implies a rise in rentals or a net transfer from wage earnings to profits. However, the part of the transfer as between *indigenous* labour and *indigenous* capital does not matter from the point of view of the *indigenous population as a whole*. We are left then with the transfer from the earnings of the influx of immigrant labour to the profits of indigenous capitalists. Notwithstanding the regressive distributional changes, this additional gain to indigenous capitalists appears as a net gain to the indigenous population as a whole, against which we must set the terms-of-trade effect suffered by both groups of the indigenous population, capitalists and labourers. Dividing this net gain, or loss, by the indigenous population as a whole gives the rise or fall of its real income *per capita* that results from immigrant labour.

The categories of labour (or labourers) and capital (or capitalists) do not, of course, purport to be a description of social realities. They form a convenient economic dichotomy for this kind of analysis and are defined functionally. In so far as an individual's income arises from personal services he contributes as labourer; in so far as it arises from the services of the assets he owns he contributes as capitalist. Most income-earners in Britain contribute to national output in both capacities, as labourer and as capitalist, although most earn the bulk of their income in either one capacity or the other.

The implication for the rest of this essay is that a statement about a transfer or redistribution of income in favour of capitalists is to be interpreted as affecting most people in both capacities, as capitalist and as labourer. If most of his income comes from the services of the assets he owns, he is made better off by the redistribution in favour of capital. If the greater part of his income comes from his personal services, he is made worse off by this sort of redistribution.

⁹ More generally, technical innovation can be relatively capital-saving or relatively labour-saving. Although on balance, perhaps, labour-saving innovations are more likely over the foreseeable future, the assumption of "neutral" innovations—those which do not alter the wage/rental ratio—is

maintained throughout the analysis. A preponderance of labour-saving innovations over time would act to reduce wages relative to rentals. But the distributional effects of immigration would not be much altered thereby.

[10] A more complete picture would require also the elasticity of export supply for the UK and abroad. As an approximation we can assume constant costs for the difference in trade made by immigration.

[11] According as wages decline relative to rentals or, what comes to the same thing, as rentals rise relative to wages, more capital-intensive goods rise in price relative to less capital-intensive goods. The greater the response by consumers to such price differentials the more limited is the resulting decline of wages relative to rentals. This substitution on the consumption side acts to reinforce the effects of substitution of labour for capital, so effectively raising the value of σ.

No estimates have been made of this so-called *product-substitution* effect and we have disregarded it in the calculations. The larger it is the more it will curb the rise in the index of regressive distribution, A, and the more it will curb the decline in *per capita* domestic product. If there were no effects on the terms of trade the B index would fall and the C index would rise.

Once we allow for the terms-of-trade effects a negative component enters into the B and C index since the relative rise in prices of capital-intensive goods could reduce demand for our exports and add to the adverse movement of the terms of trade. Nevertheless, unless this product-substitution is far more important than is generally believed, the results will not mislead.

[12] Thus the adverse terms-of-trade necessary to maintain international balance more than offset the positive transfer to the indigenous population arising from diminishing returns to labour by amounts shown in the B column for Cases *(1)* and *(2)*.

[13] Details of the sources of data and the specification of the model used in deriving these results will be found in the paper by Mishan and Needleman, "Immigration: Some Long-term Economic Consequences" (Part A), *Economia Internazionale*, August 1968.

[14] We are assuming here that the government is successful in combating inflationary pressure *and* that there is no apparent over-all excess demand for labour (which, as I showed in Part I, cannot in any case be met by immigrant labour without further adding to excess aggregate demand). In the circumstances excess demand for domestic labour in some occupations will be offset by a potential redundancy of domestic labour in others.

[15] Events that do not fit into the usual framework of formal analysis are nonetheless proper subjects for consideration by the economist. In an ideally competitive, frictionless, and informed economy, all the cost-reducing technical innovations are adopted as they appear. The adoption of known labour-saving techniques, on the other hand, takes place in response to a sufficient change of relative factor prices. Thus an influx of additional labour does not of itself *prevent* the adoption of a labour-saving device: the influx must be such as to cause a sufficient rise in the price of capital. Conversely, no reduction of labour in such an economy will of itself encourage the adoption of known cost-reducing labour-saving devices: such devices will appear economical only in response to a sufficient fall in the rate of interest brought about by a reduction in the labour-capital ratio. However, in the partly sheltered and fairly institutionalised economy of the U.K. these

propositions do not hold, except on some definition of "the long run". No casual observer of the U.K. economy would find it hard to believe that some cost-reducing labour-saving innovations are fairly readily available but, either for institutional reasons (peaceful labour-mangement relations) or because of the force of inertia, are just not adopted. Without some emergency to act as a catalyst these potential sources of efficiency will be ignored for many years. In transport, for instance, it has long been known that worthwhile economies could have been effected by the employment of one-man buses, by installing coin-operated turnstiles on underground railways, by simplification in fares, and by other labour-saving devices. In hospitals the saving of trained staff by installing patient-monitoring devices in wards is making only very slow headway. It would not be unreasonable to believe that in the absence of immigrant labour flowing into these occupations, the apparent shortage of indigenous labour might have precipitated an emergency in which the provision of such services could have been met by a change to more efficient, and already known, labour-saving methods.

[16] Symmetry would require that workers redundant in any industry emigrate from the country.

[17] It is sometimes alleged that immigrant labour is "more mobile" than indigenous labour. This is certainly true in the obvious sense that since they came into the country expressly to seek work they tend to move to areas and into occupations which offer them employment, whereas the bulk of the existing population is already employed. In exactly the same sense juvenile and unskilled labour is also more mobile than domestic labour as a whole. There is no reason to suppose that as immigrant workers settle down and acquire skills their mobility will be any higher than that of comparable indigenous workers.

[18] World population today is put at a figure of $3\frac{1}{2}$ thousand million, increasing roughly at the rate of 100 million per annum, by far the larger proportion being contributed by the poorer countries.

[19] For it is not impossible that if somehow these external effects could be brought into the calculus they would completely swamp any evaluation of the economic effects treated in Parts I and II.

[20] The possibility of immigration in large numbers creating factionalism and discord within the community, or of their forming disruptive power-groups within the host country, are consequences which formally can be comprehended by the concept of external effects. But since the range of likely consequences is better brought to the fore by harnessing the experience, specialised knowledge and judgment of the whole community, it is more satisfactory to try to reach a consensus by the democratic process.

Chapter 7. *On Making the Future Safe for Mankind*

[1] Of more immediate relevance however is the fact that our rapidly changing technology escalates the costs of the arms race while buying for nations no more security.

As Charles Schultze has pointed out, technological advance is accompanied by two developments:

"*(1)* As we learn about new technology, we project it forward into the Soviet arsenal, thereby creating new potential contingencies to be covered by our own forces; *(2)* the new technology raises the possibility of designing weapons systems to guard against contingencies that it has not been possible to protect against previously.

"Continually advancing technology and the risk-aversion of military planners, therefore, combine to produce ever more complex and expensive weapons systems and ever more contingencies to guard against." *The Public Interest* (No. 18), Winter 1970, p. 14.

[2] Though I shall not dwell on it here, the growth in population is not excluded from my terms of reference. For economic growth is one of the preconditions of the secular growth in population.

[3] *Technology and Growth: The Price We Pay* (Praeger, N.Y., 1969).

[4] Stefan Linder, *The Harried Leisure Classes* (1970).

[5] The Federal revenues alone are growing at an annual rate of between $15 billion and $20 billion.

[6] To use the suggestive term employed by Nordhaus and Tobin in their paper "Is Economic Growth Obsolete?" (unpublished at the time of writing).

[7] The slogan that "he who pollutes should pay the cost of his pollution" is not the same thing as effective anti-pollutive legislation, and can indeed act to encourage delaying tactics. It can, for example, be asked what the costs really are, on whom does the damage fall, and which firms or people can be held to be responsible for what part and with what degree of probability. A case is then made for more research into this complex question and we are back in square one.

The proposal above can, in principle, be made quite specific. It sets a time limit, say 3 years, after which a specified range of pollutants will be prohibited *entirely* (above some specified degree) unless the enterprise has a permit, renewed annually, entitling it to some greater degree of pollution. One condition under which such a permit might be given would be the existence of unanimous consent of all affected parties (for example in the case of noise). Another condition might be that the enterprise is employing an approved preventive technology and/or that it reduces its output to a level determined by reference to standard economic criteria. Any infringement of the law would bring an action by the public prosecutor.

[8] Since there is what we might call a total expenditure effect and a competitive effect attaching to any advertising campaign, it is likely to be the case that quite a bit of "successful" competitive advertising is self-cancelling —sheer waste, that is. As for entertainment and information value, better entertainment and more detailed and impartial information can be provided for a small fraction of the current resources used up in commercial advertising.

[9] There is little solace to be had from observation that after centuries of mutual antagonism, religious denominations are drawing together. For this is happening at a time when religion plays no vital part in the organisation of society. In a vain attempt to appear relevant to the needs of society, the churches are directing their appeal less to the spiritual life of the community and more towards its social and psychological needs. In adapting themselves to modern life in a bid for physical survival, they are divesting themselves of spiritual authority. They are transforming themselves into lay institutions offering society material aid, guidance and practical advice. They have little

choice in the matter. How many Protestant churchmen today believe in God?

Chapter 8. *Futurism and the Worse that is Yet to Come*

[1] See, for instance, the correspondence in *Encounter* (December 1970) between Sir Peter Medawar and Professor Paul Ehrlich; also the comments by *R* (October 1970).

[2] I need hardly remind the reader that at this juncture I choose to step down from the economist's platform. In particular, I feel no longer bound within this context to accept people's wants, as revealed by the Market or Opinion Polls, as the ultimate data in the design of the good society. Though I shall not attempt to do so here, this departure from orthodoxy can be justified by reference to the powerful influence on people's wants resulting from restricted choices and restricted experiences under existing institutions. The interested reader will find sceptical passages about free choice and consumers' sovereignty in chapters 12 and 13 of my book, *Growth: The Price We Pay* (Staples Press, London; Praeger, New York).